Bohemia Junction

by

Aimé Tschiffely

The Long Riders' Guild Press

www.thelongridersguild.com

ISBN: 1-59048-276-X

To the Reader:

The editors and publishers of The Long Riders' Guild Press faced significant technical and financial difficulties in bringing this and the other titles in this collection to the light of day.

Though the authors represented in this international series envisioned their stories being shared for generations to come, all too often that was not the case. Sadly, many of the books now being published by The Long Riders' Guild Press were discovered gracing the bookshelves of rare book dealers, adorned with princely prices that placed them out of financial reach of the common reader. The remainder were found lying neglected on the scrap heap of history, their once-proud stories forgotten, their once-glorious covers stained by the toil of time and a host of indifferent previous owners.

However The Long Riders' Guild Press passionately believes that this book, and its literary sisters, remain of global interest and importance. We stand committed, therefore, to bringing our readers the best copy of these classics at the most affordable price. The copy which you now hold may have small blemishes originating from the master text.

We apologize in advance for any defects of this nature.

THE AUTHOR

"Nous ne nous laissons pas trop imposer par les usages du monde."

GEORGE SAND

(ARMANDINE LUCILE DUDEVANT), 1804–76.

"The young man commenced his Bohemian life in London."

ANTHONY TROLLOPE

in *The Belton Estate*, 1865.

DEDICATED TO MY WIFE

who has known and loved some of the Bohemians
mentioned in these pages

Contents

Introduction

EVERY now and again we are told that someone is a Bohemian: in most cases, however, when we ask why a person is so described, we are told that he—the feminine counterpart, moreover, exists—is rather "wild," eccentric, unconventional, morally lax or even debauched. The many Bohemians, however, according to my interpretation of the term, whom I have met, associated with and in some cases known intimately for years have been very different from those which fall normally into the category of Bohemian. Most of the persons about whom I propose to write vary considerably from what is generally regarded as a typical Bohemian, frequently to be seen drifting about, unshaven, be-bearded, long-haired, unkempt, and in not a few cases, physically dirty and morally depraved. Leaving illegitimate offspring untidily scattered about or being in the grip of some vice or perversion does not make a man or woman a Bohemian, for such abnormal beings are nothing more or less than degenerates, or, to use Swift's term, commonplace "Yahoos."

Unfortunately, many of the type of Bohemian I would wish to introduce to the reader are rapidly disappearing: the cult of respectability, official restrictions and regimentation as the aftermath of two wars may be among the causes of the obsolescence of the true Bohemian.

A witty Frenchman once described *Liberté, Egalité* and *Fraternité* as "*les trois grandes blagues,*" but, as will be seen in later pages of these memoirs, biographical sketches, or whatever the reader chooses to call the contents of this book, among most of the Bohemians I wish to introduce, love of adventure, certain affinities of character, and brotherhood are realities.

As far as liberty and equality are concerned, it seems to me that, gradually, we are moving nearer and nearer towards a truth spoken in jest.

According to an anecdote, a "comrade" was holding forth in the public forum, near Marble Arch, in Hyde Park. During his fiery speech, singling out a little, meek, humble-looking man, he thus addressed him, at the same time pointing towards Buckingham Palace and a luxury hotel in nearby Park Lane.

"Yes, Comrade, when you gets your freedom, you'll be livin' in there!"

"But . . . but . . . I'd hate it," the meek one stammered.

"Never mind whether you like it or not," the orator thundered; "when you gets your freedom, you'll jolly well 'ave to do as you're told."

According to the *Oxford Dictionary*, "*the transferred senses of the word 'Bohemian' are taken from the French, in which bohème, bohémien, have been applied to gipsies, since their first appearance in the fifteenth century, because they were thought to come from Bohemia, or perhaps actually entered the West through that country. Thence, in modern French, the word has been transferred to vagabond, adventurer, person of irregular life or habits, a sense introduced into English by Thackeray.*"

In this book, I intend to use the word "Bohemian" with considerable latitude, without reference to morals, and I do not propose to unpack my full budget as Rousseau somewhat unconvincingly claims to have done in his *Confessions*. After all, most so-called autobiographies are written out of sheer vanity, even if it is of the inverted kind. A few of the people who are mentioned in these pages may have been outcasts of society, but others deliberately placed themselves outside the corral in which most of the more conventional security-seekers like to ruminate.

In order to show that in this world, whether accidentally or by design, one thing leads to another, I will endeavour to set down on paper, stage by stage, how I came into contact with the people mentioned in this book. For obvious reasons, a few names will have to be changed, several of the characters about whom I intend to write being still very much alive.

Though much of what I am about to relate concerns my activities and wanderings, I wish to make it quite clear that this is not intended to be an autobiography, but merely a partial account dealing with the "Bohemian" side of my life. I will not weary the reader with a long list of famous names which so often help the sale of books, as aces are most useful in certain card games. Instead, I will concentrate mainly on Jacks, or knaves, as the case may be, and rely on a sequence of lower cards, with here and there a joker, king or queen thrown in, trusting that, in showing my hand to those who care to peep over my shoulder, they will see, if nothing else, how a heterogeneous collection of in most cases strangely low cards may exert an influence in the game of life far greater than their playing value might suggest.

A. F. Tschiffely.

Chapter I

Odd childhood recollections.—Bad scholar becomes teacher.—Arrival
in London.—Bill and Ivy Gristin and their lodging-houses.—Happy days
in the *Maison Gristin*, and teaching in Preparatory schools.

A WRITER who enjoys fame in astrological circles very kindly
made out my horoscope, according to which, I am given to
understand, in my case "the Ascendant is Aquarius, and Saturn is
the ruling Planet, both in the sign of Scorpio."

Being lamentably ignorant in such matters, and therefore only
vaguely guessing what Aquarius, Saturn and Scorpio mean, somehow I do not like the sound of the first, there being something
watery and fishy about it. The second word makes me feel somewhat gloomy, and therefore, of the three, I least object to the last,
Scorpio, for when it comes to scorpions, I *do* know something about
them, whether they belong to the species of *Homo sapiens* or to that
of the arachnids.

The subject of this book being neither astrology nor scorpions,
but Bohemians, readers may be curious to learn how I came into
contact with the persons referred to in these pages. In order to
explain this, I will write a few words about my family, and very
briefly go back to the earliest days of my childhood. These glimpses
may possibly be of interest to psychiatrists, psychologists, and
perhaps even to alienists, because for all I know and care they may
give such learned persons certain clues as to "cause and effect," and
thus assist them in their deep-sea dives into the complexities of the
human mind.

I will not weary you, gentle and, I hope, persevering reader, with
a long account of my family history. Let it suffice that my surname
is of old Swiss origin, and that in Switzerland family history often
goes very far back. At various times the name was spelt as Tschiffely,
Tschiffeli, Tschiffeling, Gifelli and Chifelle. And who knows that
the name Chifley, if the Prime Minister of Australia agrees, may
not be another variant.

B

At some not so remote period in history, my family suffered a setback in war, when most of its male members were killed, and after that, in commemoration of the disaster, the lance in the family coat-of-arms ceased to appear intact, but was shown with the point broken off. It still retained, however, the helm, crowned by an imposing coronet which in its turn was surmounted by a golden star. Although I am not superstitious, I have often wondered whether the broken lance or the golden star would appear to have ruled my destiny. Perhaps the reader will be the best judge of whether Dame Fortune has smiled on me or not. The onlooker it is who sees most of the game. With this rough *résumé* of family history, I will start at the beginning of my life, as far back as I can remember.

Presumably I came into this world protesting, as healthy babies are expected to do upon involuntarily filling their lungs with air, of which we make much use—even of "hot air" at times—till the last breath is drawn.

How old I was when first I realised that I had parents, and what could be reasonably expected from them, I do not remember, and it was only later that it dawned on me that, besides a father and mother, I also had a brother and a sister, and that there were a few relatives, male and female. Often some of the latter made such a fuss of me that I was glad when they departed, and I was left to amuse myself in my own way.

Strange or far-fetched as it may seem, I clearly remember my parents' home burning when I was barely two years of age. In the very act of writing this, I clearly see flames leaping past the windows of the room in which I had been sleeping, and I have retained a clear picture in my mind of how I was carried to a neighbour's house, whence I thoroughly enjoyed the sight of the conflagration. After this there is a blank extending over some two or three years, until a nasty bee made such an impression on my neck and memory that I vividly remember screaming like a stuck sucking-pig as, whilst I was placed upon a garden table, my grandmother applied some ointment to the affected spot. After this experience, there is another blank space in my memory, but then came a most serious

incident which gave me my first insight into a side of human nature
of which until then I had been blissfully ignorant.

As it happened, I was the proud and happy possessor of a tin
money-box, beautifully designed and painted as a drum. Inside
this cradle of capitalism were coins, presented to me, no doubt, by
loving relatives and duty-bound visitors. One fine day, when these
came to spend the day with my parents, and several of us children
played in the garden, one of the little guests showed me how to roll
my precious drum along the ground. Its metallic contents made
such a delightful sound that, gradually, I rolled the tin with more
confidence and strength until, suddenly, it burst open scattering
coins in every direction. Before I had time to recover from the
shock, my playmates pounced on the coins like so many hungry
birds swooping down to peck up crumbs thrown to them, and
when they refused to hand them back to me, I caught hold of the
greediest of them and fought him with the fury of an angry kitten.
The next thing I remember is that a grown-up person intervened
and, for my bad behaviour, I was taken up to my bedroom, undressed, and "plonked" into my bed. Next day, upon examining
my precious money-box, I found that at least half of its contents
had gone. This happened in Neuville, a quaint old-fashioned little
town, situated on the southern shore of the picturesque lake of Biel
(or Bienne) in Switzerland.

Throughout my childhood, ever since I can remember, I was
terribly afraid of the dark. As soon as my bedroom was darkened,
I imagined all kinds of fearsome wild beasts to be prowling about
on the floor or to be lurking under my bed, ready to devour me.
Terrified, I quickly covered myself, and, rolled up into a ball under
the blankets, lay in fear and trembling until kindly Nature came to
my rescue with sleep.

At the far end of our garden I kept a number of rabbits which had
to be fed twice per day. Sometimes I forgot to do so, but, as my
parents always asked me about the welfare of my pets before I went
to bed, they never went without their evening feed. But how
terrified I was whilst through the darkness I made my way to the
hutches and back to the house!

In those days, had anyone told me that later on in my life I would often sleep out, all alone, in dark tropical forests and jungles, the very thought of it would have driven me into a frenzy of terror. Suspecting that if I told anyone about my fear of darkness I would be laughed at and probably be made the victim of practical jokes, I took good care to keep it secret, though at different times I had reason to suspect that my parents, especially my father, knew something about this childish weakness against which I fought in vain.

One day I happened to see two Italian labourers fight with knives, and one of the men was severely wounded in the stomach. This made such an impression on my mind that for several years whenever I saw Italian workers—who almost invariably wore red sashes wound round their waists—I bolted for dear life, like a frightened hare.

That, even when only a small child, I had what is often called a "bump of locality" became apparent when my parents took me to Paris, where, during some big public function, somehow I became separated from them. Finding myself alone among a mass of strange people, I toddled back, some three miles to the house in which we were staying with relatives. Everybody being out and the place locked, I sat down on the doorstep and waited.

It was getting dark when my mother and two other ladies arrived in a cab. Upon seeing me, all screamed as if I had done something wrong, and presently, to my astonishment, my tearful mother hugged and kissed me until I thought she would never cease.

Some time later, when the men returned, to my joy they took me for a ride in the *fiacre*, and when the horse stopped, I was taken into a gloomy police station where several *gendarmes*, especially a stout one who wore a long, drooping moustache, looked at me so hard that, frightened to death, I wondered what they were about to do to me.

After a great deal of scribbling on a sheet of paper, one *gendarme* growled something, whereafter we departed. Although at the time I did not know that I had been reported as lost and thought that

I was merely taken to the police station in order to prove that I had been found, ever since that evening I have disliked policemen.

When no longer afraid of darkness, on several occasions I disappeared from home, to wander about all night, or to go and sleep under some bridge, in a shed or under a haystack, and one of my chief delights was to explore the main drainage system of our town, and the woods beyond, where, for hours on end, I observed the habits of birds, animals and insects.

A little later in life, the glamour and romance of the stage, pantomimes and circuses fascinated and attracted me. But there were other allurements. I clearly remember being unable to make up my mind whether to become a railway engine-driver, the captain of a ship, a circus clown, or the hero in some stage play. It seemed to me that driving a locomotive, or standing on the bridge of a ship, dressed in a uniform with lots of gold braid, steering and giving orders, was not only dignified and romantic, but also easy, and that in the case of a clown, all that was required was to act the fool and tumble about, and that as the hero of a sword-and-cloak drama I must always be right, and therefore inevitably have victory on my side. Even at that early age I had a shrewd suspicion that tight-rope-walking, turning double somersaults in the air, doing acrobatics on horseback, and juggling with Indian clubs and plates were difficult and, in some cases, dangerous occupations, which require much practice before they can be performed with relative safety and success, and therefore, although I greatly admired and envied acrobats, jugglers, knife-throwers, flying trapeze artists, tamers of wild animals, contortionists, circus cowboys, tumblers, *haute école* riders, strong men and other breath-taking performers, I ruled them out of my ambitions.

At the age of about fifteen, I began to think that it would be grand to become a famous football star, or a world-champion boxer, but even at that age I still had such a hankering to be in command of an ocean-going ship that, whenever I was sitting in my bath tub, I turned the taps off and on, at the same time imagining I was steering a ship which took me to treasure islands and into tropical ports where, seated among the waving branches of palm trees, monkeys watched me berth my ship. When free-wheeling on my bicycle, I indulged in the reverie that I was on a fiery horse, and when I made a nuisance of myself, tumbling about on the carpet in the drawing-room, I was convinced that no clown could possibly be as funny as I. For several years the narrow space between two French windows and a large curtain in the same room had been my stage when, together with my brother and two sisters, and sometimes visiting friends, we "invented" and acted plays. Unfortunately, being younger than most of the other actors, I was never allowed to be the all-conquering hero, and therefore, after many buffetings, I began to lose my liking for the stage, and finally I cut myself adrift from the company to play football and Red Indians.

Whenever a circus came to our town, I was on the spot to watch wagons arrive, tents being put up, and to catch glimpses of the wild beasts in their cages. From outside the canvas stables I listened to the snorting and stamping of horses, and to the roaring of lions waiting to be fed. With envy I looked on as tent-peggers did their work, and with reverence and bated breath I peeped into circus wagons in which lived my heroes and heroines, some of whom conversed in strange languages, thus adding to their mystery which I tried to fathom. At such times the sight of a schoolmate brought back nauseating thoughts of the class-room and my desk. If one of my teachers had come on the scene, my normal respect for him would have given way to silent contempt, for in my childish imagination the circus people were demi-gods, not mere pedantic teachers of grammar, dull history, lifeless geography, tortuous mathematics, tongue- and brain-twisting languages and other tortures, invented only to make boys' lives miserable, and to waste their time, which could be so much more pleasantly employed in riding horses. How much more noble were my equestrian heroes than stick-in-the-muds, such as schoolmasters, business-men, professors, Government officials and politicians, who are afraid to risk their necks and skins as did my heroes, the circus artists.

My elder brother, whose ambition it was to become a soldier, hardly ever bothered to hang about the circus ground, as I did whenever an opportunity presented itself. Although he enjoyed the shows in the big tent, he was only luke-warm about the performers as persons—an attitude I failed to understand. Similarly, mine was beyond him when I refused to take an interest in Army manœuvres, parades, machine guns, howitzers, so-and-so-many-pounders, different uniforms and books on military history, tactics or strategy, which he collected and devoured as if they contained the keys to human happiness. The very thought of being drilled like an automaton, with hundreds and even thousands of my so-called comrades-in-arms doing exactly the same as I, at the very same instant, and, to my mind, for no really practical reason, filled me with impatience; but if a cavalry regiment passed, I was thrilled to the marrow, not on account of the stiff riders in their uniforms, but because the horses' looks and symmetry or graceful lines were of interest to me. Whenever an opportunity presented itself, I mixed with farmers, grooms, and even tramps, whose conversation and activities were of great interest to me, but what I liked best was to play with animals or to practise different sports and athletics.

Being red-haired, with my face, arms and hands covered with a mass of freckles, throughout my childhood I was the target of gibes and often even jeers. Although in those days I did not know the Spanish proverb that "it is better to be insulted by a Moor than to be ignored by a prince," with the passing of time, and in self-defence, I taught myself to treat all mockery concerning my appearance as compliments. As I grew bigger and stronger, and at the same time more confident, whenever boys shouted something about my red hair or freckles, this almost invariably led to fights. Some of these scraps did not improve my appearance, but with frequent practice I learnt a few tricks, thanks to which bullies thought twice before coming to grips or blows with me.

Until I reached the age of about thirteen, my brother, who was my senior by some two years, was my undisputed overlord, and whenever he lost his temper with me, all I did was to defend myself without ever daring to take the offensive. However, one day the worm turned, and to my astonishment I discovered that my antagonist was by no means invincible, with the result that after having met his Waterloo, my brother never had another fight with me.

How I·hated most of the subjects I was expected to study at school! I was fairly good at languages, utterly hopeless at maths, too impatient for humdrum essay-writing, and certain phases of, to me, totally unimportant history bored me almost to tears. Geography appealed to me to a certain extent, but as, in order to pass examinations it was almost entirely a matter of memorising names and locations of countries, towns, seas, lakes, mountains, rivers, imports, exports, etc., I preferred to read good travel books which, being alive, interested me much more than the dull set curriculum. After having suffered agonies in classrooms for seven and even eight hours per day, and on top of it all being expected to do homework for another two hours or more, I thought out various successful plans whereby, by hook or crook, I avoided such further tortures. Had I been a good and conscientious pupil, such as most of my class-mates were, perhaps to-day I would be a struggling lawyer or doctor, some sort of black-coat worker, or maybe a respected town councillor, politician or tea-cup-juggling diplomat. However, when I was old enough to observe things and to think for myself, I had different ideas about education and life, and so I did not bother one iota about examinations and what the future might, or might not, have in store for me.

Fortunately, my parents were not unduly worried about my failure as a scholar, but as far as my teachers were concerned, I must have been either an acute disappointment or a problem child to them. And so years passed, and whilst my studious class-mates— most of whom were excellent robot scholars, and therefore potential Jacks-of-all-trades—passed examination after examination with flying colours, I learnt merely to become a fairly good all-round athlete, to develop my own tastes, and not to be unduly deceived by men's outward appearances and manner of speech. This, however, has stood me in good stead.

From my father—who was remarkably strong, and an excellent horseman who had ridden over the prairies and plains of Texas and New Mexico, as well as the Argentine pampa, where my grandfather lies buried—I must have inherited my passion for horses and love of sport. My mother, who had artistic and literary tastes and played the piano better than she painted, taught me to appreciate the creative arts, with the result that, when on visits to Italy and France, I frequently went to art galleries, concert halls and theatres. Spare minutes, stolen during hours of study, I employed in making pencil sketches or slyly caricaturing my unsuspecting teachers. Drawing and painting I took up with but moderate success, but sufficient to enable me to derive great pleasure from hours thus employed when I was in the rare mood to sit still. Thrillers, sentimental novels, love stories and pornographic trash never interested me, but I revelled in books of travel and stories about people who have done things in the fields of adventure, science and art. I could never, however, take more than a casual interest in scientific matters, and the splitting of atoms never appealed to me as much as split-second decisions to do the right thing in an emergency, or giving a clever or witty reply in a verbal duel.

People often tell us that the happiest days in their lives were those of their childhood. Whenever I hear this said, I wonder what the speakers mean by "happiness." If the word implies that they were well looked after, fed and clothed, and that love, affection and even luxuries have been bestowed upon him or her, as often happens in the case of pets, as I see it, a grown-up person who considers this to be happiness has had no imagination or initiative during the early years of his or her life. Without going further into this complex subject, all I will say here is that although my childhood was a happy one, I only really began to enjoy life when I faced the world single-handed, and without ever again having to ask my parents for support of any kind. As it happened, somehow I managed to paddle my own capricious canoe before I reached the age of twenty, and when I look back to those days, although sometimes I found myself in shallow waters and in choppy seas, it was only after having attained full independence that the real happiness in my life began.

In 1912 I happened to be near Le Havre in France, when a letter reached me from a friend in London. This gave me an idea, and so,

without further ado, I packed up my belongings, and soon after
was on my way to England. Even during the train journey from
Southampton to London there was something that appealed to me
in what I saw from the train, and upon my arrival at Waterloo
Station, the peculiar smell of smoke and the light fog and fine
drizzle which reduced visibility to about fifty yards fascinated me.
The crowds of people hustling and bustling about, the quaint
hansom cabs, the heavy cart-horses bedecked with beautifully
polished brass trappings—in fact, everything I saw and heard—
seemed so friendly that I felt quite at home. As long as my limited
funds lasted, I made the best of every hour, and when the time came
to go back to the Continent, I made up my mind that at the earliest
opportunity I would return to England.

Although in the classroom I had been a distinct, though un-
ashamed and impenitent, failure, eventually I became . . . a schoolmaster!

My first position as assistant master I held under a certain M.A.
Cantab., who, as far as his teaching staff was concerned, emphatically
held that "gentlemen don't take money." Besides being a high
official on the Board of Education, as a lucrative side-line he ran a
flourishing private school. Having successfully served a kind of
glorified apprenticeship under him (at a nominal salary of £21 per
year, plus board and lodgings, for teaching, supervising games and
acting as policeman from 7 a.m. until 9 p.m., and on dreary Sundays
suffering the agonies of the damned), I had the good fortune later
to be transferred to Park Hill, an expensive and therefore exclusive preparatory school near Lyndhurst, in the New Forest.
Twenty-five was the maximum number of pupils the school ever
had in the course of a term, and among them were several
princes; and the others were the sons of wealthy social and political
figures. The buildings and surrounding parks were old and stately,
and my work light and pleasant. Although my salary amounted to
£100 per year, there were extras for special coaching, and so I was
as happy as a cricket, for besides the general friendly atmosphere in
the school, there were . . . horses to ride!

In those days, the teaching staff in "good" English schools, such as those referred to, consisted largely of young well-to-do university men who either were keen on games or who wanted a little teaching experience, in order later to take Holy Orders. With the former category the only thing I had in common was my passion for any form of sport, whereas, as far as the Church is concerned, I was, and still am, quite satisfied to be a "back-pewer," and, for my sins, a patient listener to sometimes exceedingly long and dull sermons.

With so little money to spend, I had to cut my coat according to my cloth, and therefore, when in London during school holidays, reputable hotels or residential parts, such as Belgravia or Mayfair, had to be ruled out as possibilities for my temporary residence. Instead, thanks to a friend's assistance, I found "digs" in an extremely modest and antiquated row of two-storied houses in a part of London which could almost be regarded as a slum area. There, in the company of two other schoolmasters of my financial standing, I spent many happy holidays and met a number of extraordinary characters.

Bill Gristin and Ivy, his wife, two typical Cockneys, were our landlord and landlady. By profession a jobbing builder and interior decorator, Bill had acquired several ramshackle houses, which were furnished with odd bits and pieces. The rooms were let singly, and produced a very nice side-income for the couple. Bill and Ivy had three daughters, whose ages, when I first met them, ranged from six to ten years, and they also had an adopted child, the illegitimate son of one of Bill's sisters. The Gristins were a happy family, the senior members of which were always busy raking in shillings and pence. The children, although they were allowed to do what they liked and to go wherever they chose, were, considering everything, very well behaved, though on occasions not quite so well spoken.

Dark, lean and vivacious, Ivy looked like a gipsy or a Spaniard, but she was a Cockney to the backbone. Her favourite colours were bright red or electric blue, and her hats were always adorned with flowing ostrich feathers. When Bill was dressed up to go to the races or on a trip to Ramsgate or Margate, his favourite seaside resorts, he looked quite distinguished. Fairly tall, well-proportioned, and with facial features which reminded one of the "Iron Duke," he cut a fine figure when ready for such outings. After meals he always scanned the *Daily Mirror* or the *News of the World*, and so well did he act his part, and discuss current events and scandals, that only after having known him for a few years did I discover that he was illiterate. It was Ivy who one day let me into this secret. Apparently, every morning at breakfast time she read out the news to her husband, who had a remarkably good memory; so good, in fact, that although, when working at his trade, he often pretended to be making notes in a pocket-book, he memorised all measurements and specifications of materials which had to be bought. The writing of letters and the making-out of bills was in the able hands of Ivy, who, like her husband, had many irons in the fire. Dressmaking, collecting dues for a building society, assisting a street bookmaker, buying and selling odds and ends, from antiques to rags, slap-dash housework and cooking kept her in good spirits in both senses of the word. Bill, who was a speedy and expert worker, employed two or three assistants, and these had to move fast to keep up with their dynamic boss, whose favourite occupation was the demolishing of old houses. This usually led to the acquisition of zinc water-tanks, lead and other piping, old sanitary installations, doors, window frames, tiles, wood, certain fittings, and many other things, which he piled up in his backyard, to be used later when a building or mending job had to be done. Two sheds at the back of the house were filled with cans, jars, pots and bottles containing paint, dis-temper, varnish, paint brushes, and acids, and piled high were rolls of wall-paper, used linoleum, old curtains, strips of carpet, and similar treasures, all of which, sooner or later, would be turned into money by that thrifty scrounger, Bill. In that veritable mausoleum of old building materials also were kept boards, beams, scaffolding and ladders of every size. On Sundays—especially when the weather happened to be fine—the owner of these pyramids of flotsam and jetsam could be seen scrummaging among his treasured possessions, or surveying them with crafty eyes. Though a competent builder and interior decorator, when urgently called upon to attend to stopped-up kitchen sinks or drains or to do some plumbing, Bill always found time to rush to the rescue, and when such a job was done and finished with, and he had collected his fee "without scruple or diffidence," and possibly a good tip for his timely intervention, he went to the nearest "pub" for a quick one, whereafter he hurried off to resume work on his "big job."

It was easy to tell when he was doing well or if he had made a good deal, for whenever this was the case, he hurried about, with one hand thrust into a trouser pocket, making coins jingle, whilst whistling no particular tune in high, shrill notes.

The Gristins' row of two-storied brick houses, which must have been some two hundred years old, was of very simple architectural design. Level with the ground, each dwelling place had a battered wooden door, off which most of the paint had peeled, maybe a generation before, and alongside each front door was a sitting-room window. On the first floor, running along the entire row of houses, were narrow balconies with corroded iron railings. In front, between the pavement and each house, fenced in by dilapidated cast-iron spears—many of which were missing or broken—was a small patch which, for want of another word, was called the "front garden," although in it were to be seen only sooty weeds, bits of rubbish, broken crockery and empty bottles, rusty sardine tins and other refuse. At one end of our usually deserted street was a fire station, which, in those days, meant . . . HORSES.

As far as I was concerned, I hoped, and all but prayed, for two or three fire calls to be made every day, provided, of course, it had not to be for our house. A sight for the gods it was, especially during autumn or winter nights, to see the be-helmeted fire-fighters and their snorting and prancing horses sally forth into the mist or fog. Whenever I heard the familiar noise, I rushed to my window to watch the Homeric chariots pass. If the night happened to be foggy, two men stood alongside the driver's seat, holding burning flares, the red light of which made highly polished brass glitter like gold. Hoofs clattered on the cobble-stones, bells clanked, and into the night raced the Olympians, smoke and sparks whirling and spurting out of the brass chimney of the pump's boiler, until only a rapidly fading red glare could be seen through the fog, and the drumming of hoofs and the echoes of the warning bells died away in the distance.

I salute the memory of you, brave and romantic flame- and smoke-fighters, and noble fire-engine horses of those irretrievable days!

The Gristins' "steady" lodgers were a mixed lot, chiefly middle-aged or old people. According to the weekly rent they could afford, or were prepared to pay, they were allotted rooms of various sizes, situated on the ground floor, first or second story, overlooking the street or Bill's building material deposit in the backyard. In the case of two of the "annexes," even sheds which, once upon a time, had been brick-built wash-houses, were occupied by impecunious or miserly patrons. Bill and Ivy were not particular about their own quarters and those of their children, who shifted to any temporarily unoccupied room. Sometimes, when business was particularly brisk, the entire Gristin tribe made itself fit into a fair-sized bed-sitting-room, to which its junior members only went to sleep, preferring to spend most of their free time messing about in the backyard, playing in the street, or eating in the one and only kitchen in the row of Gristin lodging-houses. Situated at the back of the *maison du patron*, this kitchen was the meeting place of Bill and Ivy's few favoured guests, among whom we schoolmasters were by far the most privileged.

In every lodger's room there was a gas-ring, or a small antiquated gas-cooker with its corresponding penny-in-the-slot meter. The last-named was a source of great joy to Ivy, for, invariably, when the Gas Light and Coke Company men called, to check up on the gas consumed and the pennies inserted through the slot, there was a nice little balance in her favour.

Weakened by age and heavy weights placed upon them, the springs of most of the beds had given way to such an extent that sleeping in them would have been a joy to anyone used to hammocks. The cotton sheets, pillow-slips and blankets were tolerably clean, though, in most cases, so full of holes and tears that it was a feat to slide into bed without getting one's feet hopelessly entangled. However, as the Gristins' sleeping contraptions were provided for the sole purpose of rest, no one complained. It would be hiding a truth if, regarding the furniture, especially some of the chairs put at disposal of lodgers, it were not set on record that, owing to the rickety state of some, several minor accidents happened, fortunately without serious consequences. As far as the tables were concerned—where such were provided—it must be remembered that, sooner or later, if we human beings live long enough to reach a ripe old age, even we are apt to get weak in the legs.

Electric light had barely been installed in the main thoroughfares of London, but already in those "early" days the mysterious current was used to give sore eyes to those who sought entertainment in so-called "picture palaces." Therefore, in order to provide his clientèle with light, Bill had fixed a gas jet in every room. In the case of his "posh" rooms, these were fitted with "stockings"—as mantles were called by the Gristins—but lodgers who did not pay more than 7s. a week for their "digs" had to be content with plain jets. These, besides giving sufficient light to read large print, had the advantage that, with patience, a kettle could be brought to the boil, or eggs and bacon and possibly even a small kipper could be cooked, if held over the narrow, fan-shaped flame in a frying-pan.

Although Bill had quite good taste in matters concerning interior decoration, in his own properties he was satisfied with the cheapest wallpaper, usually of some "loud" flower design, preferably large flaming roses. Condemned houses supplied him with old cracked mirrors, age-stained engravings, prints, and even damaged oil-paintings, which he brought home to adorn the rooms in his establishment.

Modern antique dealers' mouths would water if they could see some of the things Bill collected, and sold, during the years I have known him. Sometimes, in attics and among old rubbish in cellars, he found mouldy boxes and trunks filled with abandoned junk. Among such, not infrequently, were articles of value, for which he accepted ready cash from cunning pawnbrokers, higglers and hawkers, who at intervals called to see if he had anything to sell.

Sanitary installations were crude, but clean and quite comfortable. There being no bathrooms or hot-water taps, a battered old copper "tub" in a disused and derelict wash-house took the place of a Roman bath, and, if a lodger was fussy or could not stand cold

water, Ivy—if she happened to be in a good and generous mood—
obliged lodgers with a huge kettle filled with boiling water.

One evening, our amazing landlord returned home with a piano.
It was not just one of those tinny little uprights, but a full-sized
concert grand, which, according to him, he had bought for a mere
song. Assisted by several men, he unloaded the heavy instrument
from a horse-drawn cart, and took it into the kitchen. When it had
been roughly wiped over with a rag, he sat down to thump the
keyboard with one finger. Though the strings were badly out of
tune and a few were missing, the piano was a great acquisition. A
few days after its arrival, when it had been "fixed up" by one of
Ivy's brothers—who, besides being an ambulant fruit-vendor, also
was a bit of a banjo-player—it sounded remarkably well, considering what it must have gone through during a visibly long and
eventful life. Besides adding dignity to the kitchen, the instrument
served as an excellent table on which to place the Gristins' treasured
"grammyphone," which had one of the largest and most ornate
lily-shaped trumpets I have ever seen. Alongside the gramophone
were piled up masses of scratched and cracked records, and on
festive occasions the piano was utilised as a repository for glasses
and bottles, of which, when a party was "chucked," there were
incredible numbers; for when the Gristins entertained, especially on
Christmas Day, they did it in style. Shellfish, from lobsters down to
periwinkles, sometimes pheasants, partridges, snipe, turkeys, geese,
chickens, huge roasts, puddings, different cheeses, fruits, fancy
chocolates and sweets were handed out as liberally as glasses were
constantly kept filled with brandy, whisky, gin, port wine, stout or
ale. Friends and acquaintances were treated royally, and sometimes
local policemen, favourite firemen "from down the road," the
dustman, the lamp-lighter and even the old rag-bottle-and-bone
man were invited in for a "bite" and a few swigs. The last of the
aforementioned gentlemen was an extraordinary character, and it
was said about him that one of his side-lines was the stealing of dogs
which, according to rumours, on Sundays he sold in the street market
in Club Row, near Petticoat Lane.

Once Bill won a donkey in a raffle, and when he grew tired of feeding it in the backyard, the rag-and-bone man came to the rescue, offering, on a fifty-fifty basis, to lead the animal to Club Row and endeavour to sell it at a good price. Although the proposed business transaction was rather "steep," as Bill put it, he agreed, being anxious to get rid of the donkey. On the following Sunday, long before the man reached the East End with the poor beast, Bill had arrived there on a 'bus, in order to see that he should not be swindled.

We schoolmasters were the only lodgers who had most of our meals in the Gristins' cosy and friendly kitchen, where a fire was always roaring up the chimney and several dilapidated easy chairs provided extra comfort before and after repasts. Sometimes, especially on wet Sundays, we spent hours in this forum, where amusing local news and incidents were discussed amid howls of laughter. Very occasionally we played cribbage for low stakes, 5s. being the maximum a player was allowed to lose before he had to sit out. When only two players were left, they "cut for the lot" and the winner had to pay for the beer consumed.

It will thus be seen that, although during school holidays finances did not permit me to travel to the Riviera, or to take up residence in select and exclusive parts of London, the *Maison Gristin* provided me with sufficient comfort, atmosphere and originality to make my periodic stays there seem very short. Whenever the time came to return to my school, and I thought of Sundays with top hats and morning coats, and meals during which it was my duty to insist on good table manners on the part of the boys, I felt reluctant to start out; but on the other hand, life in the New Forest had many attractions and therefore made a pleasant change.

C

Chapter II

Glimpses of London pre-1914.—The Reverend Crimpus Jilt, M.A. and
A. Stintall, B.A.—Gristinian "steadies" and other lodgers.—Meeting the
amazing "Sophocles" who discovers a modern prophet.

DESPITE its many shortcomings, I so enjoyed my stays in the
Gristins' lodging-house that it became my second home. I loved
the free-and-easy atmosphere in it, and when I wanted a distraction,
the rough cobble-stoned street without provided me with what I
sought. There, standing in small groups, women could often be
seen gossiping, or children dancing and making merry whilst barrel-
organ men played their tunes. The new popular favourites were of
recent American vintage: "Alexander's Ragtime Band," "Waiting
for the Robert E. Lee," "Oh, You Beautiful Doll," "Hitchy-koo,"
and others that are unknown to the newer generation. The peculiar
and in some cases almost weird cries of street vendors mixed with
the joyous laughter and shouting of children, whose favourite
playground was the street. Motor cars were a rarity in those days,
and, therefore, most carriages being horsedrawn, the youngsters
were in no danger, especially so because there was but little traffic
in our neighbourhood.

When—invariably on Sundays, and sometimes also during the
week—the muffin and crumpet man slowly strolled along, his goods
on a wooden tray, covered over with a piece of white cloth and
carried on the head, and he rang his hand-bell, youngsters ran into
their houses to ask parents for halfpennies with which to buy
themselves some of the delicacies for which they longed. The
best bananas were sold at two for a penny, and with a halfpenny
one could buy two oranges. In a high, shrill note a regular visitor
to our street called "Rabbits!" Hanging from two or three wires
that were stretched above the man's barrow were displayed rows of
those rodents, most of which were skinned. These were sold at
sixpence apiece, as also were those which had not been skinned, but

in the case of the latter, if a skin was returned to the rabbit man, he gave two pennies for it.

The milkman's call, "Mee-oo-koo!" sounded like a mixture of a yodel and the mooing of a cow, and the coalman's deep hoarse "Coal!" brought to mind a voice coming out of a tomb. "Rags, bottles and bones!" was another peculiar cry, made by the Gristins' filthy, unkempt old friend, who would exchange a "windmill" for a jam-pot or bottles. Then, also, there was the man on whose barrow were heaped up shrimps and winkles, delicacies without which a Cockney's Sunday tea would have been like a joint of roast beef with no baked onions, potatoes or "bubble and squeak."

During the warm months, an old Italian—who attracted attention by striking a triangle with a short iron rod—sold ice-cream of his own and doubtful manufacture, but in winter he switched over to chestnuts and potatoes, which he baked in an oven—on wheels—which was shaped and painted so as to resemble a railway engine.

In districts of London where rich people lived, often if someone was dangerously ill, in order to deaden the noise made by iron-rimmed wheels and the drumming of hoofs on the cobble stones, straw was spread over the street.

One day there was a great "to-do" in our neighbourhood. Men, women and children stood in groups, watching, and others looked down from windows as, from a cart, straw was being unloaded and thickly scattered over the street for a distance of close on a hundred yards. About halfway along the "padded" stretch lived a miserly old pawnbroker who was disliked by all the lookers-on, probably because many of them had had dealings with the old "tight-wad."

Everybody in the vicinity knew that the "pop-shop man" had been ill for several days, but nobody felt particularly sorry for him; in fact, several of his clients had openly expressed their hope that the old "So-and-So" would "kick the bucket." But now, whilst they watched two men unload straw and scatter it over the street, what the onlookers said about the sick man is best left to the imagination of the reader. Straw was all right for the big "nobs," but who ever heard of a mangy pawnbroker put on such "side"? It was pure swank, all wrong!

·　　·　　·　　·　　·

The two schoolmasters in whose company I lodged at the Gristins during vacations were teaching in well-known public schools, one in the Midlands and the other near London. For obvious reasons, as will be seen, I am withholding the names of the scholastic institutions concerned, and on the grounds of "What's in a name?" I shall merely call my two holiday colleagues Stintall and Crimpus Jilt, "Crimpie" for short. Although in every respect we differed greatly from one another, and the only thing we had in common was restricted cash, on the whole we got on very well together.

Tall, lean, spectacled and mousey-haired Stintall was a decent sort of chap, and a competent teacher of English literature. Although older than I, in many respects he was childish and lacked a sense of humour, especially where he himself was concerned. He liked to brag that from his earliest schooldays he had always been top of his form, and that he had passed with honours in all later examinations. To use a snobbish term, of which he was very fond when referring to his colleagues, he himself was not exactly out of the "top drawer." This was apparent, and manifested itself in different ways, especially when, being a glutton, he devoured incredible quantities of food, regardless of quality. On the other hand, he was a non-smoker and teetotaller, probably because the unnecessary spending of even a penny cut deeply into his very soul. Fond of games and athletics—at neither of which he excelled—he frequently accompanied me to watch football, cricket or boxing matches. Whenever we went to theatres or music-halls, he insisted on buying the cheapest tickets, his excuse being that standing up was healthier than sitting for long periods. Despite this assertion, I noticed that whenever I or someone else treated him to a good seat, he never protested or worried about his health. Still, apart from such minor failings, Stintall was a pleasant companion, though his outlook on life was distinctly that of a Sancho Panza.

Crimpus Jilt, despite the fact that he was an out-and-out bounder, amused us immensely, especially so when he had the necessary cash wherewith to go on the spree up in the West End, chiefly around Piccadilly, Regent Street, Leicester Square, or in the Strand, which were his favourite hunting grounds. He was so well known to proprietors, waiters, barmaids and hostesses of certain establishments that, according to the plausible Crimpie, he had "struck them off his list."

About thirty years of age, he was the only son of a prosperous widowed financier, who refused to have anything to do with him. Rather too quick-witted, sharp as a needle, and highly intelligent, he had fairly sailed through Oxford, where he finished with an honours degree in classics—and in debt up to his ears, as well as leaving behind two illegitimate babies he had fathered during his spare time. Apparently he had always been a problem to his papa, who severed all connection with him after having been bamboozled for a considerable sum of money by his prodigal son, who squandered it on a hectic tour round the world. Soon after his return to England, out of sheer necessity Crimpie was compelled to descend to the depths of becoming an assistant master in a public school. For several years, the young master of arts and world traveller behaved so well that when he expressed his desire to take Holy Orders, the Church received him with open arms. However, giving preference to the teaching of Latin and Greek to the more formal, often wearisome and dull duties of a curate, Crimpie stuck to schoolmastering, but during the holidays the dapper, Roman-nosed and engaging little cad took good care to disguise himself as an ordinary well-to-do gentleman, a part he acted to perfection. His manners, cultured speech, and Oxford drawl could hardly have been surpassed, not even when he was under the influence of drink.

When in London, Crimpie was always about, doing things, or anybody he could, but his chief pastimes were drinking, running after young ladies, or looking for old Oxonian friends from whom to borrow money. If he happeend to strike oil in a big way, he would disappear for a week or even longer, only to return to the Gristins' place when he was broke. No tom cat ever looked as bedraggled, crestfallen and miserable as did that plausible bounder when he had been on the "tiles." For several days after his return, he would hardly stir out of his room, where he spent most of his time lying in bed, staring at the ceiling, or sitting near the fire in the kitchen, shaking like an aspen leaf.

"Damn my trip to Indiah!" he would stutter. "That's what I got for going tigah shooting with my old varsity friend, Maharajah Oolalah of Blahanblah. . . . No laughing mattah this, my dear fellah; I'm fwightfully suffering from malariah!"

After a few more such excuses, and a great deal of sighing, shivering and pitiful chattering of teeth, he would ask me to be a good "sport" and to save his life by going "down the road" to buy him a bottle of brandy and several of ginger ale. "Don't worry about the money," he would add grandly. "As soon as I recovah, I shall call on my solicitahs, who have written informing me that a windfall has come my way. As a mattah of fact, I half suspect that my aunt, Lady Sah-and-Sah, has pegged out at last, and that the deah old soul has remembahd me in her will."

Accustomed to hearing such and similar yarns, and having been "had" before, I would plead poverty; but, feeling sorry for the invalid, I would suggest that a short walk would do him good, and promise that, if he came with me to the nearest "pub," I would buy him sufficient "medicine" to ease his sufferings.

But to come to the Gristins' "steady" and other lodgers.

Two back rooms of one "annex" were occupied by a Greek painter, who was most original in every respect. Although he claimed to give preference to those dingy rooms on account of the light, I strongly suspected that the low rent was their occupant's chief consideration. The Gristins—who had kindly and sympathetic feelings towards artists—never pressed the reincarnation of El Greco, Polygnotus or Parrhasius rolled into one for what he owed, and, on more than one occasion, in token of money, they accepted pictures or clay statuettes from the pseudo-genius.

Sometimes, when invited, I would go to his *atélier* in order to watch him apply paint to canvas, or to be shown with explanations his latest *chef-d'œuvre*. As a rule, the tall, long-haired and bearded Hellene wore only a kind of heavy monk's robe and sandals, on which the London grime must have covered dust from Greece, Florence and Montparnasse, where their owner had previously studied and toiled. Like most men of his exalted calling, who have spent some time in Paris, he insisted on speaking to me in broken French, which he did well enough to convey to me that he had been a pretty gay dog in his time, and that, in his opinion, people in England failed to appreciate art, especially his.

In the room adjoining his "studio," he slept or cooked, though the latter only when he had money wherewith to buy food, and one or two pennies over to insert into the gas-meter. Like several other lodgers, including Stintall and the Reverend Crimpus Jilt, he constantly came to me for coppers, which, once lent, were never returned. In fairness to this modern Greek Michelangelo—for he was also a bit of a sculptor and architect—it must be stated that when, at long intervals, he sold one of his works, his debts were immediately settled, whereafter he cast aside all repression. Spirits, wine, food, and friends would be brought into his den, whence, sometimes throughout the night, emanated the sounds of drunken laughter and singing. Occasionally, when the infernal din became too loud and unbearable, causing even dogs in different back yards to voice their disapproval, exasperated would-be sleepers threw cans and similar missiles out of windows, at the same time cursing at the top of their voices. If the pandemonium in the Greek artist's rooms ceased, the ensuing silence was only of short duration, for soon, by degrees, the storm again took impetus, growing in violence until it once more reached hurricane or even cyclone pitch.

In contrast with the Hellenic genius, an old Welsh couple occupied one bed-sitting-room where they spent most of their time reading the Bible, praying, and to the accompaniment of a tiny Japanese harmonium singing hymns, or going to a nearby chapel. They hardly spoke to anyone, and when elderly people—mostly women —visited them, it was to read out chapters from the Bible, pray and do some more hymn-singing. Probably the old couple lived on a small pension, or their modest income was derived from some investment. Every Monday morning, without fail, their weekly rent was placed into Ivy's eager hands. The money was always sealed up in a used envelope which also contained a slip of paper, on which was printed a pious verse or quotation.

Music was also provided by an Italian violinist who lived in a small room on the top floor of one of the houses. For hours on end this Paganini practised irritating "twiddly bits" and scales, but when he played pieces from his repertoire, it was a real treat to listen to him. What his name was, and where he performed, I never discovered, for he was a quiet, stand-offish person who always kept to himself, though when I passed him on the stairs or in the street, he always smiled and bowed a greeting. Once or twice, when I happened to be dining in Italian "dives" in Soho, I saw him there, over a glass of wine and food of his native land, conversing with countrymen who evidently were also artists.

In one of the front bed-sitting-rooms lived two old spinsters who might have come out of a Dickens novel. Both—twins, I believe—were dressed exactly alike, usually in black, with lace collars round their vulture necks. Small, thin, with waxen faces that were furrowed with a mass of wrinkles, both wore rimless spectacles over which, when not reading, knitting or sewing, they peeped at the world with distrustful, furtive eyes. Most of their spare time was spent dusting their room, polishing furniture, or shopping in the immediate neighbourhood.

Franz and Hans, two young Austrians, also ranked among the Gristins' "steadies." Both were accountants who had come to London in order to learn English. They worked somewhere in the City, and therefore were only visible on Saturday afternoons or on Sundays. Franz—a vain little runt with a peculiar, egg-shaped head and a fluffy, toothbrush moustache—thought he was the answer to a maiden's prayer, especially when he sported his best "City" clothes, i.e. striped trousers, a dark jacket, and a bowler hat, which accentuated the peculiar shape of his noddle. It was easy to tell when Franz had received his salary, for on such occasions he always wore his favourite suit. In the evening, after having bought himself a cheap cigar, he strutted off, puffing smoke into the air, and acting as if the whole world gaped at him with admiring eyes. His vanity was such that, whilst thus displaying himself, he ignored everyone, including even his room companion and friend, Hans. The latter was a jolly, happy-go-lucky and likeable creature. Whenever he drew his salary, his chief concern appeared to be to spend it quickly. Accordingly, for a few days he lived a champagne life on a beer salary. So long as his money lasted, fair-haired, good-looking young Hans was all merriment and laughter, whereas his room companion acted the part of an industrial magnate.

Another somewhat unsteady "steady" patron of the *Maison Gristin* was a young lady who described herself as an artists' model. This Venus de Milo and the Greek artist were on snarling terms. According to confidential reports issued by the Gristinian Information Service, the rift between the two originated when the great painter had tried to make the model pose for him "on tick."

It was by accident that I discovered how this girl earned her living.

Darkness had fallen on London, and a light mist and drizzle made me pull up the collar of my overcoat. As, in the West End, I passed a stone drinking-trough, a steaming horse which pulled an empty delivery van stopped to push his velvety nose into the water. Whilst, with dilated nostrils, he drank, I watched the gulps going down his sturdy neck. He was a fine specimen of Clydesdale, whose condition and well-polished brass ornaments spoke well for the driver. Lights were reflected in the wet surface of the street, and, like worker ants, pedestrians hurried along the pavements. The driver was lighting his pipe when the horse again lowered his head to satisfy his thirst. Obviously recognising someone who had halted behind me, the man said in a friendly tone of voice, "Good evening, miss. Chilly evening, but not too bad for this time of year."

A female voice returned the greeting, and presently a girl advanced to stroke the horse's broad forehead, and to propitiate him with a lump of sugar. Whilst he chewed it, the girl exchanged a few words with the driver, and then, to my surprise, I recognised the woman.

"Well, miss, must be goin' 'ome. 'Ope to see you again soon," the driver said, at the same time gathering up the reins. The horse arched his neck as he took the strain, and soon after the wagon disappeared from my view in the thickening veil of mist and drizzle.

For some time the Gristinian Venus de Milo stood, like a statue, her unseeing eyes fixed in the direction in which her two friends had disappeared. Presently, without recognising me, she slowly walked down the pavement to give her attention to passing men.

An attractive and vivacious young Frenchman, who was studying at the London School of Tropical Medicine, was on much friendlier terms with the Greek's pet aversion. Occasionally, when she was not away on professional engagements, and the student felt in need of relaxation, he took the young lady out; thus, no doubt, improving his English, or, perhaps, giving her a few glimpses into elementary French science. So much for the *Entente Cordiale*.

Literature, philosophy and sociology had a worthy representative in our row of lodging-houses. The avid reader, thinker—and, on occasions, public speaker, who often preached every kind of "ism," from anarchism downwards—was a bespectacled middle-aged Cockney, who was in the employ of the Metropolitan Water Board. Though he himself only used water for purposes of cleanliness, and despised every form of organised society, he did not consider it to be beneath his dignity to accept wages paid to him out of funds provided by ratepayers. For years, chiefly in public libraries, he had read every book on philosophy he could lay his hands on, with the alarming result that, when holding forth, he freely quoted Plato, Aristotle, Heraclitus, Zeno, Descartes, Rousseau, Kant, Schopenhauer, Spencer, Marx, and a host of others. Despite his Cockney accent and the difficulty he found in coping with "haitches"—which he dropped and picked up to insert in the wrong places, as should be the privilege of any free man—he had an amazing command of English. With pride, he often assured us listeners in the kitchen that on more than one occasion, in debates on the public platform, he had left George Bernard Shaw "stone cold"; a statement I never doubted, considering the hours he was able to speak, seemingly without drawing breath, excepting when he had difficulty with a particularly obstinate "h." Some years later, when, thanks to hard work and ability, our anarchist was made an inspector, the extra pay that went hand in hand with promotion had such a cooling, soothing and sobering effect on the former thunderer that he became a staunch Conservative. Had it not been that cancer intervened, his ever-growing collection of rare books would have become very valuable, and after his death would have fetched a considerable sum of money if put up for auction.

Another very different type of "ist" who sheltered his body and soul under one of the Gristins' benign roofs was one of the weirdest and most puzzling characters I have ever known.

Casually acquainted with him some years previously, I had forgotten all about the young man, when, one day, he buttonholed me near the Royal Exchange. As we greeted each other, I remembered that in former years he had enjoyed quite a reputation for being intelligent, and therefore I was not surprised when he informed me that he was in an excellent position on the administrative staff of a well-known firm in the City. Having conversed for a while, we parted in opposite directions, and as I strolled down Cheapside, indulging in a little window-shopping, I remembered that my old acquaintance—whom here I shall call Sophocles—had always been a dreamer, and that his chief hobby had been the study of philosophy. Standing there, near the Royal Exchange, though wearing an immaculate morning coat and top hat, the tall, slim and good-looking, though rather pale man brought to my mind paintings of saints or martyrs. I noticed a peculiar languour and sadness in his large, dreamy eyes and, as I strolled along, I could not help thinking that he was unhappy.

Time passed, and once more I had forgotten all about him, when one day I bumped into him in Moorgate Street. He informed me that since our last meeting he had married an actress, and he insisted on my going home with him to meet her. She was a good-looking though rather "dolled-up" girl, about twenty years of age, and it did not take me long to realise that her unconventionality was merely a pose, calculated to make her appear "interesting." However, she was pleasant, and the two appeared to be blissfully happy. Before leaving, I gave Sophocles my London address, and said that I hoped, some day, they would give me the pleasure of dining with me. I took good care to tell them that my "digs" were distinctly modest, and that, in consequence, I preferred not to entertain friends there.

Several months passed after this second meeting, and when I happened to be back in London on another school holiday, one morning Ivy came to my room to announce that "Apostle Paul" wished to see me at the front door. She was shaking with laughter, and when I asked her what the joke was about, she replied, "Stroof! Just go and 'ave a look, and you'll be seein' somefink funny!"

Wondering what game she was up to, I slowly went downstairs at any moment expecting someone to play a prank on me. Upon opening the door, I, too, laughed heartily. There, of all people in the world, stood Sophocles, wearing a kind of loose, flowing Grecian gown, ultramarine in colour, with light chrome yellow borders along the seams. The long, glossy black hair of what I took to be a wig was held in place with a red cord tied round the forehead, and upon looking at the lower section of this carnivalesque apparition, I noticed that its legs and feet were bare, though sandals afforded some measure of protection to the latter.

Whilst I laughed, Sophocles stood erect, stretching himself to his full height, and stared at me with a grand look of indignation. Down the road, some firemen stood in a group, watching, and even pointing towards us, evidently highly amused, and several street urchins gaped through the dilapidated iron fence of our diminutive front garden.

In a tone of voice that reminded me of a typical French dramatic actor, the pseudo-Athenian of the Dionysian period finally spoke thus:

"Enough of this, my friend! I perceive you do not understand! With your kind permission, let us go inside. Out of the vulgar gaze and hearing of common idlers I shall endeavour to explain."

Still laughing, and thinking that a practical joke was being played on me, I led Sophocles up to my room. Having seated himself on a rickety chair, he assumed the pose of a Cæsar on his throne, and began:

"Frankly, I am disappointed with you for laughing at me as you have done down below, and still are doing now. Really, I thought you were too intelligent for such light-hearted and vulgar behaviour. But let me come to what has brought me here. Thanks to a wonderful man, one of the outstanding intellects of modern times, about a year ago I started a new life. And now I have come to put it to you in the strongest terms of recommendation to do the same. But before going into details"—(at this juncture he coughed and drew his colourful gown tightly around his chest and mid-section)—"I must tell you that I am hungry."

To make a long story short, still under the impression that all this was a joke, I merely laughed. However, at long last, realising that Sophocles was dead serious, I suggested that we go down to the Gristins' kitchen, where lunch would be served in about half an hour's time.

Having informed me that he had given up all pernicious vices, such as smoking and drinking anything containing even the least trace of alcohol, and that he had cast aside the disgusting, degrading, and even dangerous habit of eating meat or fish, he politely refused my invitation to have a meal in the kitchen. When, instead, he proposed going to a nearby restaurant he had spotted on his way to call on me, the very thought of being seen in his company made me blush.

Remembering that on the previous evening, with Ivy's permission, the Italian violinist had cooked us an excellent dish of spaghetti, of which some was left over, I suggested heating it up on the gas-cooker in my room, and frying a few eggs. Gleefully, Sophocles agreed to this, so when all the necessaries had been borrowed from the obliging Ivy, I started cooking, whilst my visitor told me all about his recent odysseys, and how and why he had started a new life.

About a year previously he had listened to lectures that were given by Raymond Duncan, the brother of Isadora, the famous dancer. Money being not only the root of all evil, but totally unnecessary in this our miserable vale of toil and tears, in accordance with the brand-new Duncanian theory, philosophy, gospel, or whatever word suits the case, Sophocles had given all his worldly possessions to his wife, and had settled down to a kind of apostolic life, preaching æstheticism, agnosticism, anarchism, atheism—in fact, every anti-ism down to inverted snob-ism. Daily he spent hours "improving" his mind by reading books on philosophy and abstract matters, or meditating deeply. His spare hours were employed in making sandals or, on a primitive loom, weaving cloth wherewith to cover his precious body.

My visitor had been talking non-stop for well over an hour when he informed me that, being penniless, and having no home, it had occurred to him that I was the person to help him overcome his self-imposed difficulties, and thus it came about that Sophocles became a temporary lodger in the *Maison Gristin*. Money being taboo, according to his newly adopted creed, I, poor unphilosophic and uncouth mortal, for my ignorance and sins had to stump up for this modern Adonis, and with strictly vegetarian food keep his body and soul together.

Ida McA.—behind her back always called Ida McUgly—claimed once upon a time to have been a circus trick-rider. Very much on the wrong side of fifty severe winters, she was tall and so lean that, when viewed in persepctive, she brought to mind some fantastic bird belonging to the realm of a grotesque nightmare. Rarely in my life have I seen a face to be compared with Ida's for ugliness. It was Ivy who once suggested that an elephant must have given that veritable scarecrow's mother a fright, for Ida's nose was almost twice as long as her tremendous, thin and practically lipless mouth was wide. A pair of watery eyes reminded one of those of a cod, and the rouge and powder she smeared and dabbed over her high cheek-bones, long, sunken cheeks and the pouches under her eyes made her look like a painted gargoyle. No wonder she had to give up riding, for surely all but blind horses must have shied when she flipped and skipped into the sawdust ring. Whenever she came into the kitchen for warmth or food—which kind-hearted Ivy always gave her free of charge—she stiffly sat down at the piano to play and sing for us.

The poor soul never realised that her antics and screechy voice had us in fits of suppressed laughter. Having treated us to some of her favourite songs, she continued her recital by playing tunes, such as "Salut d'Amour," "The Maiden's Prayer," and others she remembered by heart.

When I knew her, by profession she was a kind of free-lance nursery-maid, or a "sitter-in." If people who had no servants or children's maids intended to go away for a day or two, or to be out until the early hours of morning, they called in our Ida to mind their offspring for them. As might be expected, the pay for such odd jobs was so small, and employment so irregular, that, as a side-line, the former circus *artiste* took rich ladies' lap-dogs for walks. In accordance with her meagre income, she lived in one of the brick sheds in the yard, where, with the ingenuity typical of her sex, she managed to make the place fairly comfortable. Owing to the dilapidated state of the roof, whenever it rained and the wind blew from a certain quarter she had to cover herself and her bed with one of those gigantic umbrellas used by commissionaires outside fashionable restaurants, stores, or West End clubs.

A stately old man, some ninety years of age, was another of the Gristins' "steady" lodgers. This highly educated, widely read and, mentally, still very alert patriarch had an arresting personality, though on occasions, when an excess of port wine went to his venerable head, he could be very snarky and biting. He grew a long snow-white beard, and his hair of the same colour hung down to his shoulders in strands. Though slightly bent with age, he was tall and thin, and a delicately chiselled, slightly aquiline nose and refined features left one in no doubt that he was a person of breeding. His garments consisted of a long, shabby, black overcoat, dark trousers, a pair of leather bedroom slippers and a battered top-hat, which he wore even indoors. He possessed no jacket, underwear, socks or shirts, but, in place of the last, wore a muffler.

Another of our community was Mr. Richard John David Jones of Aberdaron, who claimed to be of noble descent and was of middle age. Evidently he had seen better days, but was quite happy to be the "toff" in the small but select Gristinian community. He was the proud owner of only one more or less presentable suit and an old bowler hat, which was so greasy round the base of the crown that, in order to take off the shine, he occasionally treated it with soot. Considering himself to be the rightful claimant to a title which had fallen into abeyance at least a thousand years ago, whenever opportunity presented itself he showed us samples out of an old cardboard box that was filled with correspondence he had had concerning the lapsed title, including a number of letters he had received from the House of Lords. With pride he would also read out to us pages of a pamphlet he had written in connection with his claim to the dukedom, baronetcy, earldom or whatever it was of Aberdaron, or some such name.

Infallibly, weather conditions permitting, flat-footed, impecunious Richard John David Jones Esquire would sally forth, dressed in his best attire, yellow chamois leather gloves, spats and all, and wend his way towards Rotten Row, where he would solemnly doff his old bowler hat to passing riders he did not know. If by any chance King George V or some well-known member of the aristocracy or sporting world happened to be out on a little jaunt, the claimant to the title of Aberdaron would doff his hat with a special flourish, and bow deeply and with carefully studied elegance.

In those days Rotten Row was one of the favourite meeting places of the aristocracy. Smartly dressed riders, both male and female, often were followed by mounted grooms who wore top-hats with cockades. Riding in the "Row" amounted to almost a ceremony which was solemnly watched, especially on fine days, by people, most of whom were driven to Hyde Park in their carriages, later to seat themselves on chairs along the "Row," whence to gaze at the equestrian parade.

There were a number of other nondescript "steadies" in the *Maison Gristin*, but lest the reader become weary of my descriptions of them, I will mention only one more: our mystery man, the secret drinker.

As far as actual residence is concerned, he does not—in the Gristinian sense of the term—qualify as a "steady," but, as every six months he paid his rent in advance, I am placing him in the category of "steadies." His name, profession, or whence he came, no one knew, or bothered to discover, but for the sake of private identification, Bill and Ivy always referred to the mystery man as the "Gent." And he certainly looked and acted his part when, at intervals ranging between three or four months, he arrived to make his temporary residence in one of the larger back rooms on the ground floor of one of the annexes. This tallish, middle-aged, well-dressed and groomed man always drove up in a cab. Soon after his arrival, one or two wooden cases, and several smaller boxes, would be delivered by a well-known London store.

After his first stay at the Gristins, he purchased his own bed, furniture and rugs, all of excellent quality, and he also brought his own linen, blankets, eiderdown and other articles which, during his absence, were stored in a large trunk, the key of which was kept by the trustworthy Ivy. Once installed in his room, the "Gent" never left it, maybe for as long as a week. All the time he kept strictly on his own, drinking until one could hear him moan, groan or snore. Upon recovering from his alcoholic coma, again he imbibed until, as sporting Bill put it, he once more "took the count." On several occasions when our landlord thought the "Gent" must be dead, he forced open the door, only to find him stretched out on his bed, or on the floor, dead drunk.

When these prolonged drinking bouts came to an end, the "Gent," who by that time was a wreck, would call Ivy to give her the key of his room, whereafter he departed as mysteriously as he had arrived. Whilst tidying up his room, she always found a number of empty champagne, whisky and brandy bottles, besides others which had contained ginger ale and Vichy water. A few empty tins and cans were evidence that all the "Gent" had eaten during his stay was lobster, caviar, crab, butter and biscuits. Having cleaned out the room, Ivy would send sheets and pillow-slips to be washed, and when they came back from the laundry and had been carefully aired, they were stored in the large trunk, whereafter the room would be locked up until the "Gent" once more returned for a "booze-up," as the Gristins called the mystery man's solo drinking bouts.

With such and similar human material available, there were no dull moments in our lodging-houses.

Chapter III

Park Hill days.—A Cockney outing to Hampstead Heath.—About Sophocles and his philosophy.—Russian wrestlers in training.— "Moonlight flits" and other escapades.—Unwritten rules and regulations of the *Maison Gristin.*

THE main subject of these recollections being "Bohemia," all I will say about life in my preparatory school is that I always got on extremely well with the boys, Mr. Charles E. Ridout, the Headmaster, and with all the other members of the staff, though one or two of my colleagues were anything but entertaining. When, after holidays, I returned to the school, I was ready to set to work. It felt good to have at my sole disposal two large and beautifully furnished rooms, besides a study filled with books, and there was also a piano wherewith to entertain myself, though, surely, to the discomfort of anyone within hearing. Servants attended to all my needs, which were so few and simple that when, on rare occasions, I asked a small favour it was done with pleasure.

One of my great joys was riding through the beautiful New Forest, where at different times I saw a vagabond-like, bearded man. Friends who knew him informed me that he was W. H. Hudson, a naturalist and bird-watcher. At the time, little did I dream that his and my trails would cross again in different parts of the world, and that in later years I was to become a great admirer of that solitary wanderer in the forest.

Lest the Headmaster should come to visit me in London and unexpectedly turn up at the Gristins', perhaps at an awkward moment, I gave him several hints to the effect that, during the holidays, I did not exactly live with the cream of the aristocracy. Evidently he fully understood, for if at any time he came to London and wished to see me, one or two days previously he dropped me a line, inviting me to have lunch with him at his club. Quite apart from wishing to avoid what, under certain circumstances, might easily have led to an embarrassing situation if my Headmaster had visited me at the Gristins, my hints concerning the modest "digs" in which I lived in London were also intended to make him realise that I would not object if he offered me a higher salary. Perhaps, whenever I mildly broached this subject, my voice was so low that he could not hear me, but the fact remains that although my hints about the Gristins' place were understood, those regarding finance fell on deaf ears.

Still, as in those days I hardly ever smoked, and only very occasionally drank a glass of beer, my expenses were negligible, though, on this, that and the other necessity, my modest funds vanished, I don't know how.

Fortunately, the father of an ex-pupil who was at Eton—where he had failed to make the grade for the Upper School—asked me if I would consider coaching his boy during my next holidays. As it happened, the boy was particularly weak in mathematics, and as I must have been even weaker in this subject than he, I explained to his father that if I took his scion in hand, it would be wasting my time and his money, besides in no way helping the backward scholar. However, nothing would convince the father that I spoke the truth, and when the Headmaster joined in the debate, taking his side, I finally capitulated. Strange to relate, owing to a miracle—for which I certainly was not responsible—the boy passed his examinations, with the result that I received a highly flattering letter from the delighted parents. In addition to the fees paid to me for my holiday coaching, I was presented with a nice little cheque, which led to a typical Gristinian celebration—namely, an outing to Hampstead Heath.

Final preparations having been completed, late one Saturday night we all went to bed, hoping that on the morrow the weather would be fine. Many pies, stacks of sandwiches, an abundant supply of hard-boiled eggs, cakes, fruit, chocolate, sweets and similar things were packed into wicker baskets. An imposing row of beer bottles and others containing lemon and orange squash having been similarly dealt with, a large kettle and a primus stove, as well as its corresponding fuel were also packed, for, as far as some of the ladies were concerned, a picnic without tea would have been as dull as a whole day's gossiping without discussing some "shockin'" scandal.

Fortunately, weather conditions were ideal on Sunday morning, and when the prospective picnickers assembled in the backyard, a more mixed *omnium gatherum* could hardly be imagined. The complete Gristin family, several of their relatives and friends, some with their children and even dogs, and a number of the lodgers were assembled when Field-marshal Bill called the roll. Prominent among the "steadies" was Ida, the ex-circus *artiste*, dressed up and painted in the most fantastic manner, and looking more hideous than ever. The Greek painter, Jones of Aberdaron (the "Toff"), the Austrians, Franz and Hans, the Metropolitan Water Board anarchist and philosopher, and one of my schoolmaster friends shouted "Present!" when their names were called out. Sophocles, the patriarch, the two spinsters, the Italian violinist, the Reverend Crimpus Jilt, and the hymn-singing Welsh couple had politely refused the invitation to so frivolous and undignified an outing.

Evidently they preferred to spend their time in deep meditation, practising their art or singing piously, as befitted a Sabbath Day. In the case of Crimpie, the French *médico* and the artist's model, we had our suspicions why they declined the invitation to join our merry and noisy throng. On the other hand, several temporary lodgers were on the spot, all looking forward to having a lot of fun, and to be at liberty to stuff themselves full of food, and to drink to their hearts' content. Two gigantic, "beefy" Russian wrestlers—who happened to be lodging at the Gristins'—were there, making the rest of us look like mere pigmies. With awe and admiration, the children looked at the Herculean figures with their shaven bullet heads and taurine necks. Despite their size and evident muscular strength, the two Russians—who spoke only a few words of English —were so shy that whenever someone spoke to them they blushed and nervously "dry-washed" their ursine paws, and, instead of replying, grinned like two animated yellow jade Buddhas.

Hobble skirts and large hats were the feminine fashion at the time, so several of the women wore such strait-jacket-like garments that walking was difficult for them. Ivy sported a very "loud" dress, the bright red colour of which struck the eye as the blare of a trumpet affects the ear. Of course, her hat was adorned with flowing ostrich feathers, without which she would have felt undressed. Bill wore a black-and-white check suit, and a grey trilby placed on his curly head at a rakish angle made him look very breezy indeed. Having commanded some of us men to carry baskets, rugs and other things, he gave marching orders, whereupon we all trooped out into the street. When an open-topped 'bus came to a halt, snorting with steam hissing out of the radiator, and shaking like a bronco being saddled for the first time, the ladies and children fairly scrambled into it, but in the case of one or two particularly tight hobble skirts, their wearers almost had to be lifted. This led to a great deal of merriment, laughter and screaming—fun the 'bus conductor enjoyed as much as everyone else. Baskets having been loaded, when everything was ready, the conductor pulled the greasy bell-cord to give the driver the signal to start. When the former came to collect fares, and beheld Ida McUgly sitting there, stiffly, like a broomstick, and had a good look at her incredibly over-painted face, he turned to me and Bill, winked an eye, and speaking through the corner of his mouth asked, "Oy, where yer goin' to shoot it?"

In reply, Bill threw back his head, opened his mouth wide, and laughed until he was red and blue in the face, but as everyone else was making a great noise, no one bothered to ask what was the cause of such boisterous hilarity. And so the old 'bus bumped and rattled along until we reached the end of the run, whence a short walk took us to our ultimate destination on the Heath, where, after some exploring, we decided to camp in a secluded hollow. Even before rugs were spread out on the grass, the children made a mass attack on pies and sandwiches, soon after to be joined by the grown-ups, all of whom acted as if they had not eaten for a week. Though most of the time mouths were so full that speech was difficult, there was much joking, good-humoured teasing and laughter. After the meal, in order to "work down" the food, a football match was arranged. Even some of the women unbuttoned their hobble skirts to join in, and it was most amusing to see the two huge lumbering

Russians being charged by boys and girls who made no more
impression on them than if they had attempted to push Landseer's
Trafalgar Square lions off their pedestals. The match concluded, a
game of blind man's buff provided more fun, and later, when the
women decided that the time had come to prepare tea, some of us
men pretended to be going for a walk. On the sly, Bill had passed
round the tip that this was to end at the "Bull and Bush," the
famous old public-house which, alas! since those days has been
renovated and modernised.

In due time, we deserters assembled at the bar, where Bill ordered
pints of beer, which the Russians fairly "knocked back" in one gulp,
to them a simple feat which they repeated every time a pint was
placed before them. Seeing the gusto and ease with which the
two giants manhandled their drinks, Bill and I thought it would be
a great joke to make them drunk, so we suggested they "lace" their
beer with whisky, an idea they took up with great enthusiasm.

Soon, tired of beer, both switched over to double whiskies we
offered them. In those days a "double whack" only cost 6d., and so,
for a while, it was a pleasure to watch round after round disappear
into the two seemingly bottomless pits. When the Russians had
dealt with about a dozen drinks apiece, Bill looked at me, amazed
and bewildered, for our guests were still as fresh as daisies, and, with
feline expressions on their Mongolian faces, silently waited for the
next round. Our intended joke turned out so ineffectual and expensive that we decided to rejoin the women and children, and to let
the wrestlers come to grips with as much of the beer we had brought
with us as they could hold. This again proved to be child's play to
the two Gargantuas, who saw to it that no food or drinks should be
wasted, or have to be carried back to Ivy's kitchen.

Sunburnt, tired and sleepy, we made tracks for home, and while
some of the women and children returned to the *Maison Gristin*, we
men went to a "local," where the Russians once more demonstrated
to us that, as far as they were concerned, whisky had no more
"kick" than water. Whilst our Metropolitan Water Board anarchist
and philosopher enlightened a group of his bar-room acquaintances
with a profound lecture, Bill and some of his friends broke out in

song, and when the time came to leave, arm in arm, forming a line across the street, we marched along, singing the at that time popular song:

> *We all go the same way home,*
> *All the whole collection,*
> *In the same direction.*
> *We all go the same way home,*
> *So there's no need to part at all.*
> *We all go the same way home,*
> *Let's be gay and hearty,*
> *Don't break up the party,*
> *And we all cling together like the ivy*
> *On the old garden wall.*

To prove to the universe that they were musical, Bill and the Water Board man reserved their full lung-power for the last four notes, which they sang "in lovely 'armony."

·　　　·　　　·　　　·　　　·

Every now and again, on Sunday mornings, a small gang of us would go to the Jewish market in Petticoat Lane, in the East End of London. In those days it was jokingly said about that picturesque and extremely lively market, that upon entering it at one end of the long and narrow street, a pickpocket would relieve the visitor of his watch or handkerchief which, upon reaching the other end of the market, their owner would see being offered for sale on some stall. Whenever Bill accompanied us, he lamented that "Dirty Dick's" bar, near Liverpool Street Station, was closed on Sundays. Formerly the atmosphere in this weird establishment was much more genuine than it has ever been since a fire practically gutted it, for after that event, in order to attract visitors, cobwebs, dust, dried-up cats, rats, and what have you were replaced by new ones.

In Petticoat Lane, almost everything from doubtful jewellery and gold watches down to old rags were sold, and in nearby Club Row, animals, poultry and caged birds of every description were on sale in great numbers. There, one Sunday morning, I bought myself a very nice-looking, though rather dirty, rough-haired fox terrier. Upon returning home, the first thing I did was to give the little chap a good bath. Whilst rinsing down the lather of carbolic soap, to my astonishment—and to the two or three bystanders' malicious delight—it dawned on me that I had been "had," for what in Club Row had appeared to be a more or less pure bred though dirty rough-haired fox terrier, now turned out to be a kind of omnibus edition of various terrier breeds. Still, I had only paid 10s. for the puppy, and as the poor little creature already seemed to have attached itself to me, I overlooked such trifles as colour and breed. Even in the Underground train, whilst on my way home, I had made up my mind to call the puppy "Chips," so when, after the ordeal of the bath and a good rub-down with a towel, I let the little rascal loose in the backyard, whenever called by his new name he knew that it was meant for him. After a spell of running about, yapping and rolling in the sooty dust, all my recent work was undone, but within a few days little Chips had improved his ways and habits. Later, when I took him to school with me, he became a great favourite among the boys, chiefly on account of his passion for football, a game at which he excelled, though his idea of it was to keep the ball to himself. Golf he also enjoyed in a similar manner, stealing any ball he saw rolling or bouncing along a fairway. Therefore, whenever I took him with me, he had to be kept on a leash, and I only let him loose in order to join in the search for any lost ball. After a little practice, he became such an expert retriever that, no matter how cunningly a golf ball hid itself, he usually found it.

Lectures given to me by Sophocles and the Metropolitan Water Board philosopher broadened my views on life in the abstract to such an extent that, whenever I could not avoid listening to them, I did not know whether I was standing on my head or on my feet. These two stupendous thinkers only met once in open debate. On that memorable occasion, as often happens when great "osophers," "ologists" and "ogians" discuss their pet subjects, the two promptly disagreed to such an extent that, as if chilled to his very soul, the Duncanian London-Greek wrapped his flowing robe tightly around himself, and with sad, compassionate eyes raised towards heaven, hurried away to meditate until I should supply him with another instalment of pure, vegetarian food. When the time came, Sophocles seriously warned me against the dangers of allowing myself to be influenced by the Water Board man's crude views, and even cruder language, and he implored me to allow him (Sophocles) to introduce me to his mentor, Raymond Duncan. He assured me that such a meeting would make me see the truth, and that, thereafter, a new life would begin for me.

As, according to my ideas and standards of comfort, the English climate is not suitable for Grecian robes such as my interlocutor wore, and I had no intention of changing my garments for any others, I kept on putting off the proposed meeting. Quite apart from fancy attire, it struck me that if I followed in Duncan's footsteps, and gave away all my worldly possessions, both Sophocles and I would have to live on philosophy and air, and as the latter can be quite chilly at times, making it necessary to heat rooms in London, it would be difficult to find pennies for insertion into the soulless gas-meter. Even if I walked out of my school and gave my few possessions to the materially poor and greedy, I could not visualise myself at a loom, patiently weaving cloth wherewith to make a Grecian robe for myself. Furthermore, where would I find, not only the material with which to make a loom, but also the silk, wool or cotton destined ultimately to be fashioned into a robe? Of course, if allowed by the guardians of law and order, I could have emulated Diogenes, making my abode in some abandoned tub in a vacant lot, but I feared that if some modern Alexander the Great came to visit me, the conversation reputed to have been held over two thousand years ago between the two great men would take a very different turn, and that, without ceremony I would be charged and run in for "wandering abroad." With such and similar fears at the back of my mind, I was not keen on making the proposed experiment, and by far preferred to look after Sophocles' physical welfare, an expense which, after all, was not exactly ruinous. As will be seen later, I was to learn a great deal about the new Duncanian movement.

· · · · ·

Some of the temporary lodgers provided us cruder and more materially-minded Gristinians with the necessary change to make life in our "digs" interesting, and sometimes even exciting. For instance, one day the two Russian wrestlers—who shared a room on the top floor of the *maison du patron*—took it into their shaven bullet heads to do something very foolish and dangerous.

I happened to be in the kitchen below, talking to Bill and Ivy when, suddenly, we thought an earthquake was about to devastate London. The whole rickety old house shook so alarmingly, that, fearing it was about to collapse and bury us under a heap of rubble, we rushed to seek safety in the open. Having recovered from our first fright, we looked round. To our relief, all the houses within view were still standing intact, and in a big old tree in the back yard, sparrows were holding parliament as usual. We were still wondering what had caused the violent tremor when, again, another terrific crash and thump shook the house to its foundation.

Thinking that, perhaps, some phenomenally noisy and boisterous poltergeist had invaded the place, I cautiously followed Bill to investigate what was amiss. As we gingerly went up the narrow, creaky wooden stairs with their prehistoric strip of worn-out linoleum—the holes in which threatened our feet with entanglement—another terrific crash shook the old house, and then we came to the conclusion that something terrible must be happening in the Russians' room. After having peeped through the keyhole, Bill flabbergasted me with a rapid display of courage, such as, hitherto, I had only read about in books, or had seen enacted on the stage. With a rapid movement, he flung open the door, and rushed into the room, just as another violent crash threatened to cause the collapse of the house. To my amazement, I saw the two gigantic Russians, stark naked, on the floor, tightly locked together in a classical wrestling position, growling and snorting as they heaved, pulled, pushed, twisted and groped for a new grip on each other.

Casting aside all caution, I helped Bill to separate the two gorillas, who, upon rising, stood puffing and panting, and looking at us with Mongolian grins fixed on their broad faces.

"Stop monkeyin' abaht!" Bill shouted. "If you go on like this,

you'll 'ave the bleedin' old 'ouse dahn. Understand? . . . Like this
. . . crash, bang!"

After a short pause during which the two continued to grin and
pant, Bill exclaimed, "If it's exercise you want, I'll give you plenty.
Come on, you so-and-sos, put on your trousers, and I'll give you
some 'ard work to do."

Saying this, he picked up the wrestlers' trousers, and with a sign
asked the two cave-men to put them on. This having been done, he
led the way downstairs, and into the backyard, where, having
fetched and handed to them a two-handed saw and an axe apiece,
he told them to fell and cut up a large old tree, the spreading roots
of which were threatening to break down a garden wall. Laughing,
and spitting on the palms of his hands, Bill went through the motions
of sawing, and then, pushing the Russians towards the doomed
tree, said, "Go on. Let's see you do your bleedin' stuff!"

When the two realised what he wanted them to do, and that he
was quite serious about felling the tree, they set to work with indescribable vigour. Within some three hours the big tree was felled,
the trunk and all its stout branches cut into sections, and these,
together with twigs and smaller branches, were neatly stacked
against the garden wall. In the evening, when Bill came home from
one of his "big" jobs, he took the two lumberjacks to the "local,"
but, bitter experience having taught him that to give the Russians
a more or less satisfactory fill of whisky worked out very expensive,
this time he treated them only to several pints of beer. After this,
until the two wrestlers returned to their homeland, whenever Bill
had some really heavy work to do, he called them to his assistance.

Every now and then, in choice language which varied according
to the seriousness of the case, Ivy would report that a temporary
lodger had made a "moonlight flit"—that is to say, that during the
night he or she had disappeared without paying the rent, or other
minor debts, such as pennies borrowed for the gas-meter.

For sheer, low cunning in "doin' a bunk," as Bill called disappearing without taking proper leave of him or his wife, a certain
well-dressed and prosperous-looking gentleman distinguished
himself above all others. Previously, some of the worst offenders

made off into the night, taking with them pillow-slips, blankets and other odds and ends. However, there was nothing like this about the gentleman who, having become almost a "steady" let his rent accumulate. After about three weeks, when Ivy tactfully reminded him that quite a bit of rent was due, he grandly informed her that he preferred to settle his financial obligations every quarter. As, according to her, he "looked ever so nice, and every bit a gent," she agreed to his proposal. After all, besides being well dressed, quiet and reserved, he possessed a large travelling trunk—the biggest she had ever seen a lodger bring into any of her houses—and, besides this, he had a hat box and two leather suitcases, the quality of which could leave one in no doubt that money offered no serious problem to their owner.

One day he informed Ivy that important business made it imperative for him to rush to New York, where he would have to remain for a week or two. He said that he would be most grateful if, during his temporary absence, she would be good enough to keep an eye on his room, especially on the trunk, which, he whispered to her in confidence, was filled with valuable articles, among them some family heirlooms which, though of no special intrinsic value, he treasured greatly.

Taking with him his two suitcases and the hat box, he hailed a cab, and soon disappeared in the direction of Victoria Station. When Ivy went up to his room to tidy up things, and to lock the door, the nasty suspicion assailed her that, perhaps, the "ever so nice gent" had done the "dirty" on her, but when she saw the large trunk, and remembered what its owner had told her about some of its contents, she reproached herself for having given way to nasty thoughts concerning so serious and polite a person. However, in order to make quite sure, whilst dusting the room she could not resist the temptation of testing the weight of the trunk. To her great satisfaction, it proved to be so heavy that she was unable to lift it, so she locked the door, and went to hide the key.

Time passed. Several prospective lodgers had to be turned away on the grounds that not a single room was vacant; and still the owner of the trunk did not return from New York. Discussing the puzzling situation with his wife and me, Bill suggested that, most likely, the absentee had done such a good deal that he had prolonged his stay in America, and that thence, in due time, he would return full of "dough."

It was only when I returned to London for my next school holidays that Bill and Ivy reluctantly decided to let the "nice man's" room to someone else; but only on the condition that, should the long-overdue traveller return, the new lodger should sleep in the kitchen, where it would be easy to "rig up" some kind of bed. In order to make quite sure that nothing should happen to the absent business-man's trunk, conscientious Ivy asked me to help her husband shift it to their room, where it would be safe. Accordingly, the two of us went to do as requested, but upon attempting to lift the trunk, we found it to be so heavy that, despite using all our strength, we could not even drag it along the floor.

With a typical Cockney oath, Bill kicked the trunk with one foot, and when this made a suspiciously hollow sound, he looked at me with a most peculiar expression on his face.

"Strewth! I wonder if the . . ." he spluttered, and with this rushed out of the room, soon after to return with a hammer and a heavy screwdriver, with which he feverishly set to work to force open the trunk's two brass locks. And lo and behold, when we gazed into it, to our amazement we discovered that it was empty, and that the "ever so nice" business man had firmly fixed the trunk to the floor with four screws. What Bill said for the next few minutes, I only remember in part, but I clearly recall the frequency with which he used his two favourite adjectives. Presently, seeing the funny side of things, he laughed with me until our ribs ached.

It must not be thought that any person applying for lodgings at the Gristins' place was received with open arms. Oh, no; Bill and Ivy were born psychologists, and they had their strong likes and dislikes for certain types of people. Tolerant and liberal in the true sense of the words, they gave credit where credit was due, but, being only human, and therefore not infallible, occasionally they mis-judged a person. When opinions and feelings concerning a "rotter" were aired—without evasion, equivocation or mental reservation of any kind—it was an education to listen to the ease and conviction with which Bill and Ivy could express themselves.

Effeminate men, masculine women, or young ladies who were just a little too feminine for the Gristins' approval were always turned away from their door with the excuse that every room in their establishment was occupied; for, as Bill repeatedly and emphatically stated, he did not want "any of that there 'ere," and so long as it was within his power to prevent it, he "wasn't goin' to 'ave no scandal on 'is pitch." Still, despite his and Ivy's good judgment of human beings, several slippery eels managed to wriggle through the fine mesh of the Gristinian psycho-analytical net. For getting rid of such undesirables, my landlord had various most efficient forms of technique. Usually, he would simply give the unwanted lodger a week's notice to quit, saying that a sister of his, who recently had undergone a major operation in some London hospital, needed the room for the purpose of convalescence.

Lest the gentle reader should get the erroneous impression that I spent most of my time with the Gristins and their peculiar assortment of lodgers, in the next chapter I shall endeavour to show that this was not the case, for during my frequent wanderings through London I associated with many other people in different spheres of society and activity. Perhaps what might be called the Gristinian phase of my education gave me a mild insight into life in the raw, besides teaching me how to enjoy it with little money at my disposal. As will be seen later, at about that time, other hitherto more or less dormant propensities were also awakened within me, chiefly due to a series of extraordinary circumstances which brought me into contact with many other people who make up the variegated scale of human society.

Chapter IV

VARIETY being said to be the spice of life, whenever I was in need of a change, London provided ample opportunities. If the cave-man within me called for entertainment, there were boxing, wrestling and football matches to go to, or if I was in a more genteel mood, admittance to art galleries was free, and theatres and concert halls not prohibitive, provided I was satisfied to go up to the "gods," or *poulailler*, as that heavenly place is more descriptively called in French. As far as theatres were concerned, there were two flies in the ointment—namely, Sophocles and Stintall, one of the two schoolmasters who lodged at the Gristins'. Whenever they insisted on accompanying me, it was always I who paid for their tickets, as well as, after the performance, for fried fish and chips or sausage, onions and mash. In the case of the vegetarian Sophocles, the finding of suitable refreshments and sustenance for his sensitive soul and body presented serious problems, besides as far as I was concerned, often leading to profound embarrassment. He himself, living on a high plane, far far above the vulgar rabble, paid no heed to rude remarks passers-by shouted at him, whereas I, blushing and with cold perspiration oozing out of my pores, hoped the ground would open and swallow me. If we found a small eating place where fruit, milk, butter, eggs and certain kinds of cheese were obtainable, Sophocles would lead the way in. Whilst patrons stopped eating to snigger, or with open mouths to gape at the Grecian apparition, he would go to the counter and ask if any wholemeal bread was obtainable. If the answer happened to be in the negative, he sadly shook his head, turned on the flat soles of his sandals, and, throwing a section of his flowing robe over a shoulder, floated out, patiently to continue the search for the only kind of bread fit for super-human consumption.

In view of such and similar trials, whenever possible I went to shows alone, but it was no easy matter to dodge my hangers-on. Occasionally, wealthy parents of pupils invited me to dine in their sumptuous homes, and sometimes to accompany them to a theatre or concert. Dressed in my "glad rags," I felt like a Crœsus, but the one fly in the ointment were the tips I had to give, for as these had to be on a level with my "affluence," they invariably "bent" my budget badly.

One night, when thus invited and, after a performance, I was waiting together with my hosts outside the Covent Garden Opera House for their carriage to pick us up, then and there I had a shock which froze me to the marrow.

We happened to be talking about the evening's presentation of *Il Trovatore*, when a voice I recognised addressed me from behind. "Good evening, friend, I hope you enjoyed the opera. Speaking for myself, I did not; for artistic reasons, I shall endeavour to explain to you in due time."

"Who is this interesting-looking man?" my hosts whispered to me, as none other than Sophocles sandalled away in the company of a well-dressed elderly lady, who gazed up at him as if he were a demi-god.

"Oh, just an acquaintance," I stammered. "He is . . . well, how shall I put it . . . a kind of crank, or idealist . . . somewhat strange. . . . I don't quite know how to explain."

"How romantic!" my hostess exclaimed. "For a moment I thought it was Duncan.

"Duncan? Do you know him?" I asked.

"Rather! I met him at Lady So-and-So's, when he gave a divine lecture in her *salon*. What a striking figure of a man! How good-looking, and how intelligent!"

By this time the carriage had driven up, and the footman, with a heavy rug folded over one forearm, held open the door for us to enter.

Until late that night my hosts and I chatted over refreshments served in their drawing-room, and whilst her husband yawned and looked visibly bored, she raved about Duncan until I almost began to believe that Sophocles must have been right in his eulogies of him. On my way home, I thought of asking Sophocles to introduce me to his mentor, but when I happened to see a poster announcing that on the morrow two well-known gentlemen in the punch and cauliflower trade were to clash in Blackfriars Ring, then and there I decided that it would be much more exciting, and less fatiguing, to watch punches being exchanged than to listen to Duncan.

Upon arriving at my "digs," I found Sophocles sitting in the darkness of my room, waiting for me to insert a penny into the gas-meter. When the miracle of producing light with a coin—which he so deeply despised—had been performed, he opened a tin of Nestlés condensed milk wherewith to prepare a cup of cocoa. Whilst this was in process of being made, he gave me a lecture on music, voice-production and décor, all of which, according to the speaker, had been massacred and prostituted by modern civilisation and commerce. When, in order to change the one-sided conversation, I asked who had taken him to the opera that night, he sadly told me that it was a rich and kindly soul, who would never learn to appreciate the really fine things in life. Having said this, he began to sip his cocoa, and whilst he deeply meditated over it, I undressed, went to bed, and turned over to dream material and shockingly concrete dreams about vulgar commercial upper-cuts, jabs, hooks, swings, "pile-drivers," and highly artistic knock-outs which I hoped to see next day.

On the assumption that every normal baby arrives in this world squealing, kicking its frail bow legs, and waving about its little arms, usually with tightly-clenched fists, soon after vociferously to clamour for sustenance, I will begin by recounting episodes connected with my fistic education.

Although, when a boy, I was a bit of a scrapper, it was only during my early twenties that I began to aspire to an honours degree in the fistic art. Whilst engaged in such "academic" studies, I was often brought into much too close physical contact with professors, by the vulgar frequently called "bruisers." Perhaps, if I wished to put the blame on someone else for the innumerable punches I received, and also dealt out, in various boxing rings, my finger of accusation would point straight at Sophocles, and at tight-pursed Stintall, from whom, for reasons previously explained, I frequently had to flee. Also, perhaps, an impartial judge and jury might censure my good Headmaster for not having paid me a higher salary for educational services rendered.

Be this as it may, the fact remains that, on the day after having attended the performance of *Il Trovatore*, instead of allowing Sophocles to lead me before his mentor, the great Duncan, I sneaked out of my "digs" into the mists of night, about half an hour later to mix with a crowd of "toughs" in Blackfriars Ring.

In two senses of the word, the atmosphere in the place differed greatly from that of the National Sporting Club, to which I had been invited on two or three occasions. By far the most oustanding boxer I have ever seen in action there—and, for the matter of that, in any of the many rings I have visited since then in different parts of the world, including Madison Square Gardens and other fistic arenas in the U.S.A., on the Continent and in South America—was that diminutive, pale-faced, and weak-looking human whirlwind, Jimmy Wilde. Those were the days of Bombardier Wells—before Georges Carpentier came on the scene—Colin Bell, Pedlar Palmer, Gunner Moir, Johnnie Summers, Willie Farrell, Bandsman Blake, Jim Driscoll, to mention only a few of the British crop. Then, of course, there were redoubtable Americans, such as Jack Johnson, Sam McVea, Sam Langford, and the "Pittsburgh Dentist," Frank Moran, who evidently found the knocking-out of teeth much more profitable and entertaining—as far as he was concerned—than the scientific extraction of such, and the "fiddling" job of filling in cavities, fitting on plates, and making bridges. But to return to Blackfriars Ring. As I took my seat among the crowd of mostly good-humoured, though exceedingly keen, spectators, little did I dream that Fate had something in store for me that night.

It all happened in a curious and most unexpected manner when, between rounds of a particularly lifeless preliminary bout—during which two middle-weights, in order not to hurt each other, all but played a game of kiss-in-the-ring—I turned to one of my immediate neighbours and told him that, if given a chance, I would not mind betting that I could beat either of the two mugs in the ring. As it happened, the man to whom I thus bragged turned out to be the father of one of the contestants; and, therefore, what he snarled at me is best left unwritten.

As he happened to be in the company of several friends, the ensuing storm of indignation and abuse to which I was subjected was such that all the spectators who were seated near us looked on and listened, but, fortunately, the time-keeper's gong acted like oil on a raging sea. For the next three long minutes, as I pretended to be tremendously interested in what was going on in the ring, I wished I had stayed with Sophocles, for had this been the case, instead of having got myself into a nasty jam, I would then have been listening to words of profound wisdom emanating from the mouth of Duncan.

When the round, and with it the preliminary bout, came to an end, and the unshaven old "plug-ugly" who acted as referee raised the victor's arm, blood-curdling yells of triumph and wild cheers greeted the decision, especially from our side of the ring where, obviously, most of his supporters were seated. When I thought the recent storm had completely blown over, the offended father at my side, caught hold of the lapels of my jacket, pulled me towards him, and growled into my face that he wanted to see me after the last fight, and that he wanted to introduce me to his son, 'Arry, who, no doubt, would be interested to hear repeated what I had said about his abilities as a fighter.

In a tone of assumed indifference—which even to me sounded most unconvincing—I replied that, being in no hurry to return home, I had plenty of time.

The main event between two mediocre "sloggers" proved to be lively, until one of the contestants had to retire owing to a sprained ankle, whereafter everybody rose to push their way out into the street. Several of the "toughs" who bore me a grudge wedged me in, and when we reached the open, led the way to a nearby public-house. To my astonishment, when one of my escort ordered a round of beer, I was included. After a while, 'Arry joined the little gathering, and when I saw him at close quarters, dressed in a shabby suit and wearing a muffler and cap, I was disillusioned. In the ring, the strong light of arc lamps had made him look passable, but now he gave me the impression of being anything but an athlete.

I still wondered what was to happen, when his father stepped forward and in most expressive words told his son what I had said in the arena.

Having wound up his speech for the prosecution, 'Arry Senior pushed a challenging, unshaven chin towards his son, and asked what he was going to do "abaht" it.

Looking at me threateningly, with a contemptuous sneer, and speaking through a corner of his mouth, Junior informed me that, were it not for the fact that we were in a "classy public-'ouse," he'd knock my something block off.

Following Napoleon's maxim that offensive is the best defensive, I agreed that the public-house in which we were was much too respectable for a brawl, and suggested that, perhaps, at some future date we might arrange to settle our differences in the only correct and proper manner—namely, in a boxing ring.

Noticing my peculiar accent, one of the bystanders, who evidently had a keen ear, interjected that he felt sure I was a —— Irishman.

At last it looked as if we were getting somewhere, so after I had ordered another round of beer, we gradually came down to real business. Eventually it was arranged that, as a novice, I should formally challenge young 'Arry to a fight. The next items to be considered were the side-stake and deposit, without which the prospective world champion flatly refused to step into any ring. At this juncture, I breathed only with difficulty, and felt as if there were a nasty hollow in my stomach. Before leaving the Gristins' place I had put only about 30s. into my pocket, and as five or six of these had already been spent, and I expected the deposit about to be proposed would be a sum corresponding to the high esteem in which the matchmakers held my opponent, I felt very uneasy.

Things became even more embarrassing for me when 'Arry Senior went away, a few moments later to return with a stout middle-aged man who was introduced to me as the proprietor of the "pub."

The appearance of so important a personage threw a solemn hush over the little assembly, but having no time to lose on ceremony, he immediately came down to business.

" 'Ow much is it to be? Come on, quick, I ain't got no time to waste," he said, impatiently.

Putting it briefly, the following agreement was reached:

1. Young 'Arry and I were to deposit one "Jimmy," i.e. one £1 sterling apiece with the publican.

2. Should either of the parties fail to appear on the date and at the time when the match was to take place, "the bloke what did not turn up" was to forfeit his deposit.

3. The side-stake was to amount to a further four "Jimmies" apiece, and this money was to be handed over, by both parties, to the referee, before the opponents stepped into the ring.

4. After the match, the winner would take the lot, deposits and side-stakes, i.e. thus winning five "Jimmies."

5. In the event of the match ending in a draw, both parties were to get their money back, i.e. deposit and side-stake, amounting, as previously stated, to five pounds apiece.

Unlike most so-called "gentlemen's agreements"—usually made between parties who distrust one another—this one was entirely verbal, and, therefore, red or blue silk ribbons, imposing seals and signatures affixed with ink out of a platinum or gold inkstand were unnecessary. Having put our respective deposits into an envelope, without further ceremony the "boss" went behind the counter to put it into a drawer, and when one of our party handed him a drink, he raised his glass and, addressing 'Arry Junior and me, said, " 'Ere's to you, gentlemen. May the best man win."

Whilst watching him drink, I could not help wondering if by "best" he meant to insinuate that someone else would take part in the proposed fight, or if, by any chance, this was merely a kind of grammatical finesse to hint that he intended to stick to the £2.

After having put their heads together, my prospective opponent and his several advisers informed me that, barring unforeseen circumstances, the fight would take place ten days hence, in a little

boxing arena known as the West London Stadium, situated in
Church Street, off the Edgware Road. Its address and the approxi-
mate time when the clash was to materialise having been scribbled
on a piece of paper and handed to me, I was allowed to depart,
though not without serious warning concerning what would be
done to me if I failed to make an appearance.

On my way home, I wondered if it would not be wiser and
healthier for me to forfeit my deposit, and simply not present myself for the fight. However, upon turning the matter over in my
mind, it struck me that it would be a pity to miss such a golden
opportunity for a little excitement and adventure. After all, I argued
with myself, if the worst should come to the worst, a good hiding
in a boxing ring could do me no great harm and, furthermore,
'Arry had not impressed me as being quite the type of young man
to punch me into a mass of pulp.

Later, whilst lying in bed, thinking over things, I decided to tell
no one about what had happened to me that night, let alone to ask
any of my friends to accompany me on the day when my first fight
in a public arena was to take place. Supposing I had underestimated
'Arry's fighting abilities, and he gave me a sound hiding? Oh no,
I would not give my "supporters" a chance to laugh at my expense.
With this in mind, I kept my secret, and on the appointed day
presented myself at the hall, outside the entrance to which the
Blackfriars gang waited for me. In a small bag I carried a sweater,
a pair of boxing boots and trunks I had bought at Gamages' store,
and as a precaution I also brought with me a clean towel, some
sticking plaster and a small bottle filled with pure alcohol.

'Arry Senior—who tried hard to look eminently business-like,
and who acted as spokesman for his chip of the old block—informed
me that, although I was a complete outsider, and totally unknown
to the "blokes in the game," thanks to his influence, it had been
arranged that young 'Arry and I should stage one of the preliminary
bouts, and that ours was to be of six rounds of three minutes each.

Presently, we made our way into a fair-sized though rather narrow
hall, in which a number of spectators were already seated, talking
loudly and smoking like so many volcanoes in eruption. Having

been guided to a dirty dressing-room, in which several young men were busy undressing themselves, I was told to do likewise. In whispers, shabbily dressed and be-muffled "trainers" were giving advice to their "pupils," who, acting as if they agreed with what they were told, every now and again nodded their heads. Whilst slowly taking off my clothes, and putting on my new boxing boots and trunks, I watched what was going on round me. What interested me most was the care and solemnity with which 'Arry's retinue attended to their protégé's comforts and needs. Bandages having been wound round his hands as if they were made of Venetian glass, he was massaged by three pairs of hands. Whilst this was going on, and no one took any notice of me, I slipped a half sovereign—which I had brought with me as a reserve—into one of my boxing boots, leaving only a few pennies to the mercy of any possible marauder who might enter the dressing-room during my temporary absence.

After a while, the first two gladiators were called out to do their "stuff," and I was about to go out into the hall, in order to see the opening bout being fought, when 'Arry Senior reminded me that we had not yet fixed up about the "brass."

"Oh, yes, I almost forgot about that," I replied; whereafter he called in a quite pleasant though tough-looking man who answered to the name of Charlie. His general demeanour, as well as his none-too-clean white flannel trousers, sweater and tennis shoes, led me to guess that the new arrival must be some kind of ring official.

" 'Ere's the bloke I told you abaht," old 'Arry said to him, pointing at me. Having introduced me to the man in white, old 'Arry informed me that the newcomer was going to act as referee, and that in the capacity of such, I was to hand over to him my side stake of four "jimmies."

Having received our respective four golden sovereigns—mine, about which I had almost forgotten were inside a knot I had tied in my handkerchief—Charlie dropped them into one of his trouser pockets, and departed. Following our treasurer, I went to a kind of stage on which was the ring. There, in a space behind it, were a number of chairs, reserved for contestants and their "managers," so I had what might be described as an excellent back-ringside seat, whence, on the other side of the roped-in square, I could see some two or three hundred spectators who filled the hall beyond. Above the ring fizzed the carbons of four arc lights, which resembled large white toy balloons. These gave the mass of faces a ghostly, pale appearance, and threw strong shadows on two novices who were dancing about in the ring, busy unpacking all the limited contents of their bags of pugilistic tricks. Encouraged by the fierce yells of their respective supporters, the two slugged away until, out of breath, they could hardly lift their arms.

Three such preliminary bouts having been fought without any of the contestants suffering any apparent bodily harm, except one who had his "claret tapped," Charlie climbed through the ropes and beckoned me to do the same. My opponent, who had remained in the dressing-room until that moment, now appeared, followed by two seconds and his father, all dressed and acting like so many well-seasoned professionals. 'Arry Junior even sported a dressing-gown, made of bath-towel material, and, for additional effect, over his shoulders was slung a sweater, the sleeves of which were wrapped round his neck. As far as appearance was concerned, my opponent and his entourage certainly looked impressive. Whilst they nimbly vaulted into the ring, I stood, alone and abandoned, watching them.

Noticing my plight, Charlie, the referee, came to ask me where were my seconds, and when I replied that I had none, he beckoned to two be-sweatered individuals, and asked them to take me in hand. This they immediately proceeded to do with such proficiency and vigour, massaging my arms and legs, whilst I sat on a stool in my corner, that I felt as might a person in the process of being dissected alive. Despite my feeble protests, dirty bandages were produced, and wound round my hands, and when gloves had been laced on, after what seemed an eternity, Charlie called young 'Arry and me to the centre of the ring. Raising his arms theatrically, after the usual "Gen-tle-men!" shouted in a falsetto voice, he introduced us to the assembly. A small section of the spectators greeted my opponent with blood-curdling yells and vigorous clapping of hands, accompanied by stamping of feet, but when the referee introduced me, the public's response was so weak that, had it not been for my two faithful seconds, no hand-clapping would have given me any encouragement. Weights were not announced, but the referee informed the spectators that the six rounds of three minutes each about to be fought were for a side stake of £5.

Next he assembled young 'Arry, his papa, me and our respective seconds in the centre of the ring, where he solemnly warned us that he would tolerate no buttin' with 'eads, rabbit or kidney punches, and that breakin' away from clinches had to be clean. After such and similar warnings and instructions which, in order to make us clearly understand what he meant, were imparted with many gesticulations, we were dismissed to return to our respective corners, where my seconds gave me final advice as to the tactics I should adopt. I was much too excited to listen to what my two "experts" told me, and my interest was entirely focused on 'Arry's corner, where I watched every movement until the time-keeper struck the gong, producing a nerve-racking sound which almost made me jump out of my boxing trunks.

As I nervously stepped towards the centre of the ring, to shake gloves with my opponent, several husky voices shouted something about knocking a block off.

It is impossible for me accurately to describe what happened during that, to me, memorable fight, save that, after having received a good old Blackfriars clout on one of my temples, I decided that it would be wiser to box, and not to fight, my opponent, who threw wild swings at me from all angles. The first and second rounds must easily have gone to 'Arry, but in the third, after I had ducked one of his "haymakers" and connected a sharp right hook with his jaw, for a few moments a glassy look came into his eyes, and as he staggered back on his heels and dropped his guard, I realised that he was at my mercy. However, being too soft-hearted to make a successful pugilistic "killer," I let the opportunity pass, with the result that, soon after having recovered, my opponent pummelled me good and hard, whereafter he even went so far as to fight me both with fists and words, making especially good use of the latter tactics whenever we happened to be in a clinch. Fortunately, during the next round he either began to tire, or acted according to his seconds' advice, for, instead of slugging as he had done up to that stage of the bout, now he tried to box me. So far, although in preference I am a left-hander—or "southpaw," to use the more "academic" term—I had hardly used my favourite weapon, and therefore my opponent treated my left hand with contempt, with the result that, in the fifth round, he fairly walked into the first hard left-hand punch I had delivered so far. It got him square on the jaw, and after this, as far as 'Arry was concerned, it was all over. Despite the yells I heard, urging me to finish the fight, I simply could not make up my mind to release the *coup de grâce*, and so what now was but a farce dragged on to the last round, at the end of which, after the referee had raised one of my arms, thus proclaiming me victor, my former opponent sulkily shook gloves with me.

In the dressing-room several "pugs" came to slap me on the back, and Charlie, the referee, after having congratulated me, put into my hands the eight pounds he had kept in his pocket. Going over to 'Arry, I asked if he was hurt in any way, and invited him and his gang to come and eat something in a little eating-place situated almost alongside the Metropolitan Music Hall in the nearby Edgware Road.

Later in the evening, as we sat together on wooden benches, eating, drinking tea, and joking, no one would have thought that only ten days before the "toughs" who were with me had threatened to "rough-house" me in Blackfriars. Before we parted, I asked young 'Arry to go and collect our joint deposits in the bar where we had left the money with the publican, and when I told him that he could keep the two pounds, he was delighted.

My new friends assured me that with practice and training I might go a long way in the "game," and so it came about that old 'Arry became my manager. During subsequent "professional engagements" he introduced me to Dick Burge, an ex-convict who, after having done a "long stretch" in jail, became the owner-manager of Blackfriars boxing arena. Despite his past, Dick Burge "made good," and became one of London's most popular and respected characters, so much so that when he departed from this world, he was given a public funeral.

In those days, another well-known "Punch Exchange" was Wonderland, situated near the Mile End Road in the East End of London. The manager of this arena—now used as a church hall—was a certain Harry Jacobs.

Masquerading under an assumed name, every now and again, during school holidays, I had a lot of fun with second and third-rate punch-traders and "rosin-inspectors," as "horizontal champions" were sometimes called in those days. For several good reasons, as far as my boxing activities were concerned, I led a kind of double life, and not even my friends at the Gristins' were aware of the fact that every now and again I was absent on "business."

In order to learn a little more about the "Noble Art of Self-defence," and to be able to train for bouts, I enlisted as a pupil under a remarkable and well-known London character, "Professor" Andrew J. Newton. Formerly, in 1888 and 1890, he had held the British Amateur Lightweight Championship, and, upon retiring from the ring as an undefeated professional, he opened a gymnasium and training centre in Marylebone Road, near the Edgware Road end. In this seat of pugilistic learning, Army and naval officers, doctors, lawyers and others sought physical fitness and instruction from the "Professor." Apart from many outstanding amateur pupils who trained under his expert guidance, he turned out several professional champions. Also, for many years the "Professor" acted as boxing instructor to Dulwich College, and at different times several world-famous "pros" trained in his physical laboratory.

Whereas Sir Isaac Newton's thoughts are said to have been directed to universal gravity by the falling of an apple, which, according to a tale, struck his head, no doubt making him see stars, his namesake, the "Professor," struck out in a different direction. His whole life was devoted to boxing, and to the study and practice of the many theories connected with the fistic art. Above the ring in his training quarters hung a board, on which, in large letters, were painted the following words, once written by a poet when in a thoughtful mood:

THERE IS SO MUCH GOOD IN THE WORST OF US,
AND SO MUCH BAD IN THE BEST OF US,
THAT IT ILL BECOMES ANY ONE OF US
TO FIND ANY FAULT WITH THE REST OF US.

Originally, Newton's gymnasium at 241 Marylebone Road was one of several homes for "Red Coat Boys," as bootblacks were called. Most of the poor youngsters were orphans or foundlings, and were employed and housed by a firm called Day and Martin, manufacturers of blacking for boots. In 1822, when Charles Dickens was ten years old, and his father was locked up in the Debtors' Prison, the little boy was sent to work in the Day and Martin factory at Old Hungerford Stairs, where, sick at heart, for two years he stuck labels on bottles and wooden boxes.

Thanks to social progress, when Red Coat Boys became but memories, the interior of 241 Marylebone Road was slightly altered. On the first floor, a gymnasium was set up, the first one in Great Britain to be specially fitted out for the sole purpose of teaching the "Noble Art of Self-defence and Scientific Boxing." A certain William Ecclestone, better known as "Jolly Jumbo," who weighed over twenty-two stone, sponsored this venture. Later the establishment became known as "Mansell's Picture Palace," for in it were held London's first "Penny Picture Shows." Despite the grandiose name, locally the "Palace" usually was called "The Penny Flea Pit." It is of interest to note that, in 1902, the world's bantamweight championship between Geo Dixon, the American coloured champion, and Pedlar Palmer—known as "The Box of Tricks"—was fought in Newton's gymnasium, and that in a hall below it— formerly the Red Coat Boys' dining- and recreation-room—many professional billiard championships were played by masters such as Gray, Inman, Stevenson, Faulkner, Reece and others.

When I went to the Professor for a few lessons, his little boy, "Andy," surprised me with the skill he showed in the manipulation of various types of punch-ball, and I never dreamt that, many years later, I would see him in very different circumstances.

·   ·   ·   ·   ·

Somehow or other, information about my clandestine activities in various boxing arenas reached my Headmaster. Though amused at my escapades, he quite rightly pointed out to me that even during the holidays I was under a certain moral obligation to the school in which I taught. Without reproaching me for what I had done, he asked me in future to keep away from boxing rings and, above all, on no account to tell the parents of our pupils that I had ever taken money for boxing.

Thus a nice little source of additional income was cut off for me. Still, it had been great fun while it lasted, and my escapades brought me in contact with a number of interesting characters whom otherwise I would never have met.

This brief summary relating to parts of my physical education must suffice to show that I went "through the hoop" in the best academic tradition, and that, although I was awarded no special honours degree, my studies opened for me many doors which otherwise would have remained closed.

Having learnt the alpha, beta, and, perhaps, the gamma of the punch trade, and boxing for money having been made taboo for me, while on my next school holidays, I decided to peep into the Valhalla of higher thought.

Chapter V

PERHAPS it was my cooking, the general atmosphere in the place, or possibly the presence of a crude, outspoken and sometimes aggressive rival in the person of the Metropolitan Water Board anarchist that made Sophocles gird up his tunic and sandal out towards an undisclosed destination. Occasionally, however, he returned for a little bodily refreshment in the shape of milk, wholemeal bread, butter, eggs, cheese, or a good tucking-in of *risotto* or *spaghetti à la Napolitaine*, for which he had a special weakness. Where he lived and slept he never divulged, but once he casually informed me that marriage, being a barbarous institution and a tyrannical tradition of the past, fit only for the *petite bourgeoisie*, he and his wife, though still the best of friends, had drifted apart, he going his way, and she hers. Between long bouts of spouting philosophy and every kind of other "osophy" and "ology," he sang the praises of Raymond Duncan, and lamented that I was so obstinate in my refusal to be introduced to him. Curiosity having got the upper hand of me, at last I agreed to go and hear the modern Messiah lecture. My announcement so delighted Sophocles that the joy he felt was reflected in his large, dreamy black eyes.

A few hours later, accompanied by my mentor, who, as usual, wore his Grecian robes, I got off a 'bus in Oxford Street, and, after a short walk—which, to me, was as embarrassing as had been the 'bus ride—entered the Doré Galleries in Bond Street, the premises of which to-day are occupied by Sothebys, the famous firm of art and book auctioneers. (Incidentally, on their catalogues Sothebys' very prettily call themselves "Auctioneers of Literary Property and Works illustrative of the Fine Arts.")

In a large room, on the walls of which hung a great number of paintings, were arranged chairs, and at one end of this auditorium a low platform had been erected. Placed on it, so as to stand obliquely from the audience, was what appeared to be a large, high-backed armchair, covered over with leopard skins. On the floor, beneath and all round this imposing throne, were spread several tiger skins, their stuffed heads, with formidable fangs, strawberry-red tongues, terrible snarling expressions and fiendish glass eyes, making an impressive sight.

When Sophocles appeared, a momentary hush fell on the people who had already taken their seats, and all eyes turned to stare at the two of us. Without taking the slightest notice of anyone, my leader "sclaf-sclaffed" (to use a musically descriptive Scottish expression) to the front row, where, without uttering a word, with a gesture he bade me take a seat beside him. During the next ten long minutes or so, with bare arms folded over his Socratean chest, he meditated deeply, with closed eyes. Not daring to do more than occasionally cast a quick, sideways glance at the people near me, I spent most of my time looking at my shoes or at Sophocles' be-sandalled feet, to which, instead of the soil of Mount Olympus and the sand of Corinth, Marathon and Thessaly, was stuck the unromantic grime and dirt of the London streets.

At long last, when I began to feel that I could no longer bear the suspense, a hush and rustle gave me hopes that the great moment was at hand. Even statuesque Sophocles must have sensed the presence of the pundit, for, like the needle of a compass when a magnet is held somewhere near it, he swung round in his chair, and, laying a gentle hand on my shoulder, whispered, "Here he comes."

Evidently I was an honoured guest, for before Raymond Duncan, the living encyclopædia of wisdom, theatrically and with the agility and grace of some celestial sub-species of panther leapt on to the platform, I was introduced to him, and also to his wife and young daughter, both of whom were dressed in pseudo-classical Grecian costumes.

I must admit that Raymond Duncan cut a fine figure, especially when, upon having majestically seated himself on his throne, he offered the audience a semi-profile view of himself. His long black hair was held in place by a fillet, and his fine-cut sharp features would have been an excellent subject for any painter. Of medium height, he was endowed with splendid physique, and that he was aware and proud of this, he showed by occasionally twitching an arm or leg muscle. Somehow, as I watched him posing there, scowling in silence, as if waiting for inspiration, to me this consummate actor looked like a mixture of a Sioux Indian, an Adonis and one of the pantomime Roman emperors. In my profane eyes, and in matters concerning classical costumes my inexpert opinion, the dress he wore was a combination of a Grecian tunic, *chlamys* and *peplum* (which, according to an outstanding French expert, in old Greece were *a l'usage des femmes et des élégants*) and a Roman *tunica palmata*. Whatever this fancy dress may or may not have been, it was every bit as striking and original as any stage costume I have ever seen, the main reason for this perhaps being the *panache* and almost *éclat* with which its fine-looking designer and manufacturer wore it.

Having given the audience time to "take in" this magnificent *tableau vivant*, the San Francisco-born Paris-London-Riviera Athenian philosopher, world-reformer, artist and prophet, brought his chin to rest on a clenched fist. Then, for some time he held this studied pose, and with eagle eyes and knitted brows stared as if minutely scrutinising something far beyond the wall facing him. Presently, as if coming out of a trance, he slowly turned his head towards the audience, and after another theatrical pause began to speak.

His measured and deliberate flow of eloquence, and the thoughts and theories he began to expound were such that I only vaguely understood odd statements. With singular modesty, he explained that, some years before, whilst standing on Mount Olympus, gazing at the universe, he had made an inward vow to teach his miserable fellow men below the technique of life, and to fill them with the desire to learn that new technique from him. He would knock at the door, if necessary, again and again, until it was opened to allow him to enter and present those living within in utter darkness with light and gems of beauty such as never before have been seen by mortals. Apparently, like Prometheus, Duncan had stolen fire from heaven, and now he generously offered it to his enraptured listeners. When, for a brief moment, he cast a penetrating glance at me, and addressed the seemingly enthralled audience as "my friends and beloved pupils," I longed to fly back to "Professor" Newton's Boxing Academy, for there I could understand what was said, and there theory was put into practice in so comprehensive and concrete a manner that if a "beloved" pupil made a mistake, heavenly constellations were made visible to him. Duncan invoked the muses, poetry, music, dance, inspiration, and, without coming to real grips with any of them during his exhibition of metaphysical shadow boxing, referred to Thales, Terpander, Erastosthenes, Polygnotus, Euterpe, Uranus, Polycletus and a host of others. In quick succession, Plato's *Republic*, Aristotle and many other Greek philosophers were mentioned, and when the lecturer had dealt with them, he turned to things more modern.

Talking about painting and painters, he said that none of the so-called great masters conveyed anything spiritual to thinking persons like him. Raphael, Da Vinci, Titian, Rembrandt, Velasquez, and many others he pooh-poohed, and musical geniuses such as Mozart, Beethoven, Verdi, Bach and others, he mentioned almost with pity.

"Close opera houses and concert halls, scrape the paint off canvases, do away with art schools, academies and universities where pupils and students are bottle-fed like babes. Renounce your luxuries, your vices, and follow poverty, simplicity, suffering and inspiration!" he exclaimed.

Without qualifying, or explaining the whys and wherefores of his statements, he talked about "real" poetry and "real" painting and music. "Yes, my friends and dear pupils," he went on to say, "maybe, some day, you will realise that this fanatical Duncan, that man with bare feet, was right. I have spoken and preached a long time; I have been taken for a madman, but there are many now who say, 'It is strange, but he is right.' To-day I tell you, you are on the threshold of a frightful, horrible life. Prepare, cleanse yourselves,

F

begin afresh, work, for life has to be started afresh. Until death we
shall agitate, with dignity, with honour and with beauty. This we
must not only say: it must be done! No longer is one permitted to
follow decayed traditions, old fashions. A new epoch must be born,
with new ideas, new works, new actions and a new humanity. Form
your ranks for this epoch, be reborn into this new world, and begin
a new life; not for your own sakes—for we are belated—but for the
little children who are going to take your place!"

Thus spoke Raymond Duncan; and, as I sat, listening, but not
trying very hard to understand, Sophocles was beside me, acting as
if he were lost in ecstacy. Being a bit of a cynic, I could not help
thinking that no one, not even Duncan, can build up a lasting
reputation by quoting reams of statements made by ancient philosophers, and I compared the speaker with a famous pianist
who, upon being asked by an admirer if he had ever thought
of writing music, replied that when he was young, his memory
was so good that he might easily have become an excellent
composer.

At long last, when Duncan majestically rose from his throne, he
was warmly applauded, and within a few moments he was surrounded by admirers who all but kissed the hem of his Grecian
tunic. At this juncture Sophocles introduced me to a number of
people, and pointed out to me several well-known personages and
members of London's budding intelligentsia. A few of the latter
"got there," and to-day their names are household words in so-
called "highbrow" literary and artistic circles. Most of the grand
ladies who graced the Doré Galleries with their presence have
passed on to regions where, I trust, lectures on second- and third-
hand philosophy are strictly taboo.

Together with Sophocles—who hoped I would join the pseudo-
Grecian fold—I met the prophet several times, and also the latter's
famous sister, Isadora, the dancer. "Strewth! Them there was the
days!" as my landlord and friend, Bill Gristin, would have said.
What with Isadora Duncan and her super-classical Grecian dancing,
and Maud Allan, the forerunner of the modern strip-tease act, a
minor artistic American invasion of Europe had begun. London

took Isadora much more seriously than Paris, and certainly much more so than New York. Perhaps it was a case of prophets hardly ever being honoured in their own countries; but be this as it may, as in the case of Raymond Duncan, his sister's ambitions were mainly concentrated on Paris and London, two cities she privately professed to detest.

Whether it was for the sake of her new art, or *pour épater et choquer le publique*, only Isadora knew, when, on one occasion, she performed a most original dance. At the time she was expecting her second love-child, and when, after the performance, a friend whispered to her that, under the flimsy costume *la Duncan* had worn whilst dancing, "it" had been plainly visible, the latter replied that this particular dance—in my profane language, a kind of "maternity hop"—was meant to express "Love, Woman, Formation, Spring-time, the fruitful Earth, the three dancing Graces *enceinte*, the Madonna and the Zephyrs, also *enceinte*." In 1921, a few years after having tragically lost her two children—who, in a motor car, were drowned in the River Seine—upon leaving for Russia, where the Government had promised to subsidise a Duncan-Greek dancing academy, Isadora exclaimed, "Farewell inequality, injustice and brutality of the Old World which made my dancing school im-possible!"

Why she returned to France, I do not know, but, as will be remembered, her end was as sudden and tragic as that of her two children, her scarf becoming entangled in a wheel of the car in which she rode, thus causing instantaneous death.

The two Duncans hailed from San Francisco, and were of Irish-American family. There were, I believe, other brothers and sisters, and their parents were divorced. With practically no money, Raymond and Isadora set out from California, some time later to arrive in London, "broke to the wide." After having started by doing a "flit" from their hotel, somehow the pair managed to "grub through," and later shifted their camp to Paris, where Raymond tried his hand at pictorial art, whereas his sister improved on what dancing she had learnt in the U.S.A. Fond of making himself conspicuous—as was the case with not a few American and English

art students who became more "Montparnasse" than the "artiest"
French Montparnassiers themselves—Raymond let his hair grow
long, and took to wearing a large black hat, open shirt, and a
"loud," flowing tie.

It was during a visit to Greece that he discarded this startling
attire for a kind of imitation ancient Greek tunic, and a fillet round
his head, and that his sister, Isadora, followed his example. If this
new guise was calculated to attract attention, it certainly succeeded,
for within a few days the two Duncans were the talk and the objects
of laughter of Athens, where, for a while, they thought of "settling
eternally and there to build a temple that should be characteristic of
us," to use Isadora's own words. It was at about that time that
Raymond—in order to earn a few *drachmas* wherewith to buy raw
materials for his work and vegetarian food—began to weave cloth,
carve wood, and model figures. Why the two Californian Greeks
returned to Paris, and later to London, I leave the reader to guess,
but the fact remains that, from that time on, wherever they appeared,
all eyes were fixed on them, and in *salons* and drawing-rooms they
were frequently discussed. No doubt, Raymond was a studious,
intelligent and fundamentally good man, and, of course, an inveterate idealist. He was fond of the theatrical in a peculiar inverted way,
and it always struck me that his main ambition in life was to be
looked up to as a second Christ, with the difference that, at his table,
instead of only twelve apostles, he wanted to see thousands seated
with him, Duncan, as the centrepiece. In Sophocles he had a kind of
apostle Paul, for, as we shall see later, my peculiar friend was
destined to do a great deal of travelling.

In Paris, Raymond could often be seen in cafés, squatting like a
Buddha, busy weaving patterns on a small portable frame; certainly
a most original setting for a neo-classical Greek philosopher and
world-reformer. Had his loathing for cities been as genuine as he
professed, it struck me as somewhat strange that he did not lead the
life of a Diogenes. But perhaps the very sight of a barrel was re-
volting to him.

After lectures I noticed that he was invariably whisked off in a
carriage, or even in a Rolls Royce, put at his disposal by some

wealthy admirer, whereas Sophocles clung to me in order to be treated to a ride in a common 'bus.

After Duncan had returned to Paris, I received pamphlets he himself turned out by hand, all the text printed in capital letters. The first I read was entitled:

LES MOYENS DE GREVE

CONFERENCE PAR RAYMOND DUNCAN

A LA BOURSE DE TRAVAIL, PARIS

STENOGRAPHIE D'ARISTIDE PRATELLE[1]

IMPRIME A L'AKADEMIA RAYMOND DUNCAN, PARIS, 1914.

I could not help noticing that he addressed his readers, presumably consisting of workers, as "*chers camarades.*" Having seen the lecturer ride in horse-drawn carriages and motor cars, which in those days were rare luxuries, even for many of the rich, the following remark struck me particularly:

"*Vous savez que les chauffeurs restent assis sur un siège du matin au soir et qu'ils passent leur temps à faire des mouvements imbéciles pour gagner quelques sous.*"

In 1914 he also published a booklet entitled *La Danse et La Gymnastique*, and in 1919 this was followed by three pamphlets, *Les Muses, Prometheus* (*Les grands crucifiés*) and *Ecos de mon Atélier,* all

IMPRIME A LA MAIN

PAR

RAYMOND DUNCAN

21, RUE BONAPARTE, PARIS.

In the last publication he makes a weighty statement, typical of himself:

"*Qui ne connaît pas le passé ne doit pas parler.*
Qui ne voit pas le présent ne doit pas parler.
Que n'est pas prophète doit rester muet."

[1] The author wonders if "prattle" is an apt translation into English.

The last line, I take it, means that only Raymond Duncan is qualified to speak and write.

At one time Raymond and Isadora visited the rocky coast of Albania, in the neighbourhood of Santi Quadrata, where he did really noble work among the poor and, at the time, starving people. To-day, I believe, he is back in the United States, where, as far as I know, next to no notice is taken of the neo-Greek philosopher.

But let me return to London and my enigmatic friend, Sophocles, whose Odyssey had hardly begun when his mentor gave those memorable lectures in the Doré Galleries.

My refusal to become a Duncanian Greek so disappointed poor Sophocles that, for some time, I saw very little of him. When, on rare occasions, he came to take bodily nourishment at my expense, he never told me where he lived, or who normally provided him with food and pocket money for fares and other incidental expenses. After a prolonged absence, one evening he again turned up, and after his usual meal, paced up and down my room, as if something weighed heavily on his mind. At last, halting before me, and having wrapped the tunic tightly around his body, he began by telling me that people in London lacked the finer feelings to enable them to appreciate his teachings, and that he had come to the conclusion that the struggle to get an intelligent hearing was hopeless. He went on, recounting how he had weaved, toiled and preached, but it was of no avail, and, to make things even more depressing, an elderly lady who had been a veritable angel to him, had gone abroad owing to ill-health.

To set on paper what happened to Sophocles after that last bitter blow would take up too much space, and so, for the sake of brevity, I will put it into a nutshell.

Deeply disappointed, with tears in his large, dreamy black eyes, one day he cut off his long hair and cast aside his beloved Grecian tunic and sandals, in order to don a neat lounge suit and other brand-new garments. Who had given him the money wherewith to buy his wardrobe, I did not enquire, but I guessed that it would not be long before I, too, would be "touched."

Having seen an advertisement in *The Times* that a Russian prince required a tutor for two of his boys, Sophocles applied for the job ... and got it. Before leaving for the Land of the Tsars, a number of things had to be bought, and money had to be raked together for the journey. Of course, he could have written to the prince asking him to advance the necessary funds, but this might have made a bad first impression, so he thought it much easier, and less embarrassing, to borrow money from friends in London. A middle-aged lady came to the rescue with a substantial contribution, which represented part of her savings of years, so when the newly-appointed tutor departed in great state, he promised to refund the money on the first opportunity. Some time later, I received a glowing letter in which Sophocles informed me that he was living in a veritable paradise, and when, in my reply, I hinted that it was high time he paid off his debts, an iron curtain was lowered on our correspondence which, on the Russian side, was left to freeze.

With the passing of time he almost slipped out of my memory, but at rare intervals when random thoughts concerning him flashed through my mind, I laughed heartily to myself, and wondered what he might be doing in this strange world, filled with even stranger people. As will be seen later, when least expected, I was to hear from Sophocles, but in the meantime we will leave him in the land of the Tsars, caviare and balalaikas.

Chapter VI

The Reverend Crimpus Jilt has several adventures.—Ida McUgly
becomes a mother.—Taxi-driver Bert Gristin turns up with a mysterious
merchant.—The First World War breaks out.—A joking jockey.—
Denny, the Irish newspaper-vendor.

SOPHOCLES' departure to Russia passed almost unnoticed in
the *Maison Gristin*, where things were always happening. The
same old "steadies" were still there when we schoolmasters arrived
to spend another holiday with Bill and Ivy, who, as usual, gave us a
most cordial reception.

For a change, or possibly to make more room in the kitchen, the
grand piano had been moved into a ground-floor room which had
been reserved for the Reverend Crimpus Jilt, M.A. Although no
Paderewsky, Chopin or Liszt—in fact, unable to pick out even the
most simple tune with one finger—Crimpie was delighted to have
the imposing instrument in his room, to which it gave a special
cachet, especially so with an "ever so nice" aspidistra our thoughtful
Ivy had placed upon it. As pointed out in a previous chapter, the
Gristins were dead against any lodger bringing in lady friends, but
as our reverend gentleman was not quite in the same category as the
rest of us earth-bound lodgers, Bill and Ivy always made it their
bounden duty to be fast asleep when, during nights, the Oxonian
Master of Arts brought in an aunt or niece, with whom to discuss
private affairs.

One evening, when I happened to be strolling down Regent
Street, near Piccadilly Circus I met Crimpie, who was in the
company of a rather too well-dressed young lady.

"Hello, my deah Count," he exclaimed, rushing up to me.
"What a pleasant surprise to meet you! Lord Oodah-Doodah told
me you had gone to the Rivierah."

Having introduced me to his lady friend as Count So-and-So,
the famous turfman and *grand viveur*, after a quick, meaning wink,

Crimpie gave me a dramatic description of how his Rolls Royce had got smashed up in a collision.

"Just too bad!" he went on. "And it *would* happen as I'm about to take this lady to spend a week-end in my villa near Brighton. Now, dammit, we shall have to travel by train; and you know, my deah Count, how I hate trains. Still, I suppose we shall survive the journey, and within a day or two my chauffeur will bring down the repaired car. Now, don't forget, my deah Count, if you have nothing bettah to do from to-morrow on, just dash down and drop in on us. Even if we happen to be out when you turn up, old John, my butlah, will look after you until we blow in."

Saying this, Crimpie bowed, and, arm-in-arm with his companion, strolled away, leaving me standing, perplexed and bewildered, wondering what the little game was about.

On the morrow, when, to my surprise, Crimpie returned to his "digs" at the Gristins, he called me into his room, where, exceedingly pleased with himself, he recounted what had taken place after he and his lady friend had left me near Piccadilly Circus.

Pretending to be suffering from a "hangover," he had accompanied his new female acquaintance to her apartments, situated in that neighbourhood. After having been given many drinks and an excellent dinner, he stayed there until next morning when, in a taxi, the two went to Victoria Station. Whilst waiting for a train to take them to Brighton, the couple went to a nearby hotel, where they ordered breakfast. When this had been eaten, under the pretext of going to buy the tickets, Crimpie left his prospective week-end guest sitting at the table, thus making his get-away and leaving her to foot the bill.

Having finished recounting his recent adventures, Crimpie laughed heartily. Upon regaining sufficient breath to speak, he slowly shook his head and said, "My deah Count, I see there's a hell of a lot you have to learn before you become a man of the world."

This is only one of several similar low-down tricks I have known this bounder play on women. Strange to relate, despite the fact that he indulged in almost every vice, besides being unashamedly dishonest, in some peculiar way he was very religious. Whenever I tackled him on this subject, calling him everything from a hypocrite down, he was frankly astonished, and replied that all he did was to have a bit of fun, and that such minor sins were typical of exuberant youth.

That his was spent in exuberance was proved to me when, one afternoon, someone knocked at the front door. Upon opening it, to my surprise the caller was a well-dressed gentleman of the type who rarely strayed into our poor neighbourhood. He wore a well-cut morning coat, spats and a top hat, and carried a rolled-up umbrella and a brief-case, the *tout ensemble* making me wonder if he was a lawyer, some high Home or Foreign Office official, or perhaps a "classy" funeral director. Evidently there was something about our dingy lodging-house which puzzled him, for, after having produced an envelope from one of his pockets and read out the address that was written on it, he asked me if he had called at the right place. Having been informed by me that, indeed, this was the street and the number of the house for which he looked, he inquired if the Reverend Crimpus Jilt was at home.

As it happened, after a hectic binge somewhere up in the West End, poor Crimpie had been under the weather for two days, so much so, in fact, that after a sympathetic and obliging cab-driver had unloaded and put his "fare" to bed, Bill Gristin diagnosed the moaning invalid's affliction as being a mild attack of the "tiddlyums."

Fortunately, by the time the man in the morning coat and top hat called, the crisis had passed, and although the convalescing carouser had by no means recovered his full physical and mental strength, when I entered his room and described the person who wished to see him, Crimpie jumped up from his armchair as if someone had pricked him with a pin. Having cursed freely, in a kind of hissing whisper, he asked me to be a good "sport" and to show the caller in, but to take my time over it.

Whilst I went to do as requested, I could hear Crimpie rushing hither and thither, evidently tidying up his unmade bed, and hiding from view glasses and empty bottles.

Having admitted the visitor, and closed the door behind me, I went upstairs to read. That the practical wisdom of life is not derived from books was proved to me some two hours later, when Crimpie joined me. For some time he stood, staring into the coal fire, evidently worried about something, and when at last he began to speak, in a mournful tone of voice he told me what had brought the recent caller to our lodging-house.

To begin with, he repeated a story he had told me long before— namely, that, whilst a student at Oxford, he had become the father of two children. At the time, he was still on friendly terms with prosperous Jilt Senior, who undertook to pay for the kiddies' education and keep. However, since the breaking-off of relations between father and son, things had taken a very different turn, for since those happy-go-lucky days at varsity, Crimpie had added six more offspring to his score.

Apparently, the gentleman who had called on him was a solicitor, and, if memory serves me right, he had informed our Don Juan that if he could raise £360, i.e. £60 for each child, and pay the money in a lump sum into some special fund which existed for such cases, he would be free of any further financial obligations, as far as the children were concerned.

For a long time the sorely distressed Crimpie told me about his worries, and when I suggested that a square meal would do him a lot of good, and I asked him to accompany me to a little restaurant, he immediately accepted my invitation. As the two of us walked down the street and approached our "local," he made a bee-line for it, saying that a hair of the dog which had bitten him would work miracles. That there is a great deal to be said for this simple remedy, I soon discovered; for, after having swallowed two large whiskies in quick succession, my companion cheered up no end, and even his hitherto pale face assumed a rosy tint. The meal and a further three or four drinks had a miraculous effect on the patient, who now treated everything as a joke, and in fits of laughter told me about some of his love affairs.

Shortly after the interview with the solicitor, in order to avoid a scandal, Jilt Senior once more came to the rescue. Although he never communicated directly with his prodigal son, he paid the required sum of money, an event Crimpie duly celebrated somewhere up in the West End whence, after three days, he returned to his lodgings, a veritable wreck.

Once, although I was the victim of one of the reverend gentleman's tricks, he amused me greatly. Here I must remark that his plausibility was such that one could hardly be angry with him. His manners were charming, and even old clothes and gloves that were full of holes he wore with such *chic* that he always looked a perfect dandy.

One fine morning, when Crimpie and I happened to be enjoying the sunshine in Hyde Park, a luxurious car drew up alongside us, and before I realised what was happening, two Hindoos jumped out of it, rushed up to my companion, and all but kissed him. Presently he introduced them to me as two Indian princes who had studied at Oxford with him. I, of course, once more became Count So-and-So. Then, for some time, the trio talked about the "good old varsity days," and before the young potentates departed, they invited Crimpie and me to dine with them that night. Fearing that such a meeting might lead to expenses far beyond my means, I made some excuse for not accepting the invitation, but my companion, evidently anticipating a princely spree, promised to be on the spot at the appointed time.

Back in his room at the Gristins', Crimpie enthusiastically set to work, unpacking his trunk in which he kept an old dinner jacket and other requisites wherewith to make himself presentable for the auspicious occasion. Upon discovering that old food stains had gone mouldy on the lapels, that his silk socks were full of holes, shirts and collars threadbare and dirty, and that moths had eaten parts of the trousers, he asked me to lend him my outfit. As it happened, being somewhat tight for me, it fitted him perfectly. When, among other things, I produced a monocle—once worn by me during a school entertainment in which I had sung "I'm Jones of the Lancers"—Crimpie was overjoyed. That evening, when fully rigged out, and with the monocle screwed into one eye, he departed in a taxi, even the two old spinsters peeped at him from their window.

Two days later, when the Beau Brummel failed to return, the Gristins and I began to fear the worst. Upon coming home after some show, I looked into his room, and as I did so, Ivy's dog slipped through the door, immediately to start barking at something under the bed. Wondering what was amiss, I bent down to have a look, and, lo and behold, there lay Crimpie, fully dressed, and dead-drunk. Despite the fact that, whilst undressing him, and dumping him on his bed, I handled him as one might a sack filled with rags, he never moved as much as an eyelid. Next morning, upon going to investigate how the carouser was getting on, I found him still asleep, blissfully smiling to himself, like the cat which has eaten the canary.

When and how it happened I never heard, but during the following night the reverend gentleman disappeared, taking with him his belongings, as well as the precious dinner jacket and other articles of clothing and the monocle I had lent to him.

Several days later, in a short note—on which no address was given—he apologised for his informal departure, and briefly hinted that, thanks to his friends, the Indian princes, now he could afford to live in respectable quarters, as befitted a gentleman of his social standing. In a postscript, he thanked me for the loan of the dinner jacket, and promised, as a small token of friendship and gratitude for all I had done for him, in the very near future to take me to his tailors in Savile Row to have really first-class "togs" made for me.

This is how the Reverend Crimpus Jilt departed from the *Maison Gristin*, and why, before returning to school, I had to buy myself a second-hand dinner jacket.

.   .   .   .   .   .

Whether it was due to mysterious psychic influences or hoodoos with which Crimpie may have impregnated our lodging-houses, or possibly because our Metropolitan Water Board philosopher did not take sufficient water with IT, I am unable to state, but, to what-ever cause, or causes, a certain event might be attributed by psycho-logists or neurologists, the fact remains that, shortly after our reverend lodger had departed to "more respectable" quarters, something strange—in fact, something bordering on the miraculous —happened to Ida McUgly. No one had noticed any visible physical change in her, and not even as much as the faintest of Mona Lisa smiles had been detected on her tortoise-like lips when she packed up a few things in a suitcase, and, after having told Ivy that she would be back within a few days, left in a hansom cab.

True to her word, after about a week, accompanied by the Water Board official, she reappeared, carrying in her arms a little bundle which puzzled us greatly. Having greeted us in passing, she went to the shed in the back yard—among us always referred to as "Ida's Room"—followed by her escort, who carried the suitcase.

The little bundle so excited Ivy's feminine curiosity that she followed the pair. When, a little while later, she returned to the kitchen—where a few of us were assembled—she flopped into a dilapidated armchair, and laughed until we thought she would choke.

Impatient to hear what might be the cause of such excessive merriment, Bill went up to his wife, and, shaking her by an arm, with a smile of anticipation asked her to tell him what the joke was about.

After several vain efforts to control herself, at last Ivy managed to splutter, "She's 'ad a ba—ba—baby!"

"What?" we all exclaimed in chorus, no one believing what she said.

In convulsions once more, Ivy sat, doubled up, and after a while, with tears streaming down her cheeks, repeated, "Yes, a baby. Honour bright, I'm not jokin'. They've just come back from the maternity 'ospital, and the brat ain't no bigger than a large 'errin'."

We still refused to believe a word of what she said, when, smiling proudly, and carrying the baby in his arms, the Water Board anarchist arrived on the scene. Even when he assured us that he was its father, we still thought he was merely joking, and possibly trying to play a practical joke on us. We knew that he was a married man, who, some years before, had left his wife, and as Ida earned her living looking after other peoples' babies and children, we refused to be taken in so easily. However, to our amazement, we were to discover that what the Water Board official told us was the truth, the whole truth and nothing but the truth.

Despite the loving care with which both father and mother nursed the baby, after having weakly gurgled and cried in this wicked world for some ten days, it departed as quietly and unobtrusively as it had arrived, leaving its mother to look after other people's offspring, and its father to continue his professional activities, and, occasionally, to indulge in bouts of tub-thumping.

Among the visitors who came into the Gristins' friendly kitchen were several who never let many days pass without dropping in for a chat and a little refreshment, liquid or otherwise. An elderly, tall and ponderous police sergeant and two hefty constables—whose beat happened to be in our neighbourhood—usually brought in exciting news and gossip, mostly connected with local happenings and rumours. From them I learnt many interesting things, among them how many pints of ale a well-trained police constable can swallow in a day without turning a hair or having to ease his belt. The street lamp-lighter, also, could be most illuminating on some subjects which, hitherto, I had let pass unnoticed. But the star turn, as far as general knowledge and information was concerned, was Bill's brother, Bert. By profession a taxi-driver, he knew his London like the palm of his hand, and, being as fly as you can make them, there were no flies on him. Quite rightly, the whole Gristin tribe looked upon Bert as the most eminent member of the family, and therefore, whenever he chipped in on a discussion, his word was final. And no wonder, for not only could he drive a car, and knew more about motors than their designers, but, at a pinch, he could turn his hand to almost anything, from bookmaking at the races down to fleecing "mugs" with the three-card trick. Furthermore, in his younger days Bert had been a professional football player, and when it came to playing the concertina, no minstrel down at Ramsgate or Margate was in the same street with him. Although he had suffered his ups and downs in life, no one had ever seen Bert look down-hearted, let alone heard him utter one word of complaint. Oh no; he wasn't that kind of bloke; he took things as they came, rough or smooth, it was all the same to him; just part of the game.

It was Bert who, one day, drove up with a new client; not exactly a lodger, but a gentleman who was looking for two suitable rooms, if possible large ones, in which to store what he described as "valuable goods." When, for such accommodation he offered to pay what, according to Gristinian standards and tariffs, was a high rent, Bill quickly put on his thinking-cap. One of the sheds at the back of one house was filled with pots of paint and odds and ends which could just as well be stored in the open, without doing them any harm, so when Bert's "fare" declared the place to be suitable for his purpose, as well as an adjoining room, Bill promised to have everything shipshape by next day. Having handed over a month's rent in advance, the new tenant departed, and when Bill asked Bert where he had picked up that "toff," the latter replied that it was at Fenchurch Street Station he had met him. Apparently, whilst being driven towards the West End, the stranger had asked Bert if by any chance he happened to know a private house where he could store a number of boxes, and so, naturally, the latter had immediately thought of his brother.

As arranged, next morning a horse-drawn cart delivered a number of wooden packing cases, which were carefully stacked up in what formerly had been the storing place for some of Bill's working materials. Within a few days, further consignments arrived, and when the two rooms were filled up to the ceiling with neatly stacked packing cases, their owner locked the doors and departed.

About a fortnight later he returned, and when one room had been emptied of its contents and these had been loaded on two large vans, the "merchant"—as we now called the new tenant—once more left for an unknown destination. Such comings and goings and deliveries and withdrawals of goods had gone on for several weeks, and the rent had always been paid in advance when, suddenly, all such activities ceased. I happened to be spending another school holiday in London when Bill told me that the "merchant's" prolonged absence began to puzzle and worry him, especially as the rent had not been paid for two months. Though the two rooms were still full of packing cases, Bill, being a trustworthy person, flatly turned down his wife's suggestion to open one, in order to investigate what it contained.

One morning, during breakfast, when, as usual, Ivy read out the *Daily Mirror* to her illiterate husband, she became very excited on seeing the photograph of a person whom she immediately recognised as the "merchant." Even I was called out of bed to go and have a look at the picture, and to hear the startling news.

Three months' imprisonment and a heavy fine our mystery man had been sentenced to, for wholesale smuggling, but, unfortunately, the caption below the photograph did not inform us what he had smuggled. We were still discussing the sensational news when Bert came rushing in. He, also, had seen the photograph in the *Mirror* and so, without losing precious time, had quickly driven down in his taxi to give us the news that the "merchant" had been "knocked off" for smuggling.

"Now, listen to me, Bill," he whispered, addressing his brother, and at the same time winking one eye and rubbing his nose with an oil-stained first finger. "Don't say a word to nobody abaht them packin' cases. If, after 'avin' done 'is short stretch, the bloke comes back to fetch 'em away, just tell 'im to be in no 'urry, and to wait till I've 'ad a word wiv 'im. If you let me 'andle the bloke, I bet we shall do well out of 'im; and, what's more, wivout runnin' the slightest risk of getting involved in any way. After all, you don't know what's in them blinkin' boxes, but I guess it ain't Bibles or 'ymn-books. Not on your sweet life!"

Bert and Ivy were all for opening a case, just to see what it contained, but Bill flatly refused to do this. Before Bert left us to pick up "fares," it was agreed that not a word was to be said to anyone about the stored goods, and that we would wait and see what would happen after the smuggler's release from "quad." In order to make entry into the store-rooms more difficult, Bill fixed a padlock to each door and hid the keys.

> .   .   .   .   .

In 1914, when war broke out, after a prolonged absence, I returned to Switzerland to serve in the Army there. The weeks I spent in training as a recruit were so delightful that upon being

G

drafted to a unit which was known as the "Foreign Legion," my enthusiasm suffered a severe setback. Most of my companions were men who had come from abroad, and as several among them only spoke languages none of us understood, sometimes this led to most amusing situations and incidents. Besides watching the frontier from the top of a low mountain range, there was nothing to do, so in order to keep us occupied, daily hours were spent doing dreary rifle-drill, 999·999 per cent. of which consisted of sloping and grounding arms. Most of the officers seemed to take a delight in this form of torture, or in chasing us about on meaningless stunts, with the result that, by degrees, I more and more loathed the very sight of my swaggering superiors, who in civilian life were mere nobodies. Fortunately, after about four months, some of us useless soft "foreigners" were given leave to return to our respective jobs abroad. When, after an eventful journey through France, I once more found myself in London, and in the Gristins' friendly lodging-house, I was a very happy man.

Shortly after war had been declared, and refugees from Belgium began to cross the Channel, an English jockey and his Belgian wife arrived from Brussels to become "steadies" at the Gristins'. The husband, an impish, jovial creature with the word "jockey" written all over him, had been riding and training horses in Belgium. Owing to the war, things in the turf line were rather slack in England, so, whilst looking for a job, the jockey and his wife lived in one of our large rooms. Our little forum was much enlivened by this little man's arrival, for, besides being an excellent conversationalist, he was a great practical joker. Often, especially on Sundays, our landlord's kitchen resembled a cageful of monkeys, everybody laughing and playing tricks on one another. In the backyard we had made a kind of cricket pitch, three sticks driven into the hard ground representing a wicket. There, with a ball made of rags tied together, we often played "test" matches among the ashes and Bill's condemned building materials. There being only one wicket, the solitary batsman had to play against all the other participants, who had their work cut out to retrieve the ball from among the flotsam and jetsam piled up in the yard. Though the Greek artist was repeatedly asked to join in the fun, and the rules and intricacies of the "King of Games" were explained to him, he failed to understand, and therefore refused to take his place in the field. However, the jockey, the Water Board official, two of us schoolmasters, Bill, and any male visitor who happened to drop in for a glass of beer, took a great delight in such games, which were played with great keenness and enthusiasm. Cricket often led to horseplay, for which the backyard and all its contents offered unlimited scope, and such romps sometimes led to minor accidents, all of which were taken as part of the game.

After such an *intermezzo*, the jockey went up to his room, shortly after to reappear, astonishingly well disguised as a little old woman. Croaking in broken English and imitating a strong French accent, he was in the act of giving us a fanciful imitation of an old hag begging, when the two spinsters—who occupied the front bedsitting room—entered through the front door. As usual, both were dressed in black, and wore their invariable lace collars.

Tottering up to them, the jockey whined, "*Mon Dieu!* Zeese people no understand what I say. Zey bad people, make fun of poor old refugee."

Listening from the kitchen, we all kept as quiet as mice, and it was only with the greatest difficulty that we managed to suppress our laughter when we heard the spinsters invite the "refugee" to go into their room and have tea with them.

About an hour later we heard the jockey totter out of the front door, soon after to re-join us in the kitchen, which he reached by entering his "annex," situated two doors further down the road, and coming to us through the backyard. The story he told us was excruciatingly funny, and before going to re-join his wife, he implored us not to spoil his game. During the next fortnight or so, the rascal regularly visited the two old ladies who, on one occasion, even took him to a "pub," where, on his instigation, they took so much harmless-tasting but potent sloe-gin that, had it not been for clever jockeying, the "refugee" would not have succeeded in steering his two swaying charges down the home stretch without mishap.

Soon everybody in the immediate neighbourhood knew about this practical joke, and, therefore, whenever the trio went out together, many eyes watched. The climax came when, during a visit to the spinsters' room, the old "Belgian refugee" suddenly lifted her skirts to show a pair of riding breeches and canvas leggings, but although the jockey now spoke in his normal voice, what the women saw and heard was so bewildering that they failed to comprehend. Thinking that the "refugee" had gone mad, both rushed out of their room and frantically called Bill and Ivy to come to their assistance. Upon dashing to the rescue, there we saw the jockey, dancing about, skirts lifted high, and waving the bonnet which had hitherto hidden his neatly cut hair.

It took us quite a while to explain that all this Belgian refugee business had merely been a practical joke, and when, at last, it slowly began to dawn on the two victims that this really had been the case, with downcast eyes they smiled sheepishly and blushed.

.   .   .   .   .

Denny, an elderly Irishman with a wooden leg, had his newspaper pitch outside our "local," near which was a 'bus stop. This living encyclopædia of London firmly believed in the strength of numbers, and, accordingly, raised an enormous family, to which he always referred as his "capital." All the children—with which two wives had presented him—did some kind of work, so pennies and shillings rolled in steadily. In order further to supplement the revenue derived from the sale of papers, Denny also acted as a kind of sub-agent for a firm of street bookmakers. Twice, when Scotland Yard men were after his employers and the latter offered the newspaper-vendor an attractive little sum of money, he undertook to act as scapegoat for them, which led to Denny taking short holidays in Wormwood Scrubs Prison whilst the real culprits carried on their business as usual.

As far as I was concerned, being no gambler, Denny never made a penny out of me, but, in spite of that, he never let me pass him without telling me an amusing story or shouting some friendly remark.

As the war continued, public-house strategists were much in evidence, eminent ones among them drawing diagrams on the counter by dipping a finger in puddles of spilt beer. Denny—who was much too practical for such indirect methods of warfare—always maintained that if the British General Staff had any sense, they would offer an extra half-crown a day to Irishmen, who would then flock to the colours by the thousand, soon to wipe Germany off the map. According to Denny, the very fact that British "Tommies" had revived and borrowed the, at the time, three- or four-year-old song, "It's a Long Way to Tipperary," from Ireland, was sufficient proof that the key to victory was lying, rusty and unused, in his homeland.

And so, abroad, the war went on, whilst in England football matches drew large crowds of able-bodied young men dressed in civilian clothes, and still, for political reasons, the Government were afraid to pass the Conscription Bill, let alone to take Denny's tip to offer Irish volunteers an extra half-crown per day. According to Mr. Asquith's newly-coined and ill-timed slogan, as far as the *Maison Gristin* was concerned, it certainly was a case of "business as usual," and, as we shall see, there things continued to happen.

Chapter VII

Repercussions of the War—A thoroughly conscientious objector.
—The Reverend Crimpus Jilt joins the War Office staff, and plays a
strategic trick.—Bill Gristin expresses his weighty opinions concerning
conscription and the war in general.—Zeppelin raids, and what happened
in the *Maison Gristin* during one of them.

BEING keen on adventure, and longing for a radical change
from school life, I considered offering my services to the British
Army, but upon mentioning this to my Headmaster, he dissuaded
me, chiefly on the grounds that if I left his school it would be very
difficult for him to find a suitable assistant master to take my place.
The vast majority of ex-university men and young schoolmasters
had joined the Army immediately after war had broken out, and
therefore schools carried on with reduced teaching staffs. In order
to help out, ladies or middle-aged men were employed, though in
many cases such substitutes lacked previous teaching experience.
My Headmaster argued that, as I was a Swiss, the war had nothing to
do with me, and that my services as a teacher were of more value to
England than they would be as a soldier, especially as hundreds of
thousands would be available as soon as the Conscription Bill would
be passed by Parliament. The war had gone on for about a year when
the inevitable happened; Park Hill School had to close down and
amalgamate with the "Priory," a well-known preparatory school
in Malvern. Mr. C. H. Giles, my new Headmaster—who had taken
my previous employer into partnership with him—was such a
charming person that I enjoyed every minute of my work, for
which, incidentally, I received £150 per year. Both my Headmasters and I were so busy teaching and looking after the boys,
numbering 120, that sometimes a week would pass without more
than cheerful "good mornings" and "good nights" being exchanged
between us. However, the flies in the ointment were one or two of
the temporary teachers, whom the boys "ragged" unmercifully.

As far as London was concerned, the effects of the war were not serious. True, there were certain shortages, and a few restrictions came into force, but there was no severe rationing. Meat was rather scarce, but otherwise almost anything could be bought without coupons at relatively reasonable prices, and in consequence there was no "black market." Owing to the possibility of Zeppelin raids, street lighting was dimmed down to what might be described as a "brown-out," but football matches and horse races still attracted huge crowds of potential soldiers. At last the Conscription Bill was passed, an historic event which, among many young men of a certain social class, started the great game of Army dodging.

One night, when I went to Blackfriars Ring to see if 'Arry and some of my old acquaintances were still in the "game," suddenly the military police appeared, blocking all exits. Stepping into the ring, an officer announced that a check-up would be made on everybody present, and politely asked Army exemption papers to be held in readiness for examination. Before his short speech was finished, there was a wild stampede, dodgers making frantic efforts to escape in every direction. Smashing a window, some reached adjoining roofs, but as one of them happened to be made of glass, several fugitives fell through it with disastrous results.

Unable to produce my identity papers, which I had left at home, together with a great number of young men I was marched to the nearest police station, where, after much palaver and a telephone call to a Cabinet Minister—whose boy I had formerly taught—I was released.

On another occasion when again I forgot to take my identity papers with me, and happened to be in the now defunct Oxford Theatre, I had an even more embarrassing experience. As we "dodgers" were marched out into the street, women hissed, booed and several even spat at us, and one—who must have been prepared for the occasion—presented some of us with white feathers. That the indiscriminate handing-out of such can have nasty repercussions to donors was proved to me when I happened to be dining with a friend in the Café Royal.

Whilst we were conversing, a most unpleasant-looking female

approached our table, and with a nasty sneer handed us one white feather apiece.

"Thanks," my companion said, rising to accept the gift, and then, with a resounding back-hander, he slapped the woman's face. As it happened, he was dressed in civilian clothes, having been granted leave from the Army in order to receive the Victoria Cross from the King.

As might be expected, a commotion followed this incident, but, upon recognising my companion, other diners became so indignant that they took the screaming woman by the scruff of her neck, and all but kicked her out of the restaurant.

A few days after this unpleasant happening, in the neighbourhood of Piccadilly Circus someone slapped me on the shoulder from behind. Turning round to ascertain who was thus greeting me, to my surprise I saw that it was a dashing bemonocled officer, whom I only recognised when he exclaimed, "Delighted to meet you, my deah Count So-and-So! This unexpected and delightful encounter calls for a drink, so let us go to the Leicester Lounge and duly celebrate it."

As we sat, Crimpus Jilt explained that, thanks to an influential friend, he had been given an important job at the War Office, and that, for the time being, he had to content himself with the rank of captain. He assured me that promotion was round the corner, and explained to me that on his shoulders rested tremendously heavy responsibilities, the nature of which, of course, he could not divulge. After having taken two or three double whiskies, he went as far as to let me into the secret that it was he, Captain Crimpus Jilt, who made the plans for the campaign in France—plans which, once put into effect, would bring the war to a speedy end.

Knowing my Crimpie, I listened patiently, and when he told me that he had not forgotten his promise to present me with a dinner jacket, I began to take a real interest in the one-sided conversation. Before departing to "attend to important duties," he invited me to meet him in the same bar two days hence, sharp at noon, in order to have a cocktail before going to have lunch at the Frascati Restaurant, which, according to him, was the only place in London where they knew how to prepare certain dishes of his fancy, and where black coffee and Napoleon brandy were better than anywhere else.

Thinking that at last I would get something out of Crimpie, I turned up at the Leicester Lounge as arranged. Upon entering the establishment, there I found him, waiting for me over a drink, and I noticed that he "wore" an ugly black eye. Before I had time to ask him where and how he had acquired such a war decoration, with a matter-of-fact smile he informed me that whilst playing polo —just for a little exercise and recreation from his heavy duties at the War Office—a rising ball had struck him.

In anticipation of an excellent meal, my mouth was beginning to water, when my companion suddenly felt the breast pockets of his tunic, and with assumed embarrassment told me that he had left all his money at the office.

"Heavens!" he exclaimed, closing the eye which still functioned, and at the same time striking his forehead with the palm of one hand. "Now I remembah that I have promised to meet Generals So-and-So and So-and-So at the Ritz, where one of the Chiefs of the General Staff is giving us lunch. Now, my deah Count, I wondah if you will be a brick and pay for the drinks. Anothah day I shall arrange a meeting, and then I shall royally make up for the inconvenience I am causing you now."

Saying this, without even waiting for my reply, he quickly rose, warmly shook my hand, and dashed out of the bar. And that was the last I ever saw of the great new military genius. However, as will be seen later, many years after he had played this last strategic trick on me, a typical Jiltian echo was to reach me.

·   ·   ·   ·

Shortly after compulsory military service had come into force, there was consternation in the Gristinian camp. Bill, who for years had done the bossing of his men, as well as in his home, shuddered at the very idea of having to join the Army. To make prospects even more unpleasant for him, he feared that, being illiterate, he would be put into an Army unit where he would have to mix with a rough crowd. Though, as we have already seen, Bill was not exactly an angel, he shunned "toughs" and hated discomfort.

" 'Oo in 'is right senses," he exclaimed, "wants to wade through trenches filled with mud and water, when so much work is waiting to be done in London? And supposin' I'm disabled for life, or even killed, 'oo will take me place in me 'ome, or as a builder and decorator?" For hours Bill argued that it was all very well for professional soldiers and idle rich men to fight, for, after all, surely the former didn't expect to be paid for only turning out on parades and for seeing to it that brass buttons were kept well polished? No, if a bloke made the Army his living, he had to expect to be called upon to fight, even if only once in his lifetime. As far as rich young men were concerned, if they were killed or maimed, there was plenty of money knocking about to smooth things over; so he didn't see why, of all people, the Prime Minister should pick on hard-working builders and decorators like him, Bill Gristin, to help professional soldiers out with the war, which, anyway, he hadn't started. Of course, if he had "pull," as, for instance, that parson-schoolmaster Crimpus Jilt appeared to have, and could get himself the job of redecorating the War Office and the Admiralty, he wouldn't mind doing a spot of work up there; for them generals and admirals have plenty of dough at their disposal, and he wouldn't say "No" if he were offered a little slice of it—mind you, not for doing nothing, but for making a posh job of them there buildings, which could very well do with a bit of expert touching up.

As, by degrees, the different age-groups were called up, Bill began to take an ever-increasing interest in the progress of the war, which, according to him, should have been won by the Allies long before. The Belgians, Froggies, Wops and Russians just weren't pulling their weight, and even the British Guards regiments weren't doing their stuff, and it really looked as if that Frenchman, Foch—or however you pronounced his name—purposely delayed the Big Push until Bill Gristin should cross the English Channel to do the dirty work for him.

Thus, more or less, my good landlord protested and argued for hours on end. Early every morning, when, as usual, Ivy read out for him the news from the *Mirror,* and still the end of the war was not announced, Bill went to his work with a heavy heart.

Shortly after the outbreak of war, the two Austrian "steadies," Franz and Hans, had been rounded up and sent to the Isle of Man as prisoners of war. Kind-hearted Ivy felt so sorry for the two young men that she kept up a regular correspondence with them, and frequently sent cigarettes and what she called "little bits of fancy food," as well as old magazines, to relieve the monotony of their existence behind barbed wire.

The two Austrians' internment was another source of annoyance to the thrifty Bill; for not only did the parcels his wife sent them cost money, but he lamented such wanton waste of manpower on the part of the authorities. True, in the case of Franz and Hans this did not amount to much, but, nevertheless, they had to be housed and fed at the tax-payers' expense for doing nothing all day long, when they would have made two quite useful assistants for him, especially since most able-bodied men had been "pinched" by the Army. Yes, there was a lot to be said for Bill's summing-up, which he always concluded by saying that it was a "cryin' shame!"

Those were truly heroic days. When the military authorities decided that London must be defended against possible aerial attacks, especially by Zeppelins, volunteers—mostly elderly men—came forward to man the guns which, in most cases, were of naval types. At the time, the range of aeroplanes was too short for flights from Belgium or northern France to London and back, and it was only later that the first "flying machines"—Fokkers, I believe—reached the Metropolis, where, particularly in a daylight raid on the City, a number of people were killed.

One of my friends, Sir Richard Harington, a retired judge from India, offered his services as a defender of the London skies, and I vividly remember when he came to me, asking if I could help him with mathematical calculations connected with range-finding. Unfortunately, I was of little or no assistance to him, but, nevertheless, he carried on the good work, regularly taking his turn at manning the gun, which, if nothing else, looked imposing, and, when fired, made a great and reassuring noise.

Zeppelins made two or three mild attacks on London, and it was during one of them that, to use Ivy's own words, "somethin' un'-eard-of an' shockin'" happened in one of her houses. It may have been due to the bad example set by our Water Board anarchist and the Reverend Crimpus Jilt, or possibly to "nerves," that the exemplary Richard, John, David Jones Esq. strayed from the straight and narrow path. Whatever the cause or causes may be ascribed to, the fact remains that the "Toff" got himself into a nasty jam.

Something strange and electric must have been in the atmosphere, for one evening the two old spinsters—who hitherto had lived together in peace and harmony like a couple of love-birds—had such a row that half the neighbourhood listened. After a while, one of the two women rushed out of the front door, and, shaking a feeble fist at her companion within, called her such names that most of us listeners blushed. Before turning to leave, the infuriated spinster shouted, "And I hope to-night the Germans will drop a bomb on you!"

Yes, incredible but true, those were her parting words. Even when Bill came home from his work, it took Ivy and several of us quite a while to convince him that we were not joking, and that what we told him about the two old spinsters' verbal battle was true.

After dinner, the "Toff," all dressed up, and holding his old bowler hat in one hand, peeped into the kitchen, and in a whisper told Ivy that he was going out for a little fresh air, and that, therefore, should anybody call for him, he would not be "at home" until next morning.

It must have been well after midnight when the sound of gunfire awakened me from my slumbers, and upon going to the window I could distinctly see, high up in the moonlit sky, a cigar-shaped Zeppelin coming from a north-westerly direction.

Two doors away from the "annex"—in which I occupied a first floor room—I could see the whole Gristin family craning their necks towards the sky, but after having shouted to me a few remarks expressing his opinion of air-raids, Germans and the war in general, Bill went back to bed, and I did the same. Although for some time afterwards I still heard voices and occasionally a thump, soon I once more dropped off to sleep.

Early in the morning I was awakened by someone knocking at my door, and when I asked who it was, in a loud whisper Ivy asked me to hurry to the kitchen, where she would tell me something interesting.

Wondering what this secrecy and early morning alarm might signify, I quickly dressed, and upon entering the kitchen found Bill and Ivy giggling and tittering like mischievous girls.

"Blimey! You missed somethin' last night," Ivy said. "There was a shockin' do. The 'Toff' ain't 'arf got 'isself into a mess!"

"The 'Toff'?" I asked. "What has he done?"

"Stroof!" Bill interrupted. "If to-day I fall off a ladder for laughin', and break me bloomin' neck, it will be Stintall's fault."

"Ssh, not so loud, Bill. If the poor blighter 'ears you, he'll get peeved. So shurrup, and let me tell the story," Ivy commanded.

Presently, whilst she spoke he listened, and every now and again laughed until tears streamed down his cheeks.

"Would you believe it," Ivy began in a shocked tone of voice, "but last night, on the sly, the 'Toff' brought 'ome a bird. I never saw 'er, and I knew nothin' abaht it till this morning, when one or two lodgers and neighbours told me the 'ole scandal. Oo, an' a shockin' to-do it must have been, but I can't 'elp laughin' all the same."

According to my landlady's story, this, briefly, is what had happened during the previous night.

Having successfully smuggled a girl friend up to his room, the "Toff" and she were having a rest when the guns started booming. Thrown into a state of hysteria and panic, the modern Eve dashed out into the street only half clad, and, upon becoming a little more composed, to her utter dismay realised that she did not remember the house in which she had been. Crying like a babe lost in a wood, she slumped down on the kerbstone where, fortunately, the old Welsh couple—who lodged at the Gristins—took compassion on her. Taking the unfortunate girl—who also happened to be a native of Wales—into their room, throughout the night the three prayed and sang hymns. From her the two good Samaritans got such a good

description of the man in whose company she had been prior to the
air raid that the finger of accusation pointed at one person in our
neighbourhood: Richard John David Jones Esq.; the "Toff."

How the would-be imitator of the Jiltian technique spent the rest
of the night, and what thoughts must have passed through his
bewildered brain, is best left to the imagination. In the early hours
of morning, when the old Welshman called to collect the garments
the girl had left behind, the "Toff" handed them over without
uttering a word.

A little later, having been given a cup of cocoa and some biscuits
by her two protectors, the hapless girl departed, whereafter the
indignant old Welshman made it his duty to report so unheard-of
a scandal to his landlord. Hardly had he finished his tale than other
eyewitnesses came to recount to Bill and Ivy certain parts of the
same "shockin' to-do." As far as the culprit was concerned, all that
day and during the next two or three he was an invisible man.

But to come to the strangest part of that memorable Zeppelin
raid.

It will be remembered that the two hitherto inseparable spinsters
had a serious disagreement, and that, before departing in a fury, one
had shouted at the other that she wished a German bomb would fall
on her that night.

Though, for some unaccountable reason, no one had heard or
noticed it during the raid, a bomb very nearly fulfilled the old
woman's curse. In the course of the following day, whilst the
Gristin children played in front of their house, in the very middle
of the little "garden," some five feet away from the window of the
ground-floor room in which the other spinster must have passed a
miserable and lonely night, the youngsters saw something strange
sticking out of the ground. Fortunately, their father happened to
pass, and when he examined that strange object, he immediately
guessed that it was the tail-end of an unexploded bomb.

The reader will be glad to learn that, after a night separated from
each other, there was a tearful reconciliation between the two
spinsters. During a short evacuation of several houses in our row,
whilst the bomb was being dug out by firemen, the two old ladies

stood round the corner of the street, locked in a tight embrace, probably praying that their treasured possessions should come to no harm.

To the whole neighbourhood's relief, the bomb was removed without mishap, and the two loving spinsters lived together happily ever after.

As different age groups were called up for military service, Bill's apprehension grew, and, with it, the anxious interest he took in the progress of the war. Hitherto, France—a peculiar country, in which, Bill had it from good authority, people lived on frogs and strange grub called "homlets"—had seemed to be far away. But now, as the war dragged on, Froggieland drew ominously nearer and nearer. Occasionally, when in a merry mood, or in order to disguise his inner feelings, in the back yard Bill imitated rifle drill and bayonet charges with a broomstick, chasing me or any bystander over the stacks of old building materials.

One night, after he had given us another lecture on waste of manpower and how the war could easily be won in a few days, we all retired, soon after to be awakened by the noise of anti-aircraft guns. This time, I did not even bother to get up, but, upon hearing excited people in the street shout, "Hurrah! He's burning!" and "Look, he's coming down!" I rushed to the window, just in time to see what might have been the afterglow of a red sunset. Next morning, the newspapers informed us that Lieutenant Robinson of the Royal Flying Corps had set fire to a Zeppelin with tracer bullets, and that the airship had crashed in flames at Potters Bar, all the members of its crew having been killed. A few days later, Robinson was awarded the Victoria Cross, and, strange to relate, some years later, when the airman died, he was laid to rest in the same cemetery where his victims were buried. And so, side by side lie the mortal remains of victor and vanquished.

·   ·   ·   ·   ·

Time passed, and still the "merchant"—who had been sentenced to three months' imprisonment for smuggling—failed to make an appearance, in order to claim the packing cases which, all that time, had been kept carefully locked up in two rooms. Bill's brother, Bert, the taxi-driver, must have kept an eye on the calendar, for now his visits became more and more frequent, and his interest in the "valuable goods" increased. However, every time he hinted that it could do no harm to open a box or two (of course, only just to see what they contained) Bill flatly refused to do so, and even when Ivy seconded her brother-in-law's proposal, the boss of the house firmly stuck to his resolution not to tamper with the "merchant's" property. During my next vacation, when the matter was again discussed *in camera*, and *in absentia* of the smuggler, and I sided with Bert and Ivy, the hitherto unswaying keeper of the keys to Ali Baba's cave began to waver.

Chapter VIII

The Gristinian Criminal Investigation Department makes important discoveries which are duly celebrated.—Bill Gristin's departure to the back of the Western Front.—His participation in the "Big Push," and subsequent retirement from active service.—Move to South America.

ONE Sunday, after we had eaten a good lunch, and we were sitting in the kitchen, discussing the "merchant," suddenly Bill rose and announced that the time had come to make an investigation.

Those were moments of suspense when he removed the padlock and inserted the key into the lock of one of the two back-rooms in which the "valuable goods" were stored. His brother Bert, Ivy, Stintall, the Water Board anarchist and I were there, watching in silence. When, accompanied by the creaking of rusty hinges, the door was pushed open, Bert—who was holding a hammer and a screwdriver in his hands—rushed forward, like a cat about to pounce on a mouse, but Bill stopped him, pressing the palm of a hand against his over-enthusiastic brother's chest.

"Whoa!" Bill exclaimed. "Don't be in such an 'urry. Give us the tools. *I'm* goin' to prise open a box, so stand back, all of you!"

Having lifted a large packing-case off a pile, he set to work, until nails began to squeak, and with an ugly snarl the lid gave way. Necks were craned, and eager eyes followed every movement as Bill removed the straw with which the inside of the box was padded. Presently, something shiny appeared, and to our astonishment that something turned out to be a bottle. Holding it up for our inspection, Bill asked what it "said" on the label, and when several voices informed him that it was champagne, he gave a drawn-out, significant whistle.

" 'Arf a mo'!" the taxi-driver said, looking very wise. "Don't you be too cock-sure that what's in this 'ere bottle is fizz. I 'aven't knocked abaht London for all these years wivout learnin' a thing or two. Never mind what it says on the label. Perhaps, inside the bottle the cunnin' old smuggler 'as 'idden pearls or even diamonds. Come on, Bill, 'and us the bottle. I'll 'ave a good look at it."

Having wiped the dust off the object of our curiosity, Bert held it up to the light. The glass being thick and dark green in colour, a proper examination was impossible, so our Sherlock Holmes suggested that we open the bottle, and thus continue our investigation.

It was no easy matter to make Bill give in to this suggestion, but, eventually, he fetched a pair of tongs and with them began to remove the wire with which the cork was secured.

"Look out!" Bert shouted. "If the cork comes out with a pop and 'its you in the eye, you're for it. Come on, let's 'ave the bottle; I'll show you 'ow to hopen it."

Gingerly, the dangerous object was handed over to the speaker, and as he twisted off the wire, and expertly began to wobble the cork to and fro, Bill and Ivy, with hands raised to protect their blinking eyes, stepped back a pace or two.

When, with a mild report, the cork blew out, and froth and liquid squirted over Bert's hands, he quickly licked up some of it.

"That's the stuff, all right!" he grunted, smacking his lips, and then, handing the bottle to Bill and Ivy, asked them to taste some of its contents.

"No fear," the latter replied. "For all you know, the stuff is poison."

Bill fully agreed with his wife, and went on to say that after what it had "said" in the *Mirror* about the smuggler, he wouldn't put anything past the bloke.

At this juncture the Water Board man—who knew something about other liquids besides the one which indirectly provided him with his bread and butter—came forward and heroically offered to act as a human guinea-pig. When the bottle was empty, and a careful examination of its interior revealed that it contained no jewels or other insoluble matter, it was replaced into its bed of straw, and the lid of the packing case was once more nailed down. Despite the protests voiced by the majority of the investigators, Bill locked the room, and went to hide the keys.

A few minutes later, when we reassembled in the kitchen, in order further to discuss the investigations, only so half-heartedly begun, Ivy and Bill cast searching glances at the Water Board expert, and when, after about an hour or so, he showed no signs of being any the worse for having experimented on himself with the champagne, Bill suddenly announced that he would fetch another couple of bottles. But he made it quite clear to us that the sole motive which prompted him to do this was of a purely scientific nature, and for the sake of criminal investigation.

Having said this, Bill left, shortly after to return with two samples, the contents of which we immediately began to analyse. This time, our landlord and his wife took an active part in the work, and when the empty bottles proved to contain no hidden treasure, two more were fetched.

We were engrossed in the study of the subject under our inquiry when the Greek artist came to ask for a penny he needed for the gas-meter. Although he knew nothing about the important investigation which was being made by us, Bill not only presented our El Greco with a few coppers, but also offered him a tankard filled with champagne. Noticing the look of astonishment on the recipient's face, Bill exclaimed, "Honour bright, it's real fizz. Come on, drink up. We're celebratin' Ivy's birthday."

That evening, Bill and his brother were in such a merry and generous mood that they treated all the members of the investigation committee to seats at the Shepherd's Bush Empire, where Marie Lloyd was performing. Bert himself drove us down in his taxi, and after the show took us for a ride along the whole length of the Embankment, stopping only at " 'ouɔoo" where he knew they served good beer.

Next day, although Bert and the Water Board expert urged Bill to make a really thorough search among the "valuable goods," the store-rooms remained locked, and it was only some time later that, after much pressure on the part of us technical advisers, he decided to reopen the Sesame.

Nothing had been seen or heard of the "merchant" for all that long time, so Bill felt more than justified, once and for all, to ascertain what the stacks of wooden cases contained.

In order to speed up operations, this time all of us were provided with suitable implements wherewith to prise open the boxes, and when Bill gave the word of command, we set to work like Trojans. All the packing cases in the first room proved to contain champagne, but upon tackling lot No. 2 we discovered four cases of *fine champagne*, which greatly puzzled the investigators, until I explained that, in plain English, the two mysterious words meant "brandy." Having opened a bottle, and tasted a little of its contents, everybody was satisfied that my statement was correct, whereafter investigations proceeded, until two smaller boxes were opened. These proved to contain an assortment of flasks, some embedded in satin-padded leather cases, which profoundly puzzled my collaborators, until, once more, I came to the rescue in the capacity of translator.

"Oh, look. Ain't these lovely!" Ivy exclaimed. "Well, I never. 'Ow pretty, and what fancy cases!"

" 'Ere, you 'ave a look, and tell us what it says on the labels. I can't make it out," Bert said, handing me one of the ornate little flasks. "I bet that's a drop of fancy booze what's in 'ere."

Though knowing very little about perfumes, I immediately guessed that the different brands submitted to me for examination were most expensive and rare, and that every flask almost represented its weight in gold.

Scents being of no interest to anyone present, except Ivy—who only very occasionally bought herself a tiny sixpenny flask in some bazaar—at this stage the Water Board man suggested that we open a couple of bottles of bubbly wherewith to quench our thirst. Bert enthusiastically seconded this proposal, but without even putting it to the vote of the assembly, Bill immediately prised open the case, out of which, some time previously, he had taken several samples.

"Come on, boys," he shouted. "Let's 'ave a good drink and a rest. We might just as well polish off the rest of this case."

As we sat on packing cases, drinking and smoking, I had another good look at the perfumes, and when I was asked to tell my fellow investigators what it "said" on the different labels, the conversation took a most unexpected turn.

Nuit d'Amour was the first I translated, and by the time my listeners knew the meaning of *Rêve d'Orient* and *Pour Exciter*, they had a great deal to say about the French and their peculiar ways.

Curiosity getting the better of Ivy, she opened a flask to have a smell. Delighted with the odour, after having taken a few sniffs, and made noises of ecstasy, she fairly soaked her handkerchief with scent, with the result that soon the strong smell in the room became nauseating. This circumstance and the "bubbly" consumed, made the conversation grow lighter and lighter, until it became distinctly frivolous.

Encyclopædic Bert, who claimed to know a great deal about the sons and daughters of "lah bell Frangce"—having driven many in his taxi, especially to and from Victoria Station—gave us such an interesting and spicy lecture that Ivy, who, like the rest of us, was in fits of laughter, left the room, doubled up, and, holding her aching sides, spluttered, "For 'eaven's sake, shurrup, Bert, I don't believe a word of it, you dirty 'ound!"

And so we carried on until the time came to replace lids on boxes, but before the store-rooms were once more locked, Ivy sneaked out with several flasks of scent. Later, when Bill found them on the kitchen mantelpiece, he fairly smothered everybody with scent, finishing by pouring the rest of the flask over the cat and Ivy's mongrel dog.

It being Christmas-time, and the ball having been set rolling, soon other champagne and brandy bottles were opened, and anybody who dropped in was given as much of it as he or she cared to drink. The ponderous police-sergeant and several of his subordinates became daily visitors, and any lodger or friend who popped into the Gristins' kitchen were offered as much champagne as they could drink. Even after the festive season, when Bill and his assistants resumed work in the building and decorating line, they never set out with their push-cart without putting a few bottles of champagne into it. With the passing of days, the smell of scent became so obnoxious that, without saying a word to his wife, he took away all the remaining flasks of perfume, and sold them to a second-hand dealer for a few shillings. Straw packing having been burnt in the back yard, and boxes broken up to be used as firewood, not a trace of the "valuable goods" was left. And as for the "merchant" and what became of him, none of us ever discovered. But, anyhow, who cared?

.   .   .   .   .

At long last the military authorities awakened to the fact that Bill Gristin was the man to bring the war to a speedy and victorious end. Accordingly, the hitherto overlooked strategic genius was enrolled as a private in a labour battalion. Even if there is any truth in the Napoleonic maxim that every common soldier carries a field marshal's baton in his knapsack, Bill, for one, being an eminently practical sort of man, did not bother to search through his kit to ascertain if any such trifle was hidden in it. Instead of thus wasting his and the Army's time, he looked for an opening which might lead to a position whence, from afar, he could follow operations in the various battlefields. Being a bit of a plumber, his services soon became invaluable in an Army laundry, and when his "outfit" moved over to France, his chief concern was how and where to hide his money. Banks he did not trust, and War Loan certificates were too mysterious for words, so he did the next best thing with several hundred golden coins he had saved; he buried them. This "hush-hush" operation was carried out with such cunning that not even his wife knew where Bill hid the bulk of his treasure; but, being a good husband and father, he saw to it that his family should have plenty of "dough" wherewith to carry on during his absence. All gold coinage having been called in by the Bank of England, before going abroad he asked me to change a hundred "quid" for him; for, as he explained, it would never do to be seen in the Army carrying about so much gold.

There was nothing heroic or sentimental about Private Bill Gristin's departure to the back of the Western Front. A pint of beer having been dealt with in a soldierly manner, he firmly deposited the empty glass on the counter in the station refreshment-room, and with a cheerful, "So long, chums, I'll be seein' you," marched towards the platform.

Ivy carried on with her housework and other activities as usual, and Bill's foreman did his best to live up to the reputation his boss had made for himself in the building and decorating trade. Over in France, friendly laundry warriors wrote letters for the illiterate Bill, who every now and again reported that all was well on the steam and hot-water front, and that, French beer being no good, or worse, he had sampled wine, which, to his surprise, did not make him feel queer.

Besides being skilled in different branches of manual labour, Bill was also a bit of a clairvoyant. Of this he had given clear proof when, long before being called up for military service, he had predicted that the day would come when the Allied General Staff would have to call on him to do the dirty work for them. These prophetic words were fulfilled when, after a prolonged spell of assisting in the washing of Army shirts, socks and underwear, Private William Gristin was whisked out of his laundry and rushed to the Western Front, where, for a most unpleasant change, a big demolition job awaited his expert attention. Shortly after his appearance on the scene of action, when cracks and fissures were beginning to appear on old Hindenburg's wall, Ivy was officially informed that her husband had been wounded, and that he was lying in a military hospital near London.

How it happened, Bill never divulged to anyone, but when Ivy, together with a few intimate friends, went to see him, and the surgeon explained that the wound was not serious, a bullet having shattered the first metatarsal bone where the big toe joins it, the invalid listened with tremendous interest. When the doctor turned to the wounded hero and informed him that this injury would incapacitate him for further participation in the war, and that, in consequence, upon recovering sufficiently to be sent home, he would be dismissed from His Majesty's Forces with a small pension, it was only with the greatest difficulty and a supreme effort at self-control that Bill succeeded to repress whoops and tears of joy.

.   .   .   .   .

The foregoing chapters are intended to show the reader that, by
the time I decided to shift my camp to South America, my general
education had reached a level sufficiently high to enable me to face
most situations that might arise.

In some respects, I felt genuinely sorry when the time came to
leave the two Headmasters who jointly ran that very delightful
preparatory school in Malvern. I was still only a very young man,
and the world was open to me, so it was my determination to see
as much of it as possible, and, should I spot an attractive green twig
during my migratory flight, to alight upon it. My only capital
consisted of the money I had saved, perfect health, and the determination to open a path for myself. Among a few parting gifts,
both Headmasters presented me with excellent and most flattering
testimonials, one stating that, during the time I had been in his
employ, I had "won the affection and respect of the boys," that I
was "a keen, painstaking and good teacher and disciplinarian," and
that he regretted that I had decided to move on to a wider sphere of
activity. "I am sure," he concluded, "that he will be a valuable
acquisition in whatever work he takes up."

The other testimonial was even more flattering. Among other
nice things, this Headmaster—who subsequently returned to Eton,
where he had formerly taught—wrote:

". . . I can with the greatest confidence recommend him for a post
of assistant master. I cannot speak too highly of the help that he
gave me. I consider him to be an excellent teacher in the subjects
which he undertakes. . . . He is very keen, painstaking and method-
ical, and has a high ideal as to discipline. He is very good-tempered
and unselfish, and is always ready to join in the boys' games and
recreations in the most pleasant way, which gains him popularity
among them. He is a fine athlete and is a good deal above the average
in intellectual ability. . . ."

As will be seen later, in comparison with what was in store for me
in the New World, my practical experiences in schools, and life in
general, amounted to no more than any lively young lady can
acquire in a finishing school.

Chapter IX

Arrival in Buenos Aires.—An eventful railway journey into the heart of the Pampa.—Romantic gaucho abode near a lagoon.—Cattle-work and bronco-riding.—Pampa night.—The "Argentine Eton."

A NUMBER of people have told me that, upon arriving in various parts of the world where they had never been before, they felt as if they vaguely knew them. This is what happened to me upon landing in Buenos Aires, and shortly afterwards too, when I went out into the pampa to visit my brother, whom I had not seen for many years. True, in the city there were noises which sounded strange to my ears: the hoarse, throaty cries of newspaper-vendors and street merchants, the clanging of tram-car bells, the shrill notes of small pan-pipes played by ambulant knife-sharpeners looking for clients, and tango orchestras playing in cafés filled with crowds of arguing and gesticulating men, many of whom acted and vociferated as if they were about to fly at one another's throats.

My first long railway journey out to the central pampa was an unforgettable experience. The train left Buenos Aires as it was getting dark, so, after having enjoyed an excellent dinner in the restaurant-car, I made my way to a sleeping-compartment built to hold four passengers. Fortunately, the train was not very full, and therefore I hoped to get a compartment to myself. It was no easy matter to make the guard understand my, at the time, bad Spanish, but after having slipped the man a tip, he assured me that I would be the only occupant of the compartment, in which were two top and two lower bunks. I was unpacking a few things from a hand-bag when the guard returned, with profuse apologies and much gesticulation to inform me that there had been a slight mistake, and that in consequence I would have to share my compartment with someone else. Naturally, I raised no objection to this, and when my cabin companion turned up, I was glad to see that he was a well-dressed, affable and pleasant young man.

Soon after the guard retired, the two of us were in our respective lower bunks, and after the electric lights had been switched off, I listened to the monotonous rhythm of wheels chattering over joints of the rails. Unaccustomed to travelling in sleeping-cars, I could not sleep, and when, at long intervals, I was about to doze off, invariably the train arrived at a station where people shouted and trampled up and down the corridor, dogs barked, horses neighed, klaxon horns were sounded, and motor-car engines back-fired, burred and spluttered. When, at long last, the locomotive's whistle shrieked as if it had a bad cold, and, soon after, with jolts and jerks the train once more began to move, my struggles to catch elusive sleep would be resumed. Several times during the night, when some wandering skunk was frightened or was run over by the train, he squirted out defensive liquid, with the result that the overpowering smell diffused itself throughout the interior of the carriages. Again, I heard peculiar shrill cries of night birds, or hollow metallic clanking when the train passed over a bridge.

I was glad when the first daylight filtered through the shuttered and mosquito-wired window of our compartment, and the time came to go to the restaurant-car for breakfast.

An amazing and almost overwhelming sight greeted my eyes when I looked through the window. From a cloudless azure sky, the rising sun cast its brilliant rays over a vibrating sea of grass, dotted here and there with cattle, horses and sheep. So this was the pampa, the plain so flat and vast that it passes monotony; the pampa with its ever-changing lights and subtle shades, the immense expanse, beautiful, incomprehensible, bordering on the abstract; a kind of sublime temple, erected by Nature, for us mortals to catch a glimpse of infinity.

Whilst gazing at the indescribable *mise en scène*, again, as had been the case when I arrived in Buenos Aires, a feeling overcame me that I had been in the pampa before. Perhaps the peculiar, vague affinity that seemed to draw me towards that immense plain was due to the fact that I remembered stories I had heard about my paternal grand-father, who had roamed over it in the time when Indians were on the warpath, and because I knew that my ancestor's mortal remains lay buried somewhere in that ocean of grass and sky.

As I sat, musing, but unable to concentrate my thoughts on anything in particular, my cabin companion joined me, and soon afterwards the two of us sipped aromatic coffee and milk and enjoyed crisp rolls, butter and marmalade. After breakfast, the warm sun and the motion of the train began to make me feel so drowsy that I returned to my cabin in order to rest, and thus to make up for the sleep I had missed during the night. The attendant had already taken away sheets and blankets, and, leaving the pillows on the bunks, had transformed them into comfortable couches. The top bunks having been folded against the wall, the cabin now looked like a small sitting-room, and shortly after I had stretched myself out to read a book, I fell into a deep, heavy sleep. How long it lasted I do not know, but the next thing I remember vaguely is hearing a noise as if a door had been slammed. Upon being shaken by someone, I awoke with a start, wondering if I was being called because the train was approaching my destination. To my surprise, the guard and the sleeping-car attendant were in my cabin, whilst several people peeped into it through the open door. Presently, a man who looked as if he might be a rancher, said to me, in English, and with a wry smile playing over his face, "You seem to be a heavy sleeper."

Taken aback by this remark, I gabbled something about not having slept a wink all night, whereupon the man, pointing at the bunk opposite mine, drily remarked, "Just have a look at that."

There, sitting up, leaning against a corner of the wall, was my cabin companion, apparently also having a snooze. However, upon looking at him more carefully, to my astonishment I noticed that in his right hand—which rested on his lap—he loosely held a revolver, and upon casting a searching look at his face, I saw that it was pale and that blood trickled out of his nose. On his right temple was a dark, circular smudge, and in the middle of it a tiny hole. The young man, in whose company I had taken breakfast, and with whom I had shared the cabin, had committed suicide.

The rancher, having introduced himself to me as an Englishman, spoke again. "You don't want to get involved in this," he said, "for if the police grab you as a witness, you're in for an endless rigmarole; so let me help you shift your things to my cabin. Leave the guard to me, I'll see to it that he tells the authorities that no one was present when that young chap bumped himself off."

At the next station, the corpse was taken off the train by what appeared to be two Indians dressed in shabby brown uniforms. Both had slightly curved swords, and in holsters they carried one revolver apiece, which, together with a pair of shiny handcuffs which dangled from their belts, made the two *vigilantes* look extremely business-like. When the *autoridades* arrived on the scene in a rattle-trap "whisker" Ford car, the pow-wow started, but, fortunately, I only looked on from the window of the train. Fountain-pens, pencils, notebooks and sheets of paper were produced, orders were shouted, curious onlookers were barked at to stand back, the railway guard gesticulated so fast and excitedly that it was surprising that his arms and hands did not become disjointed, secretaries scribbled furiously, and horrified women lamented loudly, and all the while the corpse lay stretched out on the platform, looking as if wondering what all this fuss was about.

Eventually, sheets of paper having been filled in, the train was allowed to proceed. As it drew out of the little station, *investigaciones, anotaciones, protocolos, sumarios* and the *conmoción* proceeded over what might have been mistaken for a tailor's dummy lying in a horizontal position.

When I told my saviour, the English rancher, that this was my first railway journey in the Argentine, he smilingly remarked that I certainly had made an original start, and put it to me in strong terms of recommendation always to make myself invisible should anything happen for which the police might require witnesses.

Upon arriving at my destination, I waited on the platform until most of the people had gone. I had not seen my brother since I was a boy, but eventually we recognised each other, whereafter there was a happy reunion.

Outside the station, in a wide, sandy road, baggy-trousered

gauchos leapt on lively horses which had been tied to hitch rails, trees or fences, and whilst some people drove off in rusty and dusty cars, others did likewise in horse-drawn vehicles of every type, size and description.

I liked the atmosphere of that little pampa town, with its one storied, flat-roofed, brick-built houses, and picturesque stores, in which anything from motors, pianos and cradles, down to rat poison, toothpicks and coffins could be bought. But what struck me most were the people, all of whom, despite the fact that I spoke but little Spanish, had a friendly smile and word for me.

Unlike many Englishmen and Americans who, taken *en masse*, are atrocious linguists, no one in the Argentine ever laughed at my efforts to make myself understood in Spanish. Instead of being amused by my, no doubt, often laughable mistakes, they took great pains to help me out of my difficulties. Even children did the same, and, therefore, feeling at my ease, I jabbered away merrily, thus rapidly improving my knowledge of their language.

About a mile out of the town was a beautiful lagoon, where I often went to watch flamingos, ducks, black-necked Magellanic swans and other water birds which abounded there. In those peaceful surroundings, it was a joy to swim or sit for hours on end, day-dreaming and admiring the scenery. On the far side of the limpid waters, stood a little ranch, owned by a family of gauchos with whom my brother was very friendly. Whenever I went there, I was given a warm welcome, and anything those good people had to offer was at my disposal. The two low, mud-built dwellings, with their quaint thatched roofs, stood on the brow of a low, grassy undulation (*loma*), and from beneath a few weeping willows which afforded shade, one had an impressive view of the lagoon and the rolling pampa beyond. Sitting on a rickety wooden stool, or on the sun-bleached skull of a horse or cow, I liked to chat with my new friends, who made great efforts to improve my Spanish, but what I enjoyed most, was when we saddled horses on which to canter over the plain.

At first, if we happened to be chasing some elusive steer, and my pony twisted, or suddenly turned to head off the truant, I frequently lost my balance. At such times, to my companions' amusement, in order not to fall, I grabbed my mount's mane or the sheepskins with which pampa saddles are covered. No twist or sudden turn of a horse made the slightest difference to the gauchos, and when they lassoed a steer, any greenhorn, such as I was at the time, might have thought it would be child's play to do the same. Lassoing an animal, throwing it to the ground, and tying it up into a helpless bundle was only a matter of seconds, and when the victim was released, the gauchos leapt on to their mounts with ease and grace, presently, while cantering along, to gather up the lasso in coils, thus making ready for the next throw.

All the horses were neck-reined, and the rather heavy bits were only used when absolutely necessary, usually in order to check the wild gallop of some "flighty" mount. How marvellously those sturdy stock ponies responded to the slightest touch on the neck or in the mouth! It did not take me long to realise that alongside those centaurs I was a mere babe, and that there was a great deal for me to learn before I should be able to join in their work without making a fool of myself.

It was near that pampa lagoon that I made up my mind to forget all about the riding I knew, to start learning again, from the beginning, and to try to copy the gauchos' manner of bestriding and handling a horse. That this would take time, and that the apprenticeship would not be an easy one, I fully realised, but, on the other hand, it promised to be interesting and, above all, great fun and most exciting.

One Sunday, for my benefit, three broncos were rounded up and driven into the corral. One of them was particularly famed as a wicked buck-jumper, so it looked as if a good show were in store for me. My brother—who previously had done a great deal of rough-riding—offered to mount the beast. First it was lassoed, and when, after a tremendous struggle, the saddle was placed on it, he leapt on. Presently, as soon as the ropes, with which the animal's legs were tied, were released, the pampa war dance began. Squealing with rage, snorting and grunting, the bronco bucked, spun round and round like a top, sun-fished, kicked and bit at the stirrups, and when these and other methods failed to get rid of the rider, the beast threw itself over backwards, only to find that the intended victim, having anticipated the danger, had slipped off. When the bronco rose, my brother quickly leapt on him, and so the tussle continued, until, beginning to feel tired, and realising the futility of thus trying to shake off the rider, the horse adopted new tactics. Racing off at top speed, and at short intervals suddenly propping, or bucking from side to side, the four-footed demon fought desperately, but it was of no avail; my brother remained firmly stuck to the saddle. Two gauchos who were riding alongside now wedged the bronco between their mounts, and thus, describing a vast semicircle, forced him back towards the corral, where, out of breath, dripping with perspiration and groggy, he surrendered. (In the Argentine such assistants are called *padrinos*—god-fathers.)

Gauchos rode the other buck-jumpers, and, even to my inexpert eyes, it seemed that they did it with an ease and confidence my brother had not shown. When the last bronco had been ridden to a standstill, and the rider leapt off him, he turned to me and said that it was now my turn to show what I could do. Seeing an orphan calf, which was kept in a nearby enclosure, in my best Spanish I replied that if someone saddled the little animal for me, I would mount without hesitation. This made everybody laugh heartily, and after that my friends in that picturesque little ranch often called me *domador de terneros*, meaning "breaker-in of calves."

That evening, after having eaten meat roasted on a spear, as well as excellent pastry prepared by the women, we went to sit on our favourite spot under the weeping willow trees. Whilst one of the gauchos played simple tunes on his guitar, and sang a few songs in a high, falsetto voice, I envied no one in this world.

Resembling a huge crimson balloon, the moon rose out of what might have been taken for a prairie fire at the horizon, gradually to change its colour until it became a large, silvery disc, the pale light of which bathed the mysterious pampa. When, in order to light a cigarette, the guitarist interrupted his playing, the only sounds which broke the silence were the soft rustling of leaves as a gentle breeze blew through them, or, from afar, the bellowing of cattle, the neighing of horses, and the shrill cry or mournful hooting of some night bird.

As I sat there, little did I dream that, some day, I would be riding over that pampa, hundreds and hundreds of miles, from the far south to the northern Andean shore of that vast inland ocean, and thousands of miles beyond, over snow-capped *cordilleras*, down into steaming jungles, across burning deserts, on to the United States of America. But the first seed which led to that adventure was sown, unknown to me at the time, on such a night, under the weeping willow trees outside that friendly gaucho family's modest but romantic abode near the pampa lagoon.

I could have stayed there for ever, without wishing for anything better in this world, but, like the vast majority of my fellow men, I was born to work.

I was in a quandary, trying to decide what to do, when a Scottish rancher—whom I had befriended in the town—told me that English schools in Buenos Aires were understaffed and that, if I advertised in a newspaper, headmasters would fairly jump at me to help them out of their difficulties.

Thinking the matter over, I came to the conclusion that, if I went to teach in a school, and in my spare time studied Spanish, after a year or so I could take up ranching, and thus lead the kind of life for which I longed. Although the very idea of going back to classrooms filled me with gloom, I returned to Buenos Aires, where, shortly after my arrival, I put an advertisement in the *Standard*, an old newspaper printed in the English language. Twenty-four hours after my "bit" appeared, I received several replies, among them one written by a headmaster who signed himself Canon J. T. Stevenson. Among other things, he informed me that his was the largest English college in South America, and that it was situated in ideal surrounding on the outskirts of a suburban town named Quilmes, about ten miles from Buenos Aires. The writer furthermore informed me that all his pupils were full boarders, and, as a kind of bait, in singularly modest words added that certain discriminating members of the British community in Buenos Aires often called his scholastic institution the "Argentine Eton."

Apart from this tremendous attraction, the salary offered for my services was such that, two days before the boys returned to school from their long summer holidays, I travelled out to Quilmes—so named after an Indian tribe which, about half a century before my arrival, had camped there. After a bumpy ride in a rickety, horse-drawn coach, a little beyond the outskirts of the town I arrived at a gate, on which, in three-inch letters, was written ST. GEORGE'S COLLEGE.

The last few hundred yards of the dirt track we had followed, had severely tested my nerves. The deep ruts along which the coachman —who strongly smelt of garlic—had steered his two old nags, had been so tortuous and tricky that more than once I held my breath. The "road" was overgrown with high grass and masses of camomile plants, which were in full bloom at the time, and it was evident to me that in wet weather no vehicle could possibly reach the "Argentine Eton." The last few human habitations we had left behind us were ramshackle, brick-built huts and tin shanties, but the college playfields, surrounded by tall, stately eucalyptus trees, looked quite attractive.

When, shortly after my arrival, I met the Headmaster, he looked me up and down, as might a crafty horse-dealer who has bought an animal on the "blind."

White-haired and fairly broad-shouldered, Canon Stevenson was a pompous and distinguished-looking man. About fifty years of age, he was slightly above medium height and inclined to be stout. There was something of the bird of prey about his clean-shaven face and penetrating, rather closely-set grey-blue eyes.

Having greeted me in a manner which suggested that he approved of my appearance, he led the way to my quarters. To my surprise, upon reaching a small square building, on the ground floor of which was the college laundry, he proceeded to climb up a kind of exterior iron staircase, which reminded me of a ship's ladder. Upstairs there were two small rooms, one of which, my leader informed me, was occupied by an assistant master who was due to return from his vacation on the morrow. A narrow passage and a primitive bathroom, with a badly chipped hand-wash basin and

I

rusty bath tub with a shower above it, completed the accommodation for two. The furniture in my room reminded me of the Gristins'
very worst, but this I did not mind as much as the smell of steam and
soap which rose through the floor boards from the laundry below.
However, I refrained from making spoken criticisms, but as the two
of us clambered down the metal ship's ladder, and I was shown the
buildings and classrooms with their dilapidated wooden desks,
the lids of which were pock-marked with initials which pupils in
search of immortality had engraved in them, I began to wonder
if what I looked at was a museum of the early Spanish colonial
days.

The place in which, presumably, profound learning was imparted
was a kind of low wooden shed with a corrugated iron roof. At the
back end, behind a wooden screen, was the science laboratory,
which contained a few jam-jars, empty bottles, a methylated spirit
cooker, and some other odds and ends. At the opposite end of this
shed was a stage with a filthy dark-green plush curtain, behind which
was another classroom. A movable wooden partition, which ran
along the full length of the "auditorium" from the stage to the
laboratory, divided the intervening space into two sections, both of
which were also classrooms. Alongside this shed was a large chicken-
run and a wooden pergola, some fifty yards in length, and overgrown with vines. This connected the shed with the main building,
in which were the dormitories and dining-hall. A long, corrugated-
iron shack served as an extra classroom and library combined, and
alongside this construction, a rectangular concrete pit, covered over
with a tin roof, was the swimming pool.

In startling contrast with the buildings described, the chapel was
magnificent. Built of solid stone, with its excellent organ, stained-
glass windows and oak pews, one might have thought St. George's
College to be an ecclesiastical training centre. The Headmaster's
private house, situated among splendid sub-tropical gardens, was
beautifully furnished and most comfortable, as befits the mighty.
Standing on the edge of a bank, among palm, orange, lemon and
eucalyptus trees, the house had a veranda from which one had a
splendid view of the imposing River Plate in the distance.

The "Argentine Eton" was so ramshackle and depressing that I was glad when the pupils returned from their holidays, and I had to work from the early hours of morning until late at night. Every morning, when the chapel clock struck seven, the heavy oak door was closed by one of the big boys who acted as sacristan, thus shutting out belated stragglers who usually were only half dressed, as were some of the luckier ones who had managed to squeeze in, during the service to complete their *toilette*. At 7 p.m., once more we assembled in the chapel, and on Sundays the full Communion was celebrated and morning and evening services were held. On wet Sundays, during the afternoon, the wretched boys were made to go to dull organ recitals which were torture to everyone save the organist.

I took good care to take possession of the seat in the pew nearest to the door. Thus, whenever a boy felt unwell and left the chapel, acting the good Samaritan, I accompanied him out, not to return until the next session. This happened so frequently, that, when the other masters saw through my game, I almost had to fight them to keep my "pitch."

Canon Stevenson was a good, though often most aggressive and offensive preacher, but after having heard half a dozen of his sermons, the rest were more or less the same. If he happened to be in a bad mood, whilst hymns or psalms were being sung he fairly galloped away from the organ, choir and congregation. At such times, his normally loud voice sounded like the bellowing of an infuriated bull. I used to enjoy such interludes, but the poor organist took a very different view of such musical stampedes.

The Canon's gift for resisting knowledge was remarkable. Despite the fact that he had lived in the Argentine for over twenty years, his Spanish was such that it was amazing with what ease he could make himself misunderstood. Any English word with an "o" added to it was good enough Spanish for him, and the few words of Cervantes' language which he knew were pronounced so badly that this frequently led to highly amusing situations and incidents.

Most of my colleagues on the teaching staff were "imported"

directly from England. Whenever a new candidate was engaged in London (by one of the Headmaster's friends who acted as a kind of whipper-in) the Canon loved to tell us that a wonderful teacher was about to arrive. In his pompous voice, he always pronounced the qualifying adjective "wurnderful." In several cases such geniuses of modern education never reached their destination, but others blew in and out of the college like autumn leaves being whirled along in a gale. On their voyage to the Argentine, on board ship they met beef, textile, or sanitary engineering kings, who were so democratic and liberal with their money that our innocent lambs—who had never travelled in such company, let alone spoken as man to man with millionaires—lost their heads to such an extent that they tried to drink the ship dry. Upon arrival in glamorous Buenos Aires, several of our new candidates went completely "off the rails," cabarets and gay night life causing them to slither as if on ice, with the result that, after having spent a few hectic days in the city, these wurnderful men had to be sent back to England, sometimes in the same ship in which they had arrived.

Most of the really good and serious masters who joined our staff did not last long, for either they resigned after a term, or the Headmaster grew tired of them; with the result that on the "Road to Buenos Aires" masters travelled forwards and backwards in such numbers that the humorous captain of an English ship once remarked that, were it not for St. George's College, he would have no passengers to carry.

Without telling anybody where I spent my vacations, three or four times I returned to the little ranch near the lagoon, and from there set out, on horseback, to jog over the pampa. Besides the gauchesque clothes I wore for convenience and comfort, all I took with me on such expeditions were my shaving tackle, a toothbrush and a banjo, which I carried slung over my back. Thus, avoiding big *estancias,* where people might have recognised me, or thought it strange for a more or less respectable *gringo* to have turned tramp, I went from one small ranch to another. Everywhere I called, people received me as an honoured guest, and when I picked out a few tunes on my instrument, or to its accompaniment hummed songs, my listeners were delighted, or, perhaps, out of innate politeness, pretended to be.

Some of our pupils came from distant parts, such as the Falkland Islands, Tierra del Fuego, Patagonia, Chili, Uruguay, and one or two even from Bolivia and Brazil. Others hailed from different parts of the Argentine, but the main bulk came from Buenos Aires, where their fathers were in business.

During both world wars, a great many Old Boys from St. George's offered their services to the British Army, and several of these volunteers rose to high rank, and a considerable number of others were killed in action.

Taking them by and large, the pupils at St. George's College were a most pleasant lot, and, on the average, they were fitter and stronger than English public school boys. Probably this was due to the fact that a great many of our pupils came from ranches where they led open-air lives, with plenty of riding, swimming and other exercise. Having lived among rough diamonds ever since their early boyhood, they were much more grown-up and worldly-wise than boys of a corresponding age in England. It was fortunate that most of our pupils were so understanding, and that, in consequence, in having to put up with the peculiarities of some members of our teaching staff, like the Scottish poet they more or less held that "a man's a man for a' that."

Chapter X

IN the happy-go-lucky days before life in the Argentine became
officially organised, more strange characters and "oddities" were
to be found there than, I dare say, anywhere else in the world, with
the possible exception of certain parts of Africa. Buenos Aires—
often called "Queen of the Southern Hemisphere"—was the
favourite hunting ground for remittance men, adventurers, mounte-
banks and immigrants determined to "make good." If a person of
the last category had a level head and the will to get on, the chances
of success were highly favourable.

Among my many casual acquaintances were several remittance
men. No doubt they had made themselves impossible at home, and
therefore, in order to save the reputations of their respective families,
the gay young gentlemen were dispatched abroad with tidy sums
of money to give them a start, or, perhaps, to precipitate their
sinking beneath the muddy waves of life on which they had chosen
to frolic. Upon arrival in Buenos Aires, these lively sparks usually
lived like princes, and, in some cases—especially if they were
bearers of titles—so impressed some of their *nouveau riche* countrymen that the latter tumbled over one another in order to invite the
newcomers to their homes. It was wonderful while it lasted, but,
sooner or later, the inevitable happened: princes became paupers,
and eventually faded out of the picture, usually leaving behind a
trail of debts.

Whenever I was in need of a change, I went to certain cafés or
bars where I met some really interesting characters, with some of
whom I became friendly. It did not take me long to pigeon-hole
my acquaintances, and to classify them in my mental social register.
Solid substance I learnt at a glance to differentiate from liquid, and

I soon became aware that gas has neither volume nor shape. Here I must remark that most of the "smarties' " conversation amounted to nothing but "gas," as is the case with similar people, including the vast majority of politicians, all over the world.

The old Hotel "Universel," situated in the very heart of Buenos Aires, was a favourite bachelors' establishment, where "camp men" (as ranchers are called in the Argentine) used to stay whilst on visits to the city. Besides these often wild men from the pampa, all sorts of English-speaking guests made the kind of glorified hostelry their home from home. Even in 1870, the place was famed for its often lively clients, and readers who are familiar with the late Cunninghame Graham's works will remember how delight-fully he described the "Casa Claraz," as the "Universel" was called in those days. The tall and bearded Claraz was a Swiss who took much more interest in botany and ornithology than in the running of his hotel, which, after his death, passed into other hands.

The old building was square, box-like, with a *patio* in the middle. The three floors were arranged in galleries, all rooms facing the *patio*. As in the case of many buildings of similar type, the rooms had no windows, but, instead, large glass doors with wooden shutters. In the *patio*, below two tiers of inside balconies, were placed a few garden benches and palm trees, which gave the place a pleasant aspect. A small and primitive Turkish bath was a great asset to the establishment, for after stormy nights on the tiles, weary patrons frequently assembled in the hot rooms, before once more sallying forth into the fray of gaiety.

Everybody was friendly in the "Universel," and if any known client required money, there was no need to go to the bank; all he had to do was to ask the porter, who without hesitation produced the cash. Sometimes, especially in the early hours of morning, when revellers returned home in a boisterous mood, there was pande-monium, and more than once lights were shot out, and, for a little additional amusement and physical exercise, furniture and crockery were thrown down into the *patio*. Such playful interludes were taken for granted by most of the guests, and caused no ill-feeling with the proprietor, who knew very well that, in due time, damages would be paid for with compound interest.

It was a sad day when the "Universel" had to move to new premises, and it is to be lamented that no one ever wrote the memoirs of that old establishment, for such a work might easily have become a classic of its kind.

To-day, a modern building with its offices and lifts stands as a tombstone to the old Casa Claraz and its variegated assortment of inmates, most of whom have vanished behind the curtain of oblivion.

A new "Universel," more or less modelled on the original hotel, was opened near the Royal Mail Building, in which the British Embassy and Consulate have their offices. Attached to the new establishment was a small, cosy and well furnished restaurant and bar, in which Embassy secretaries, Scottish cattle-dealers, business-men, captains of ships, and all sorts of other men, including, sometimes, a small contingent from St. George's College, assembled to make conversation over drinks. Though officially named "The Criterion," clients usually referred to this bar, as well as to the hotel, as "Dirty Dick's," so nicknamed after the famous old tavern in London.

So many were the extraordinary and unconventional men I met —and in some cases befriended—in this establishment, that here I will only briefly refer to two or three of the most remarkable or amusing ones among them.

Ever since I can remember, I usually associated with people who were considerably older than myself. In Buenos Aires, one of my best friends was an Irishman who was close on eighty years of age when the two of us met for the first time.

Near "Dirty Dick's"—where the old man lived—was the "Britannia" bar, run by a certain Bill Carey. Late one night, after I had been at the opera and was waiting for the last train to take me out to the College, I thought of having a glass of beer and a sandwich. The "Britannia" being near, I entered and sat down in a corner. A number of English seamen were at the far end of the long room singing songs to the accompaniment of a tinny piano played by a countryman of theirs who had seen better days. Whilst sitting on my own, enjoying my food and drink, I watched and listened, and it did not take me long to realise that some of the sailors were in an exceedingly merry mood. How it started, I did not see, but before I knew what was happening, several of the songsters began to fight, and when the proprietor of the bar went to intervene, the whole gang turned on him.

A tall, powerfully-built, though slightly bent old man, who had been sitting on his own in a corner, adjusted his large black hat, and I noticed that his clean-shaven bull-dog face assumed a most determined expression.

Finding himself assailed by a number of sailors, who resented his intervention, Bill Carey slowly backed down the room towards the corner where the old man sat. Presently, when one of the ruffians picked up a chair, and with it attempted to strike Carey, the old man with the black hat rose, and with a terrific punch knocked down the sailor, in the nick of time to prevent him from crashing the chair down on his intended victim's head. With astonishing speed, the tall and massive old man picked up another chair, and, swinging it round as if it weighed but a few ounces drove the sailors out into the street, down which they fled, helter-skelter, as if the devil were chasing them. It all happened so quickly that I merely sat, watching what was going in. When the bar was clear of disturbers of its peace, the old man readjusted his hat, sat down, and, having to some measure recovered his breath, lit a pipe, and calmly sipped his beer.

"You're a tough customer," I said to him, for the sake of saying something.

What, in reply, he growled, referring to the sailors, is best left unwritten. Having finished airing his opinion of them, in a friendly tone of voice he asked me to join him at his table, where he introduced himself as Dennis Long. From that day on "Daddy"—as I later called him—became one of my best friends, and whenever the two of us met, we had great fun, and this remarkable old man told me many fascinating stories connected with experiences he had had during his long and adventurous life.

My colleagues at the college were not interested in operas, concerts or what they called "Dago" theatres, so whenever I went to a show, I had to go alone. Once only, a certain member of our teaching staff joined me, but finding the Colon Theatre's luxurious refreshment-room much more interesting than the opera, during the first interval he did himself so well there that, when he staggered back to take his seat beside me, I decided to take him home.

As a rule, rainy spells came on during the opera season, with the result that the wide dirt track which led towards the college, was transformed into a river of mud. Therefore whenever, after evening chapel, I set out to go to some show, I put on rubber top-boots, which I left in a café near the railway station. Having changed into evening shoes, I took train, and upon returning, sometimes in the early hours of morning, picked up my rubber boots, in order, with them on, to wade through the deep mud. The walk home was close on two miles, so by the time I reached my den, I was ready to hit the hay.

Needless to say, after such outings I felt somewhat tired, especially so after lunch, when the sleeping of a good *siesta* was my heart's predominant desire. This being out of the question, I usually made my pupils do written work, whilst I, seated at the master's desk—which stood on a dais—leaned on my elbows, shaded my eyes, at the same time supporting my head with both hands, and pretended to be reading a book. After a while, the classroom seemed to be floating away into space, and then, suddenly, I would wake up with a start. Again and again this would happen, and between short snoozes I made almost superhuman efforts at pretending to be engrossed in the book before me. Experience had taught the boys never to distrub me on such occasions, but if ever a new pupil was foolish or innocent enough to do so—perhaps with a meek "Please, sir, may I leave the room?"—my reply was curt and very much to the point. If the class had asked me for permission in a body to leave the room, such a request would have been granted with pleasure, for at such times, had King Richard III been in my place, even he would have changed his famous desperate cry for: "A sleep! A sleep! My kingdom for a sleep!"

After about 3 p.m., when classes were finished, games, swimming and gymnastics soon got rid of my cobwebs, and by the time I had eaten a hearty evening meal, I was ready for another late night. Such is youth when it goes hand-in-hand with perfect health.

But to return to my new friend, the fighting octogenarian, "Daddy" Long.

Born in Cork, Ireland, he had gone to sea in windjammers when a mere boy, and, in the course of years, had visited most ports in every part of the globe. With pride he often told me that during his early days at sea he had worn a tarred pigtail, and he loved to relate how hard but romantic life used to be on board those sailing vessels. Modern seamen—including many captains of ships who never came to Buenos Aires without visiting him—he always called "brass-polishers." After having gone through the mill as a deck-hand and ship's officer, Long became a master mariner, and as such reached the Argentine, where he settled, soon to make a considerable fortune.

"Daddy" took a delight in grumbling and contradiction, and therefore, no matter what one said to him, he heartily disagreed. If someone praised any country, including Ireland, or perhaps some person, he immediately proceeded to run him down, and if it was the other way about, he also contradicted, and this in no uncertain terms. Though he was advanced in years, there was nothing old about him, and he enjoyed life to the full. It was said of him that he knew the difficult River Plate, with all its treacherous sand-banks and currents, better than any pilot alive, and that on several occasions he had sailed to the rescue of grounded ships, through blinding storms or complete darkness, without even bothering to take a compass with him.

Often, when the two of us got into a really hot argument and I refused to give in to him, with a curse he would rise, and shuffle out of the hotel, shortly after to return, as if nothing had happened. Once, however, I made him really furious; so much so that, for several long hours, I had to keep well out of his reach, lest he belabour me with the walking-stick which was his inseparable companion. This is how it came about.

One Sunday afternoon when, as usual, he sat on a bench in the hotel *patio*, having a snooze, I happened to be on the top gallery, reading outside my room. The hotel valet was nearby, cleaning out some cupboards, and, to my surprise, I saw him take out of them masses of top and bowler hats. Astonished at this sight, I asked where they all came from, and who were their owners. The valet explained that the hats were the property of "camp men" who, at different times, had purchased them in order to be properly dressed for weddings, funerals or social functions, and that, before going back to the pampa, these clients had asked him to take care of their hats, in case they would again be required on some future occasion.

Seeing "Daddy" below, still snoozing peacefully, I had an idea. Having piled up as many hats as I could lift, I threw them down into the *patio*, where they landed with a terrific clatter, scattering all over the stone floor.

"Be Jaysus!" Daddy shouted, jumping up and scurrying for safety. Upon realising what had happened, and who was behind this prank, he flew into such a rage that, until late that evening, he waited for me at the bottom of the lift, ready to teach me a lesson. Past experience having taught me to be cautious, I stayed upstairs until a waiter came to give me the tip that the coast was clear. Fortunately, by next morning the storm had blown over, and "Daddy,' who by that time began to see the funny side of my joke, invited me to have lunch with him.

Whenever there was a show in which the chorus girls happened to be particularly pretty, the old boy could be seen sitting in the front row of the stalls, enjoying himself thoroughly. Once, when the then famous Mack Sennett girls arrived from the U.S.A. in order to perform in Buenos Aires, Daddy took a whole bevy of them out to dinner, much to the envy of numerous young *caballeros*, who thus were given the "bird."

Though he was as strong as an ox, old age had affected my friend's herculean hands, which had such a shake that he found it most difficult to drink out of cups and glasses. In order to overcome this handicap, the crafty old sailor always asked for a straw through which to suck his favourite drink—namely, hot milk and rum.

Often, when, after having made several abortive attempts, eventually he managed to get the straw into his mouth, he gleefully mumbled, "If my mother had given me such milk, I'd never have left Oireland."

Though Daddy professed to hate priests, in the past he had been a generous benefactor and liberal subscriber to benevolent funds, especially so to one which was managed by a certain Irish Order in the Argentine.

Once he fell seriously ill, and had to be taken to the nursing-home run by a well-known Irish doctor who was an old friend of his. One of the poor old boy's legs was terribly swollen and ulcerated, and eventually gangrene set in. Every time I went to visit him, he looked worse, and only sheer courage and grumbling seemed to keep him alive. Though he pretended to be at loggerheads with everybody in the nursing-home, it was easy to see that he had only two pet aversions there—namely, the middle-aged and rather "bossy" Matron and her over-fed lap-dog, who followed his mistress everywhere, including on rounds of inspection into Daddy's room, intrusions the old grumbler resented deeply.

Things took such a bad turn with the patient that the doctor sent for a dear old Irish priest, to whom, in the past, Daddy had often given considerable sums of money in support of different charities. In due time, when the padre appeared at the door, and the invalid recognised him, he immediately guessed what had brought the unexpected visitor to his bedside.

"Good evening, Father So-and-So. What can I do for you?" Daddy asked in a peculiar, somewhat suspicious tone of voice.

Knowing his old friend, Dennis Long, the white-haired priest started cautiously, and when, after many most diplomatic twists and turns, he made him understand that it was never too late to turn over a new leaf, and went on hinting about the eleventh hour, the atomic bomb was detonated.

Struggling out of his bed, the infuriated old sailor bellowed that his Blue Peter was not yet hoisted, that he was not prepared to pull in his hawser, and that, if the priest thought Old Nick was knocking at the cabin door, he was very much mistaken.

The saintly visitor, realising that he was dealing with a difficult case, beat a hasty retreat, whereupon, having rung a bell, the invalid proceeded to upset his night table, in doing so smashing glasses, medicine bottles and other crockery. By the time the nurse and doctor arrived on the scene of destruction, Daddy was threatening to wreck the universe.

Having yelled that he had come to the nursing-home for medical treatment, and that, if all they could do for him was to try to save his soul from eternal damnation, he demanded that his clothes be brought at once, and announced that, instead of dying, he was going to get drunk.

Naturally, suitable nautical adjectives were freely used to give weight to these statements, for, without their aid, Daddy could not express himself, even when in the best of tempers.

As bad luck would have it, attracted by all this noise, the Matron came rushing into the room, followed by her lap-dog, who immediately flew at the old man, yapping hysterically. With a quick movement the old man bent down, caught Fido by the scruff of the neck and flung him out of the window, which, fortuately for the victim and its owner, was not high above the ground.

No time was wasted in bringing the clothes, and when Daddy was dressed, he hobbled out into the street, and after a typical sailor's farewell to the nursing-home, its staff, and especially the horrified Matron, hailed a taxi, and told the driver to take him to "Dirty Dick's."

True to his word, upon arrival at the hotel, the grizzly old sea-dog proceeded to carry out his promise, consuming so much hot milk and rum that extra deliveries of "cow juice" had to be made in order to keep the invalid in steady supply.

But now comes the strange part of the story. With all this "medicine," his condition improved so rapidly that after a fortnight the sores on his legs were practically healed, and the painful inflammation and swellings decreased to such an extent that he was able to walk about with ease.

His friend, the Irish doctor, called several times to see how his difficult ex-patient was getting on, and when I asked the former how he could explain this amazing recovery, he told me that it was just one of those freaks—a thousand-to-one chance. According to the doctor, alcohol, and possibly excitement, had so stimulated Daddy's heart that circulation to the affected leg was retored. He went on explaining to me that no sane doctor could possibly have prescribed alcohol as a cure, but that an exceptionally strong heart, as well as other factors, had worked the miracle.

Within a couple of months Daddy was his old self again, and it was only after several years, when he was well over ninety, that he hoisted his Blue Peter, weighed anchor, and, under full sail, set out on the cruise from which no mortal returns.

It was in "Dirty Dick's" that he introduced me to a striking man I had seen there at different times. The tall, broad-shouldered and handsome stranger—who was about forty years of age—usually sat in a corner on his own, watching other clients, without speaking to them. Like Daddy, he wore a large wide-brimmed sombrero, from beneath which protruded a rebellious tuft of black hair. I was not in the least surprised to learn that this man—whom I shall call Bob Appin—hailed from Texas. Whilst with a firm grip he shook my hand, a friendly smile played round his penetrating black eyes.

During the next few months, at intervals, I again met Bob, and always enjoyed his company. It never occurred to me to ask him what was his profession, but, for various reasons, I thought he was in the cattle business. Quiet spoken and reserved, he nevertheless could be most entertaining, especially when recounting experiences he had had during his extensive travels through Latin America.

One evening, after dinner, my Headmaster at St. George's College expressed his wish to have a few words with me. When the two of us were alone, he informed me that someone had warned him that I had been seen in very bad and even dangerous company Naturally, I pleaded complete innocence, and when I asked my interlocutor to be more explicit, he told me that he had heard a most alarming report regarding a certain Bob Appin, with whom I appeared to have become friendly. Canon Stevenson went on to inform me that, according to the rumour which had reached him, Appin was an outlaw who had the very worst of reputations in several South American republics, where, besides card-sharping, rustling cattle, and holding up travellers, he was reputed to have killed several men.

My reply to this was that I could not believe these reports, and that, ever since I had known the man in question, his behaviour had always been above reproach. I flatly told the Canon that I was in the habit of taking a man as I found him, and that, unless Appin gave me reason to keep away from him, I would continue to associate with him.

My Headmaster—who in such matters was what is sometimes called a "square-shooter"—fully agreed with me, but added that he considered it his duty to pass on to me the information concerning my new acquaintance, and thus to put me on my guard.

At about that time, an American troupe of bronco-busters, led by the then well-known film cowboy, Art Acord,[1] came to Buenos Aires in order to give a show, together with a number of gauchos. When I went to see the display, to my astonishment, Bob Appin, dressed in full cowboy costume, rode into the arena. The way he sat on his horse, and the ease with which he handled it, left me in no doubt that he was a highly skilled rider, and made me wonder if by any chance there was a shred of truth in what I had been told about him. That evening, when I met Bob in "Dirty Dick's" and bluntly told him what I had heard concerning his past, he listened with a peculiar merry twinkle in his eyes. Presently, after having laughed heartily, he said, in his soft, southern drawl, "Friend, let me tell you just one thing. Whatever you've heard about me ain't half the truth; but don't let that worry you. There's so many suckers about who think themselves smart, and take me for a greenhorn, that there ain't no need for me to pick on friends. For years I've specialised in out-smarting smarties; and, let me tell you right now, it's derned good fun. But let's forget it, and talk about something else."

[1] Art Acord, a tall, lithe, fair-haired and good-looking man, was a great rider of broncos. According to rumours which reached me, he was shot and killed in Mexico, where he made the great mistake of throwing his weight about. When I met him in Buenos Aires he was very quiet and modest.

Chapter XI

Bob Appin's "excursions," and how Tex Rickard side-stepped him.—
Paraguayan interludes.—The delightful game of "Bad Man."—Versatile
Andrew Ewart meets explorer "Teddy" Roosevelt.—Introducing Dr.
Primo and Captain Heydey.—*Viva la revolución* and the International
Two-Man Brigade!

WITH the passing of the years, I was to hear a great deal about
the redoubtable Bob Appin, whose activities by no means
ended when he came to Buenos Aires. Whilst in the city, he did no
one any harm, excepting when, somehow or other, he managed to
get himself invited to exclusive gambling clubs, where, over games
of poker, he "fleeced" those who hoped to "skin" him. He soon
became so feared among gamblers that they took good care to steer
clear of him. With no victims available, Bob made what he called
"little excursions" to different provincial towns, whence he invariably returned with his pockets stuffed full with wads of banknotes.

With me, he was absolutely frank and outspoken concerning his
skill at "stacking" cards, and he often told me that, for this purpose,
his big, hairy and clumsy-looking heavy hands were a great asset,
no one suspecting that with such veritable legs of mutton he could
possibly manipulate cards. Several times he demonstrated to me his
uncanny skill, and explained that years of practice—often before a
mirror placed on the table—had perfected his technique.

Once, upon returning to Buenos Aires from one of his "excursions," he told me that in a small pampa town he had nearly got
himself into very serious trouble. With a cunning smile playing
over his handsome face, he recounted how he had fallen in with a
bunch of crooks, and how he was beating them at their own game
when, suddenly, a bystander—evidently one of the gang, who had
been looking on—pushed a piece of "hard-ware" into Bob's ribs,
and at the same time ordered him to go on playing.

K

Under such trying circumstances, having to shuffle cards, and having to deal them out, would have "rattled" the most seasoned of gunmen, but not so my friend. *Calmo e sostenuto*—to misuse a musical term—he kept up his trickery until even the man who pressed a revolver against Bob's ribs came to the very false conclusion that it was only due to phenomenal beginner's luck that the *gringo* won so much money. Before departing, Bob promised that during his next visit to the town he would give his "friends" an opportunity to win back what they had lost; but, of course, he had no such intention.

Bob was one of those men who do not feel properly dressed unless a gun is "packed" away somewhere under their jackets. No doubt, he had ample reason for not going about unarmed, for men of his calling are apt to bump into old clients when least expected, and therefore it is advisable to be prepared for such and similar eventualities.

Once, when a friend drove us out into the country for a picnic, Bob took with him a fair-sized mahogany box containing a number of what he called his "pet shootin' irons," with which he gave us an amazing demonstration of "lead-pumping." Oranges, or empty tins, thrown into the air, were hardly ever missed, and coins, stuck into a barbed wire fence, he shot off from the hip as if by magic. There seemed to be nothing he could not do with six-shooters, from juggling to firing them upside-down, and among other tricks he showed us how to draw the weapon out of his holster and "fan" six shots in rapid succession.

Some time after this picnic, I happened to be sitting with Bob in a famous tavern, known as "Fanny's Bar," situated opposite the Casino Music Hall, in the centre of Buenos Aires. This establishment was the favourite meeting place for "camp" men and British sailors, who never came to town without calling at "Fanny's." Sometimes, as will happen in such places, fights occurred, and although these were never of a serious nature, as a rule the police intervened. The carrying of firearms being illegal—but nevertheless very common—the police usually searched all patrons, even if they were not involved in the disturbance.

As bad luck would have it, whilst I sat quietly talking to Bob over a glass of beer, at the far end of the bar some over-hilarious customers came to fisticuffs, and presently several policemen and officers in plain clothes rushed into the tavern to arrest the trouble-makers and, at the same time, to make a search for hidden firearms. As it happened, I was not molested; but, to my consternation, a detective went up to my companion to pass his hands over his clothes, from the chest down to the hip-pocket, where, I knew, Bob carried a formidable ·44 Smith and Wesson. I could hardly believe my eyes and ears when, with an apology for having had to disturb us, the detective departed without having found the weapon I knew Bob had on him when we entered the bar.

The whole thing was over in a few minutes, and, peace having been restored, everybody acted as if nothing had happened.

"But, tell me, Bob," I whispered. "How the devil did that tec miss discovering your gun?"

With a sly wink, my companion asked me to wait a while. Presently, he told me to drop my match-box on the floor, and then, whilst stooping down to pick it up, to have a look at the underneath part of the table top.

When I did as instructed, to my amazement, there was the revolver, suspended from a doubled-up penknife, which was stuck into the wood. Bob explained to me that, as soon as he became aware that fighting had broken out, he had quietly removed the "shootin' iron" from his hip-pocket, to make it fast as I had seen. Before we left to go home, without anyone noticing his movements, he transferred his pet to its proper place, whereupon he rose and quietly strolled out into the street.

City life was not to my friend's liking, so when he heard that Tex Rickard, the famous American Jack-of-all-trades and promoter of boxing matches, was financing and setting up a land development company in Paraguay, Bob successfully applied for a job. Wire for fencing, tools, supplies, and many other essentials having been purchased in Buenos Aires, to be shipped some hundreds of miles up the mighty River Paraná, in due time he sailed with one consignment.

Some time later, when Tex Rickard arrived in the Argentine and heard that a certain countryman of his named Bob Appin had been given a job in his company, he became very agitated. Without travelling up to Paraguay—as had been his intention—he took the next ship back to the U.S.A., leaving friends and acquaintances in Buenos Aires perplexed as to what could be behind his hurried departure.

Later, it became known that, years before, when Rickard was the "Honky-Tonk King" during the rush on Goldfield in the U.S.A., he and Bob had had a serious dispute. Apparently, upon being chased into a neighbouring state by the police, the latter had made a public vow that, if ever again he came across Tex, he would shoot him full of holes.

Rickard was in such a hurry to put distance between himself and Bob that it did not even occur to him to give orders to dismiss his arch-enemy from his job. Some time later, when, owing to floods —which often inundate the regions Rickard had hoped to develop in the interior of Paraguay—the venture failed, Bob was assigned the task of supervising the carting-out of materials that could be salvaged, later to be resold, in order to reduce the heavy financial losses.

As it happened, my friend, the late Anglican Bishop, Edward Francis Every, was on his way to inspect an Indian mission. His diocese extended from the cold, windswept regions near Cape Horn up to the torrid zone, comprising the republics of Argentina, Uruguay and Paraguay, and, if I remember rightly, also parts of Chili. Bishop Every was a grand sportsman and tireless worker, and when it came to roughing it, despite his gentle appearance and manners, he could compete with the toughest "leather-necks."

As, sitting on a huge-wheeled cart drawn by several bullocks, he was bumped and jolted through the inundated parts of the Para-guayan Chaco, in which only scattered palm trees and clusters of thorny bushes were to be seen on the watery plain, he noticed that another cart was slowly coming towards him from the opposite direction.

After a long time, when the two vehicles with their Indian drivers met, for all the world resembling two rafts with shipwrecked mariners on them, the Bishop saw that the other cart was loaded with rolls of wire and on the top of it was perched a white man who had plenty to say about Paraguay and life in general.

Part of the conversation that ensued between the two white men when the two conveyances drew level I will set down on paper exactly as the Bishop, later, told me.

"Hell's bells and rattle-snakes! Guess I wasn't ordained to be no goddam navigator!" the tall, sun-burnt man who was perched on the rolls of wire drawled. Having finished airing his opinion on things in general, the grumbler inquired, "And who may you be, stranger?"

"I'm Bishop Every, and I am on my way to the Chaco Indian Mission."

"My name's Bob Appin. Mighty glad to meet you. Shake, Bish," the other exclaimed, at the same time holding out a hand, which the liberal-minded Bishop shook with delight.

When Bob returned to Buenos Aires, he was a changed man. His pretty, vivacious wife—whom he had not seen for several years—arrived from the U.S.A., not to re-join him, as he had expected, but to tell him that she had decided to get a divorce. After she left, he warned me to keep out of his way, it being his intention to drown his disappointment in whisky. This he proceeded to do with such determination that, whenever I saw him, he was in a terrible state. After about two months' of drinking, he suddenly cut out all alcohol and took to wandering about on his own. Then, one day, without telling anyone a word about his plans for the future, he left for another South American republic. That was the last I saw of him. However, with the passing of time, reports concerning his activities reached some of us who had known him; and no one was in the least surprised to hear that, once again, he had become an outlaw. Rustling cattle, mules and horses, and driving them across the borders from one country to another, and there to sell the animals to unscrupulous buyers, became his chief hobby. Between such expeditions and incursions he looked for "suckers" on whom to practise his skill with cards, and when business was slack, revolutions helped him out. During one of these, he was lucky in being able to supply the winning side with many mules he had stolen in the neighbouring republic, with the result that he became *persona grata* with those on whose "black list" he had formerly been. An old friend of mine who was in charge of a pioneering concern in a certain South American republic, informed me that, for a time, he used Bob as strike-breaker. All the feared "two-gun man" had to do was to walk up and down outside the company's headquarters, which was quite sufficient to make prospective trouble-makers keep well out of his way. In one shoot-up, however, Bob lost two fingers, and the bullet which did the damage also left a nasty scar on his face.

Recently, when my friend who had employed Bob in the capacity of strike-breaker came to London and visited me, he was delighted to hear me recount some of the tough *hombre's* adventures and escapes. When I finished, he informed me that Bob had taken to ranching, and that advancing years have had a sobering effect on him. My visitor also told me that several other "hard-boiled babies" have settled in the same sub-tropical region, and that, every now and again, when members of the gang meet in order to celebrate some special happening or occasion, things are apt to become exceedingly lively, especially so when one of the merry party suggests playing "Bad Man," a game Bob once told me about in Buenos Aires, but which we never played there.

The following are the simple rules of this most original game.

One of the party having been blindfolded, he loudly and slowly counts up to a number fixed by the players, and then, shouting, "Ready . . . go!" he draws his six-shooter from its holster, presently to fire in any direction where the other participants in the game are hiding and occasionally making noises to attract his attention. A player who seeks safety behind a too solid object is considered to be "yellow" and therefore no sportsman. Listening intently, the "Bad Man" slowly turns round on his heels, and when he has fired his sixth shot, his "innings" comes to an end, whereafter another player is blindfolded to take his place.

Surely this game should be introduced and popularised in the

House of Commons and in parliaments all over the world, for it would make a pleasant change when speeches get too long and dull or tempers rise too high.

With this I must leave Bob Appin and his merry friends, trusting they will continue to prosper as ranchers, and that it will never occur to a "Bad Man" for a mild joke to cheat with a blindfold through which he can see.

.   .   .   .   .

A splendid man, whose real name was Andrew Ewart, was one of the *habitués* at "Dirty Dick's." In his time, Andy, as we called him, had been a stock-breeder in Scotland, but later he shifted his camp to South America, where, at different times, he earned his living as a prospector, explorer, and rancher, finally to become a journalist, working for the Buenos Aires *Standard*, for which he wrote up the live-stock section. Often his articles were accompanied by photographs, many of which, owing to lack of proper materials and machinery, reproduced so badly in print that it was impossible to guess whether a picture was supposed to represent prize-winning Leghorn fowls or a herd of Aberdeen Angus cattle on a pitch-dark night. But such trifles did not worry Andy, who was always the first to see the joke, especially when linotype-setters made misprints which, upon publication, were the delight of the whole English-speaking community in Buenos Aires.

One of the funniest mix-ups for which poor Andy got the blame was when the captions of two pictures were reversed. As it happened, that day, side by side, two photographs appeared in his paper, one representing a champion shorthorn bull, held by the breeder's beaming wife, and the other was a snapshot of a happy bride and bridegroom coming out of a church. It can easily be imagined how readers laughed when, next morning, below the picture of the bull and the lady they read, "Mr. and Mrs. X, the happy couple, leaving the church," and under that of the bride and bridegroom, "The champion shorthorn bull led by Mrs. Y."

When Andy was in the right mood, and recounted some of his adventures, and the experiences he had had during his trips through the interior of Bolivia, Paraguay and Brazil, it was a treat to listen to him. When Theodore ("Teddy") Roosevelt was supposed to have discovered the "River of Doubt," he and his party must have been surprised to meet a solitary young Scotsman who was on his way down towards the South Atlantic coast from the headwaters of that river. Andy never criticised Roosevelt for all the ballyhoo subsequently made about that very tame expedition, but blamed the American Press for all the nonsense that was said and written in connection with it.

In modern times, there has been only one genuine and really great explorer of unknown Brazil, and that is General Rondón. It is said that whenever an expedition worked its way towards parts of the interior, intrepid Rondón could be met coming in the opposite direction, with plans made for the construction of roads and for the setting up of telegraph lines.

But to return to some of my friends in Buenos Aires.

So many were the interesting and strange characters whom, at different times, I met there that several most entertaining chapters could be written about them, but before passing on to still higher spheres of my Bohemian education, I will only refer to two others, who, despite their minor failings, ranked among my best friends. One of them, an Argentine, I shall call Primo, and the other, a most lovable Englishman, Captain Heyday.

Being the son of wealthy parents, in his youth Primo enjoyed an excellent education, and later he became an accomplished linguist. When roused, this usually most affable and quiet little man became an utterly fearless demon, but, fortunately, his fits of temper never lasted long. Though ever since his youth he had shown signs of having the necessary talents to become a painter or sculptor, his parents decided that he must become a doctor. However, upon having taken his degree with flying colours, young Primo preferred to do more entertaining things than to attend to the sick. Accordingly, he made several extensive tours through Europe, including Great Britain, but, being a gay bird, and equipped with the necessary funds wherewith to buy his amusements, Paris naturally became his favourite hunting-ground. Though Dame Nature had endowed him with many talents, with typical carelessness she omitted to provide him with perseverance—an oversight which may have given some evil spirit the opportunity to implant within the doctor a violent dislike for any kind of work, the very mention of which made him feel positively ill.

Being a spasmodic dabbler in art, science and literature, Primo had a wide range of conversation, which he freely interspersed with many witty asides. At long intervals, his favourite pastimes were drawing and painting, and when in a rare mood to concentrate for a few days he could be an excellent sculptor. But, after all, there are only twenty-four hours in a day, so if a man has many social and other engagements, little time is left over to dedicate to creative art.

In Buenos Aires, towards midday, a busy *caballero* of leisure such as Primo must go to meet friends in his favourite barber's shop, where politics, racehorses, women and many other things of vital importance have to be discussed. After about an hour of exchanging views and opinions, or imparting the "low-down" on this and that, it is high time to adjourn the meeting, and to stroll to a café to shake dice for several rounds of cocktails. This exercise is so tiring that, after a belated lunch, Nature calls for a long *siesta*. Towards evening, when the sleeper awakes and realises that a lady friend is waiting to be taken for a drive through some park, there follows a tremendous rush, but in the end all's well, and after such romantic *tête-à-têtes*, more friends have to be met in order with them to discuss important matters over cocktails. Then comes the *aperitif* session in some cabaret, and later, until after midnight, some theatrical show or opera. By the time the final curtain falls, spectators of Primo's social standing are ready for just one or two more cocktails, to be followed by an excellent dinner, the effects of which are worked down by dancing and drinking champagne. Perhaps, if in a different mood, the nocturnal wanderer calls on some lady friend, or strolls into some gambling club to try his luck until daybreak. Sundays are most tiring. For how can a man really enjoy going to the races, when, after six solid days of such strenuous social life, he is in sore need of a rest?

Despite his sixty years, most of which had been spent on such fast-revolving merry-go-rounds, Primo looked like a man of forty, and usually behaved like a lively spark of twenty. If ever somewhere trouble was brewing, it attracted him as light does a moth, and therefore he often got himself into tight jams, which he enjoyed like a fighting-mad Irish terrier. Thus, at different times, he was clubbed, knifed, kicked unconscious, and even shot at, but such incidents my friend took as being part of the game.

.   .   .   .   .

In 1919, after having been demobilised, ex-Captain Heyday—who before the war had earned his living as a scientist in England—blew into Buenos Aires with a tremendous alcoholic *éclat*. He was such a jolly and companionable soul that, within a week of his *début*, his stentorian laugh was known in most bars and cabarets, where he made friends with everybody. Unlike the majority of Englishmen (especially if they hail from Suburbia), who look upon the "natives" as inferior beings and therefore turn up their noses at them, the newcomer to the Argentine immediately became almost overwhelmingly friendly with all who accepted his invitations to tilt glasses with him. In one respect, however, Heyday was very English—namely, in his almost uncanny powers to resist even the most elementary knowledge of Spanish. For his purposes, a few words, such as "oo-eesky," *muy grande* (meaning "very large") and *otra vuelta* (another round) were quite sufficient, and therefore, upon having memorised such a reduced "working vocabulary" of basic Spanish, he was perfectly satisfied.

The ex-warrior's prolonged spree came to a logical end in a police station, whither two sturdy *vigilantes* carried him, *incapacitado*. Boiled down into plain English, this high-sounding official Spanish term means that as a result of a particularly long forced march, Captain Heyday collapsed in a state of utter exhaustion. Fortunately, the two guardian angels of public security rescued our hero from the dangers of the heavy traffic, and, as stated, took him to a place of safety where, with traditional Argentine hospitality, a cell was put at his sole disposal, and he spent the night as guest of the nation. Next day, upon having recovered sufficiently to answer the roll-call, the candidate for a fine was placed before a desk, behind which sat the *Señor Comisario*. As it happened, this important warden spoke a little English, and therefore was able to deliver a short lecture, which he prosaically wound up with a charge of drunkenness. When informed that the fees for transportation, no bed and no food, amounted to ten pesos, Heyday fumbled through his pockets, and a worried look came over his face. Upon being asked by the *Comisario* if by any chance he had been divested of everything metallic and valuable—such as watch, coins, banknotes, fountain pen, etc.—prior to being locked up in his cell, with an elongated face poor Heyday replied that, apparently, this must have been the case. After having done some quick and, most likely, painful thinking, the poor and distressed victim assured the man behind the desk that if someone telephoned to a friend of his—who was the manager of a certain British shipping company—no doubt that gentleman would immediately jump into a taxi and bring the required money, which was the fee for initiation to the discomforts of an ancient police station, known to thousands in Buenos Aires, and to seafaring men, as the *Primera*, or "Number One."

The telephone call having been put through, within a few minutes the friend in need arrived. The official bill having been settled, the *Comisario* escorted the Captain and his saviour to the door, where, with a sympathetic and understanding smile, he asked the former, "Having been detained for a considerable time, what in your present condition is the predominant wish of your heart?"

To this, in a husky tone of voice, but with soldierly candour, the Captain replied, "Oo-eesky *muy grande*."

And so the trio went to the nearest café, where Heyday had the proverbial hair of the dog which had bitten him ever since his arrival in Buenos Aires.

After this short but expensive sojourn in the *Primera*, the Captain turned over a new leaf; but, with the passing of time and as the wind veered, this leaf was blown forwards and backwards several times. Being a born humorist and an excellent "mixer"—in more than one sense of the word—he soon made numerous friends who, rightly, said of him that he was a "grand fellow," or *un gran tipo*.

One day, after a particularly nasty crash, he cut out all alcohol. During the next three years, although he still did the "rounds" with friends and entertained liberally, he never touched an alcoholic drink. However, despite this, he continued to be the life of parties to which he went; but then, one fine day, when least expected, it happened—Heyday fell off the "water-cart" with such a thump that he remained beneath it until the last of his accumulated capital was spent.

A friend, who had been watching what was going on, came to the rescue of the impecunious soldier-scientist, who, when offered the job of supervising the distribution to restaurants of free samples of a new type of mustard, was glad to accept it. Driving about in a car, and merely having to see to it that assistants delivered the samples, was not exactly strenuous work, but with so many bars and restaurants *en route*, the temptation occasionally to have a "quick one" was too great to resist.

It so happened that, during this distribution of mustard, a revolution broke out, and that, when things became really lively in Buenos Aires, Heyday and Dr. Primo accidentally met. Both were so delighted with the stormy political weather that, whenever they heard a rumour that things were happening in certain parts of the city, they hurried thither. Rushing from one place to another is apt to give a man a thirst, and so, between such races, Primo and Heyday refreshed themselves in bars. As it happened, they were thus occupied when a crowd of rioters stormed a gun-shop which was situated in the close vicinity. Without even finishing his drink the doctor fairly flew out into the street, presently to fight his way into the armourer's shop, whence, after a while, he emerged, triumphantly brandishing a shot-gun. In a matter of minutes, the mob looted and wrecked the shop, and before soldiers and policemen arrived on the scene, little Primo marched off, shot-gun shouldered in military style. Behind him, wearing his old trench-coat, his unfastened regimental tie fluttering in the breeze, and a battered Trilby hat at a dashing angle on his head, briskly stepped the tall, lanky ex-Captain Heyday, shouting, "Left, left; left, right, left . . .!"

Thus the International Two-Man Brigade paraded through the principal streets and avenues, which were thronged with masses of excited men. Every now and again, the little doctor led the way into some bar, where, having grounded his shot-gun to his companion's expert command, glasses were filled, and raised to the insurgents. Who these were, and what the revolution was about, Heyday had not the foggiest idea, nor did he bother to find out. However, Primo, who hated President Hipólito Irigoyen and who was related to several leaders of the Army who were behind the insurrection, knew only too well what all this turmoil signified. Therefore, although he had no ammunition for his newly acquired shot-gun, he was in the seventh heaven to be, as it were, on "active service."

Moving on, still followed by Heyday, Primo led the way towards the building in which the deposed President's pet newspaper was edited and printed. Upon approaching, the little man with the formidable weapon on his shoulder gruffly ordered the surging crowd to make way for him. The doors of the building were closed, and steel shutters had been lowered, so upon reaching the main entrance, to the delight of the onlookers, Primo spat against it. When he called upon the people to help him smash in doors and to take the building by storm, those of the onlookers who stood nearest to him began to move backwards. As they pushed and struggled, there ensued a *mêlée* during which Primo and Heyday became separated.

Laughing and shouting, "Whoopee! Up and at 'em!" and "Give'm hell!" Heyday enjoyed himself thoroughly, but, upon finding himself alone in the centre of a circle of wide-eyed onlookers, who pushed for all they were worth to make this circle larger, he began to wonder what was amiss. Whenever he staggered in some direction, those of the people whom he approached fought frantically to get away. All this marching through the city and halts for "re-fuelling" purposes had such a tiring effect on the ex-Captain that his thoughts became rather blurred, but when his eyes succeeded in getting into focus a solitary figure inside the ever-widening circle of people round him, and he came to the conclusion that this lone figure was a police officer who shouted something, Heyday pulled himself together with a great effort.

When it became evident to the man in uniform that the solitary Englishman did not understand Spanish, he gingerly approached him, and pointed at the bulging pockets of his trench coat. After an agitated conversation, most of which was held in sign language, Heyday began to wonder if by any chance he was being suspected of having stolen something. In order to give ocular proof of his innocence, he thrust a hand into a pocket, and from it drew forth a square shiny object, the sight of which made the police officer shield his eyes with his hand.

Despite the lamentable fact that Heyday was in a physical and mental state which made it most difficult for him to see and analyse things clearly, this protective movement suggested to him that he was suspected of being in possession of explosives. In order to show that, even in a revolution, he "played cricket," and to allay un-founded suspicions and fears, he attempted to unscrew the top of the square shiny object he held in one hand, as a jeweller might whilst displaying a diamond-studded snuff-box to a customer, or a con-juror showing his audience that there is no deception in the trick he is about to perform. When he proceeded to exert pressure on the circular lid, the crowd made a frantic effort to bolt, but, being squeezed together tightly like sardines, another wild *mêlée* ensued.

By means of signs, the valiant police officer made Heyday under-stand that his bulging pockets must be emptied forthwith. This having been done, the latter made another effort to unscrew the lid of one of those mysterious objects. As it happened, this one came off with ease, whereafter, inserting a first finger into the "bomb," Heyday withdrew it, covered with a thick, semi-liquid substance. Then, to the amazement of the police officer, and those of the onlookers who were still near enough to see, he licked the stuff off his finger, at the same time rubbing his stomach with one hand, and gleefully exclaiming, "Mustard! Very good!"

With heroic confidence, the police officer then approached Heyday, who presented him and some of the bystanders with samples of the new type of mustard.

Whether or not this incident is responsible for the popularity which, to this day, that product enjoys in Buenos Aires, I do not know, but the fact remains that, ever since that revolution, any good restaurant or bar stocks what a number of my friends and I call "Heyday's Mustard."

Upon returning to "Dirty Dick's," the weary "grenadier" found that corrugated-steel shutters had been lowered, and that the heavy iron grating at the front door had been closed. Having been let in, he made his way to the bar, there to recuperate strength and energy. Heyday was thus occupied when a cavalry regiment passed outside, so he rushed to the iron grating, whence, like an excited monkey in a cage, waving his arms, he shouted, "*Viva* revolooshion!" and "*Viva* Ereegoyee!"

He had not the foggiest notion what the latter exclamation meant, but, having heard people shout a word which, to him, sounded rather like it, it was good enough for him. As it happened, what everybody in the streets shouted that day, was not "Viva Irigoyen" (the desposed President's name), but "Down" and even "Death to Irigoyen!" However, such trifling differences were immaterial to Heyday, who continued to shout "*Viva* Eereegoyee!" to the troopers, who, fortunately, merely rode past, smiling to themselves.

Little Dr. Primo's adventures did not end when he became separated from his companion-in-arms outside the newspaper office. Until late that night he marched about the town, eventually to seat himself on a bench in the square in front of the Government House. He had been snoozing there for some time when he awoke to see what he took to be rockets exploding overhead. However, upon realising that, instead, these were shrapnel shells which were being fired by a warship from the River Plate, despite feeling very tired, he jumped high into the air, and, forgetting all about his precious shot-gun, hastily retreated to more sheltered parts. Thus, as far as the Primo-Heyday two-man International Brigade's participation in the revolution was concerned, operations came to an end.

The scientific distribution of mustard led to Heyday getting an excellent job, and he did such outstanding work that, in time, he became the owner-manager of an important commercial enterprise. Working like a Trojan, without ever touching an alcoholic drink, he went from strength to strength, until, one day, he was again tempted to smell a cork—a little slip which led to another turning of his tide.

As I am writing this, little Dr. Primo continues to hold forth over dry Martinis, and, when in one of his rare moods, occasionally to dedicate spare moments to creative art.

Chapter XII

The urge of wanderlust.—News from Sophocles and Stintall.—Horses,
gauchos and cattle.—An ex-major of the Indian Army holds forth on
horsemanship, and a stock-pony teaches him a lesson.—A sheep-stealer's
cunning trick of deception.—Gaucho pride—The red horse.—A certified
gentleman joins the brotherhood of globe-trotters.

BESIDES teaching at St. George's College, practising athletics
and occasionally "doing the rounds" with friends, I had many
other interests. When in a more serious mood, I often spent hours in
the National Library, where historical works were my chief attraction. As none of my colleagues could be bothered with conversations on such matters, whenever time permitted, I called on my
friend, the late Dr. Debenedetti, a great scholar who, at that time,
was the Director of the Ethnographical Museum in Buenos Aires.
It was he and several archæologists who first made me long to visit
certain remote regions in which they had carried out scientific
work. But how could I hope ever to go so far afield? Travelling,
even if it be through the wilds, costs money, and in my case it
could lead to nothing but a waste of time. Thus, with a strong urge
smouldering within me to see more of the world, I had to carry on
with my duties at the College.

I could hardly believe my eyes when, one morning, I received
a letter, to the envelope of which were affixed postal stamps of a
certain country in the Far East. A further examination of this
envelope revealed to me that it had been addressed to the Gristins
in London, and that Ivy had re-addressed it to the Argentine.

Like a dog carrying away a bone to gnaw it in peace, I took the
letter to my room, in order there to read its contents undisturbed.
Whilst slitting open the tattered envelope, I wondered who on
earth it might be who wrote to me from the Far East. Well, well,
wonders never cease. The letter was written by none other than . . .
Sophocles. After the usual preambles he informed me that, shortly

L

after the outbreak of the Bolshevik Revolution, he had managed to "skin out" of Russia, and that, after many adventures, he had reached the Far East, where he had settled down. I was not in the least surprised to learn that he held a very important position, and that he was earning more money than he knew what to do with. He furthermore informed me that he had married another woman, who suited him much better than his first wife—whom, as the reader may remember, he had left in London. Upon reading about the sumptuous Oriental mansion in which the writer now lived, the yacht in which he cruised about druing the hot months, his Rolls Royce cars, servants, chauffeurs, valet, and even a French *chef* who attended to the inner man of the former vegetarian crank, I felt very poor indeed.

Apparently this letter had been written shortly after Sophocles' return to the Far East from a business tour through Europe. He apologised for not having had time to look me up whilst passing through London, and very kindly invited me, should I ever happen to visit his part of the world, to be his guest. In order to show me that comforts and luxuries would not be lacking for me, he enclosed photographs of his residence and yacht, as well as several snapshots taken of him in various positions and attires. By the time I had finished reading his letter and had scrutinised the photographs, I was left in no doubt that Sophocles had thrown overboard all Raymond Duncan's theories and teachings, and that he had gone to the other extreme as far as mode of living and ideology are concerned. That some of the old Sophocles was still left in him, he proved to me by stating that Eastern philosophies appealed to him immensely, and that Western civilisation and all that goes with it was doomed sooner or later to disappear through internal decay and disintegration.

In my reply to his letter, I wrote that I was in the Argentine, where, though in a material sense not doing over-well, I neverthe-less thoroughly enjoyed life. *En passant*, I also gave him a gentle hint that the elderly lady who, prior to his departure from London to Russia, had helped him out with money, could very well do with what he owed her, and that I hoped he would send her a cheque, with, perhaps, just a little extra added to the sum he had borrowed from her at the time. Perhaps my letter was lost in transit, but whatever happened to it, the old debt was never settled, and Sophocles' epistle which Ivy Gristin forwarded to me to the Argentine was the last I ever received from him there. However, as we shall see later, the two of us were destined to meet again.

Here, once more, we must leave this strange character, this time wining and dining in super-Brillat Savarin style, or, perhaps, on the deck of his yacht, reclining on an Oriental couch, blowing fragrant cigar smoke into the balmy air and occasionally stretching out a languorous arm in order to get hold of a glass of *fine champagne* wherewith to wet his formerly Spartan lips.

Another old Gristinian who, after several years' silence, wrote to me from London was Stintall, the tight-wad schoolmaster. True to type, after the usual rigmarole of enquiring after my health and expressing his delight at hearing that I was prospering, he came to the point. To put it in a nut-shell, he informed me that, besides having been left a small legacy by an old aunt, he had saved enough money to feel secure, provided he went "slow." He also gave me the news that he had had the good fortune to meet a charming young lady, whose parents appeared to be very well off, and that wedding bells would be ringing in the near future. Stintall furthermore informed me that he was getting tired of living in England, and that, once married, and his and his wife's money was pooled, he would very much like to buy a small ranch in South America where the sun was said always to be shining, and where cantering over the prairies would be much more pleasant than having to spend the rest of his life teaching in a dreary English public school.

A few months later Stintall wrote again, informing me that he had married the girl of his choice. But, apparently, there had been a hitch, or, rather, a disappointment, as far as he was concerned; for, shortly after the wedding, it turned out that the bride's parents were so heavily in debt that they had to sell their house and everything they possessed. In his long and pathetic epistle, Stintall bitterly complained that, despite this serious setback, his wife had not changed her expensive tastes. Some two years later, in the next letter I received from him, he gave me the news that, after great expense, he had obtained a divorce, and that, although he had to pay his wife alimony, this worked out much cheaper than having to keep her in luxury, without which, whilst still his legal wife, she had flatly refused to live. So poor Stintall had to go on teaching in his school, looking forward to the day when he would be pensioned off. Let us hope his last wish has been fulfilled and that, as I am writing this, he has ample time for sitting in a tiny cottage somewhere in the English countryside, carefully checking up on his banking account and counting his loose change.

.　　　.　　　.　　　.　　　.

At St. George's College we rarely had time to feel dull. New masters blew in and out so quickly that before we knew one another well enough to drop the formal "Mister", they were on their way home to England.

During the long summer holidays I went further and further afield, seeing the country and getting to know its people. Twice, for several weeks, I stayed with a friend, Bill Norris, an old English pioneer, whose chief passion in life was concentrated on horses. What he did not know about them is hardly worth knowing, and therefore I took the chance of learning from him as much as possible. In my book, *This Way Southward*, I devoted a long chapter to this old centaur's activities and exploits, so here I will not repeat what has already been written about him.

During the hot months when, especially in the northern province, in which he owned a ranch, flies were a pest and laid eggs in any cut or open sore on animals, from early morning until late in the evening we lassoed and cured fly-blown cattle and horses. If left unattended, the flies' eggs turn into maggots which literally eat their helpless victims alive.

In the corral we had some terrific struggles with such patients, but stocky, deep-chested, and herculean-armed Bill was such an expert with the lasso that within a few moments of having lassoed an animal, he deftly threw it to the ground, and tied it into a helpless bundle. Then, having located the affected part, we slapped a swab soaked with chloroform on to it, and in other cases treated the animals with certain disinfectants which almost immediately killed the maggots. This done, with spoons or knives the pests were carefully removed, and the crude operation was finished by washing out the cavity with warm water, whereafter, having painted it over with some strong-smelling disinfectant to keep flies at a distance, we turned the patient loose and immediately started to cure another. All this rounding-up of sick animals involved much galloping over the region and strenuous physical exercise when work was being done on foot. Bill taught me many things connected with horsemanship, and when I made prolonged visits to other ranches, including some in Uruguay, my knowledge, based on experience and sometimes hard knocks, was further enlarged.

By that time I had learnt to ride and handle horses in South American style, which, as previously explained, differs greatly from the European. All mounts being neck-reined, they are not guided by the mouth. A sturdy, agile and well-trained stock pony is a gift from heaven, and, therefore, for no money in the world will a gaucho sell such a companion, who knows the work to be done every bit as well as the rider. If one happens to be driving along a herd of steers, and one of them contemplates escape, the pony anticipates the would-be truant's intention, and fairly flies to nip the break-away in the bud. Like sheep-dogs ranging up and down behind a flock, good stock ponies are ever on the move, with quirking ears and alert eyes looking out for trouble. If a greenhorn happens to be riding such a pony, and is not careful, a sudden twist or turn will surely send him flying to the ground.

Gauchos ride entirely by balance, and they hardly ever grip with their knees. Indeed, a great many do not use the stirrups, and they are perfectly at their ease with only a loose sheepskin on the horse to prevent sweat from soiling their trousers. Should a stock pony gallop along at full speed and happen to put one or both forelegs in a hidden hole, and as a result turn a somersault, an agile gaucho will never fall, but will land on his feet. Before his animal has time to rise, he will be alongside it, ready to leap on when it rises from the ground. No real gaucho ever sits bolt upright on his sheepskin saddle, but usually with a slight, restful stoop. Therefore, no matter what his horse does—without warning, jump forwards, prop, or, perhaps, shy sideways—the rider goes with it, as if he were part of it.

. . . . .

I happened to be staying on a big ranch belonging to a friend of mine when an ex-major of an Indian cavalry regiment came to spend a few weeks with us. He was a typical cavalry man of the old school, and *India* was written all over him. Accustomed to living and travelling about in great style, he brought with him sufficient equipment to fit out the officers of a squadron. One enormous wooden box contained several saddles, girths and other "horsy" paraphernalia, and in another were masses of different bits, martingales, bridles, whips, spurs, hunting crops and other equipment. Of course, he had also brought with him two or three shot-guns, fishing rods, golf clubs, polo sticks, tennis and other racquets; in fact, everything but a field kitchen, swords, lances and white elephants to carry the load. When the servants finished unpacking his boots, shoes and slippers, and these were lined up, two deep, in his bedroom, this footwear brigade on parade made an impressive sight. But on the morning after his arrival, when the Major came down to breakfast, dressed for a ride, we saw something that beat tailors' illustrated advertisements in fashionable sporting magazines clean out of the field. Everything fitted the fairly tall and lithe visitor like a glove, and he certainly knew how to strut about in his almost over-elegantly cut riding breeches. When he looked at me through his monocle, I felt as unshaven recruits must on parade when confronted by a grumpy inspecting colonel. All I wore were a checked shirt with only half sleeves, a scarf, wide baggy *bombachas* (as pampa trousers are called), and none-too-clean rope-soled slippers.

My host—an Anglo-Argentine who had spent most of his sixty years in the pampa—was dressed more or less the same as I, with the only difference that he wore black riding boots. Having acquired the gauchos' manners and ways, normally he was very quiet and reserved, but, nevertheless, a keen observer whose seemingly unseeing eyes missed nothing.

After breakfast, whilst we made ready to set out on horse-back, we watched the Major select a girth, martingale and fancy bit—to which none of the neck-reined horses were accustomed. Whilst he was saddling up, several times when our host happened to catch my eye, he gave me sly winks, for now we were really seeing things in the horsy line.

The gauchos had been working cattle ever since daybreak, so when we met them, far away from the *estancia* house, they were on their way home to have lunch. The countryside in this province differs from the flat pampa, for where we were, in parts the undulating ground is covered with bushes, trees and big patches of thistles, through which our horses nimbly wound their way.

The Major sat his mount in true cavalry fashion, upright and rather stiffly, and although our host repeatedly told him not to pull on its mouth, he could not resist doing so, with the result that his horse, unaccustomed to such treatment, fought the bit.

That evening, as we sat on the veranda, the Major expressed his disgust at the "slovenly" way in which the "gawchos" (as he pronounced "gauchos") sat on their horses, and told us that if only he could hand them over to his former Rough-riding Sergeant-major, and let him put them through the hoop, in time they might become decent horsemen. To this and similar statements we listened in silence, and after the Major had helped himself to another whisky and soda, he started to give us a long and most interesting lecture on horsemanship, hunting, tent-pegging, pig-sticking, and so on.

As usual during the hot season, every day after lunch the gauchos had their *siesta* until about 4 p.m., some choosing shady spots under trees, where they slept on the sheepskins of their saddles. Whilst we were having tea, several English visitors who were spending a holiday on the ranch remarked that they had always heard that people in South America are lazy, and went on to express their surprise that the gauchos should be paid for spending the best part of the day sleeping.

To these remarks our host calmly replied that, by the time his guests rose in the morning, his men had ridden many miles, and had done several hours' work among the cattle. He explained that, during the summer months, his gauchos rise at 3 a.m., and that, after a few sips of *maté* (green tea), they set out on horseback. He went on telling his surprised listeners that, before daylight appears, the men are ready to start work, which is carried on until about eleven o'clock, and that, after lunch, they sleep until it gets a little cooler, whereafter they change horses, and once more set out to ride fences, or to "revise" cattle, until the sun sets.

Indeed, during the summer season, gauchos only get about three hours sleep during the night, and two more at *siesta* time. When one considers the great distances they ride and the hard and often dangerous work they do, surely these "Mañanalanders" are not as lazy as they may appear to holiday-makers, who only rise in time to have breakfast between 9 and 10 a.m.

About a week after the jovial Major's arrival, when cattle had to be rounded up and he rode out with us, mounted on an excellent stock pony, he met his Waterloo.

For some time all went well with our friend and his monocle, but during a wild chase after some elusive steers, things began to happen to him. Sitting stiffly upright in the saddle, he dashed into some bushes, where his clever pony showed that it had its own ideas about which way to turn in order to head off a dodging steer. When, whilst tearing along at full speed, the Major's mount suddenly whipped round a bush, the rider was shot off, head first into its thorny embrace. Fortunately, beyond tearing his jacket and slightly scratching his face and hands, no harm was done, so, when the gauchos had caught his pony and the Major had once more screwed the monocle into his eye, he mounted. However, soon worse was to befall him, for when we galloped in and out among thistles, over which he expected his pony to jump like a hunter taking a fence, it again whipped round to one side. Thus, several times within an hour, the rider was unseated with such bad luck that, with every fall, he landed like a swimmer taking a "belly-flop" off a springboard. As one gaucho slyly remarked to me, it looked as if the Major were determined to plough up the region with his nose.

That evening, when, as usual, we sat on the veranda, the man from India looked like a schoolboy after a disastrous fight. Both his hands were bandaged, and his face could hardly be seen for sticking-plaster. However, despite his discomfort, he saw the funny side of things, and, after a lull in the conversation, confessed that in having so prematurely criticised the gauchos' riding, he had made an ass of himself.

The Major was a grand sport and a first-class horseman, of which, after a few days, he gave us full proof, sitting and handling his mounts in gaucho fashion. No matter in which direction a pony twisted whilst galloping at full speed, he "went with it" without ever again "buying a league of land" (*comprar una legua de campo*), as the gauchos say when a rider falls off his horse. Very wisely, he never tried his hand at bronco-busting or lassoing, though I guess that if he had ventured on to the hurricane deck of a buck-jumper, he might possibly have weathered the storm.

Why the Major had left the Indian Army, and what made him come to South America, he never divulged to any of us; but I do know that, for well over a year, he had a rattling good time. Eventually, when he quietly slipped away to Brazil, his remaining possessions fitted into a dilapidated hand-bag. Months later, when last seen by a friend of mine, the Major was about to sail—as a deck hand—up the mighty River Amazon, near the head-waters of which recruits were wanted on rubber plantations.

Those remote and little-known regions used to attract all sorts of down-and-outs and strange characters, most of whom never returned to civilised parts, where, for various reasons, they were misfits. A few of these wandering souls became tropical tramps, and for the rest of their stormy lives roamed about among Indian and half-castes, anywhere between latitude 10 north and 25 south, until alcohol or disease brought them to their final rest. Strange to relate, most of the tropical trampo I met during my travels through the wilds of South America were highly educated and intelligent men. The majority of these wandering children of the sun hailed from the U.S.A., England, Central Europe, Poland and the Baltic States, and, as will be seen later, I only came across one Frenchman who had taken to a somewhat similar mode of life.

·   ·   ·   ·   ·

With the passing of time, the picturesque, partially wooded and undulating parts of northern Uruguay became my favourite region in which to spend the long school holidays. I had the good fortune to be invited to stay with a grand old English gaucho, Edmund Griffin by name, who had come to South America when he was a boy. His Anglo-Uruguayan wife (née Childs, a niece of Colonel Childs, who at the time was the Chief of Scotland Yard) was as charming and delightful as her husband, who, throughout the region, was known as Don Edmundo.

Besides riding, swimming, and trying to catch big fish in various most attractive sub-tropical rivers, we had a lot of fun tinkering with this and that. Every other day, one of my delights was to drive to the distant railway station in an old Ford car, in which to bring back supplies and mail. Such outings always meant one or two halts at quaint, low-roofed pampa inns, where I soon made a number of friends.

There was no village near the tiny station, but only two square brick-built stores, besides a few thatched adobe huts which were scattered over a wide area, dotted here and there with palm trees. In one of the huts was the post office, run by the local *comisario* (chief of police). He was a truly extraordinary man, perhaps not much to look at, but with a tremendous sense of humour, and, above all, when it came to facing danger, he did it with the heart of a lion. Short and stocky, he hardly ever wore his uniform, much preferring to go about in gaucho clothes. In his time, this remarkable man (Rios by name) had been shot so often that it was one of his favourite jokes to tell people that it was not food that made him so corpulent, but lead, which in the course of many years outlaws had "pumped" into him. In this yarn there was a great deal of truth, for it was only after having been particularly badly wounded in the abdominal region that Rios had begun to put on weight. Whenever urgent work had to be done, he was always ready to ride out, at any time, day or night, into the forests along the rivers, which he knew like the palm of his hand.

Though this splendid man died some years ago, in the region where he lived, and even far beyond it, his name has become almost a legend, and over camp-fires gauchos still repeat many of his witty remarks and humorous stories.

Rios and I soon became friends, so every time I went into his hut in order to collect the mail, a friendly verbal duel ensued. His repartee and knack of playing on words were so quick and devastating that invariably I retired laughing, and when he called me back, it usually was to tell me something more serious or interesting about local happenings.

One day, he had such an amusing story to tell me, that he did not even bother to begin by humouring me, so whilst the two of us split a bottle of warm beer, he told me what had happened on the previous Sunday.

Rios had ridden over to a solitary inn, situated on the brow of a long, low hill. He was talking to a number of friends who were assembled there, when a man whom he recognised came along the wide sandy road, leading a horse by the halter rope. Doubled up, seated on the animal was what appeared to be a drunken man, wearing a flowing poncho, and a large neckerchief wound round his head to protect him against the hot rays of the sun, and, pulled well down over the ears, a battered hat.

"*Amigo, por amor de Dios*" ("Friend, for the love of God"), the man who led the horse said to the limp rider, "pull yourself together. Can't you see that the *Señor Comisario* is watching you, and that the disgraceful state into which you have got yourself reflects shame on me?"

Saying this, the speaker led the horse and its rider past the inn, but when the trio had gone some distance, it suddenly struck Rios as odd that only one horse was with that party of two men, and that the animal belonged to the one who led it. As it happened, the latter was a good-for-nothing, who, despite being the father of a family, had never been known to do an honest day's work.

Getting suspicious, Rios cantered after the mysterious one-horse cavalcade, and presently, upon raising the poncho to see who the drunkard beneath it might be, to his amazement he discovered that it was a dead sheep, which had been cleverly tied to the saddle.

The cunning rogue was busy, trying hard to convince the *comisario* that, upon seeing a sick sheep, he had killed it out of sheer pity when the owner of the ranch from which the animal had been stolen came cantering towards the inn. As it turned out, this chance arrival proved to be lucky for the impenitent thief, for when the rancher heard about the recent happening, he was so amused that he asked Rios not to arrest the culprit, but to allow him to go home to his family, taking the sheep with him.

In the same region I saw a perfect example of gaucho pride. Throughout the pampa, among the sons of those vast plains it is considered a disgrace for a man to work afoot, unless it be in a corral, or in an emergency whilst handling cattle. In former times even beggars rode about on horseback, and no self-respecting gaucho ever walked far. Agriculture never appealed to those centaurs, let alone gardening, and therefore both these occupations were left to the *gringos*, most of whom were Italian and Spanish immigrants.

On the ranch where I stayed lived a grizzly old gaucho who for many years had been famous as being what is often called a "hard case." What with old age, with its accompanying infirmities, and *caña* (rum) on which most of his hard-earned money was spent, gradually he had to reduce his radius of activity, until, finally, he could no longer join in when cattle work had to be done afar. Thus the old boy spent most of his time at home, mending harness, bridles and saddles, or with raw-hide making lassos, halters and similar horse gear. Often, time lay rather heavy on his gnarled hands, and as the boss continued to pay him his full wages, one day he asked him to go and cut thistles which had begun a pernicious invasion of a nearby paddock.

Though deeply hurt by this request, the pensioner made no reply, but slowly shuffled away, like a tortoise or an alligator walking on dry land. Sad at heart, with drooping shoulders he made for the tool-shed, and some time later, upon emerging from it, he triumphantly carried a hoe, for which he had made a long handle. Going to the hitch-rail, he unfastened a pony, and presently rode forth to begin cutting thistles, without having to dismount. For many days after, despite the fact that the long handle and the position in which the old chap had to work made his task rather difficult and tiring, he carried on contentedly. His gaucho honour was saved.

Every now and again another old character came to visit the same ranch. Many years before, in consequence of a nasty fall, sustained whilst chasing a steer he intended to kill for consumption, his mind had become deranged, so ever since that accident the victim had done no work, but merely rode from ranch to ranch, where he was given food and hospitality. Throughout the region, people were firmly convinced that the man's mental affliction was a judgment of God. Apparently, despite warnings given to him by friends, he had insisted on slaughtering a beast on a Good Friday, when the accident happened.

The old horse, which was the unfortunate victim's inseparable companion, happened to be white; so upon seeing it tied to a shady tree, whilst its owner slept a *siesta*, two naughty boys decided to play a trick on the half-crazy old gaucho. Taking a stick of the soapy red dye which is used for marking sheep, they painted the animal all over. Strange to relate, in due time the visitor departed without noticing the startling appearance of his mount. The sheep dye being waterproof, for a long time after a wild-eyed and long-haired gaucho could be seen cantering through the region, seated on a bright-red horse.

.   .   .   .   .

By degrees I grew heartily sick of school life with no prospects for the future. My conversations with archæologists, and books I read about early Spanish expeditions and explorations, more and more made me long with my own eyes to see the interior of the continent, and to get to know something about the Indians living there.

There was only one thing to do: screw up courage, burn all the bridges behind me, and start a new life, no matter whither it might lead. Convinced that he who has not lived dangerously has never tasted the salt of life, one day I made up my mind to take the plunge.

How it came about that I set out with two Patagonian Indian mustangs, after two years' riding through every imaginable climate and type of country, eventually to reach New York, is partially described in my book, *Tschiffely's Ride*, so I will not repeat what has already appeared in print. Instead, it is my intention to deal with some of the strange characters I met along my ten-thousand-mile trail. However, before we come to them, for a few moments let us return to St. George's College, near Buenos Aires.

When I told my Headmaster that I had decided to undertake a ride through the three Americas, and after some difficulty convinced him that I was quite serious about it, he looked at me as if wondering if I had gone mad.

When the day came to say goodbye, Canon Stevenson jokingly told me to write my will, and in it to bequeath my bones—which I would surely leave somewhere in the Andes—to the College museum, where they would serve as a warning to students never to be foolhardy. Before we parted, he handed me a testimonial, the last lines of which read: ". . . He gave entire satisfaction. He has always acted as a Gentleman and was very popular with the boys. He takes with him our best wishes for the future."

Apart from the "hes" with which these three short sentences begin, the document amused me immensely. Remembering what Stevenson had said about the bequest of my bones to the College museum, I wondered what he meant by the last statement; but what I liked best was the bit about always having *acted* as a Gentleman. (The Capital "G" did not escape my notice.) In view of my intended travels through the wilds, this was of such paramount importance and incalculable value, that I felt inclined to have the testimonial framed, in due time to have it dangling from my horse's neck. Perhaps hostile Indian Chiefs or ungentlemanly cut-throats I might easily meet would be deeply impressed by such a document, and, on the strength of it, spare my life; for surely it is not every day that certified Gentlemen stray so far from the comforts and relative safety of civilisation. Not only this, the testimonial was adorned with a crest depicting St. George and ye wicked olde dragon, and was signed by a live Canon—a combination which should impress even starving cannibals.

Having given away some of my possessions and stored away the rest, I travelled out to the pampa, and there made the acquaintance of two exceedingly wild mustangs. Their heart-felt appreciation for the honour of being given the names of "Mancha" and "Gato" they immediately proceeded to show by trying to buck the guts out of me. However, after a few days, when the three of us more or less reached a compromise on spiritual and corporeal matters, in relative peace and harmony we set out, heading towards the distant Andes and vast wild regions beyond them. Suddenly the world seemed to become mighty big, whilst, on the other hand, day by day I felt smaller and smaller. Thinking over matters—and there was plenty of time for reflection—I came to the conclusion that these disconcerting feelings must be part of the peculiar game I had chosen to play. Sometimes, when assailed by a sickly feeling, as if my stomach were a vacuum, I tried to comfort myself by thinking that this was merely a kind of initiation trial all candidates to the brotherhood of globe-trotters have to undergo before qualifying for full active membership of that ancient—though by conventional citizens not honoured—society.

Chapter XIII

SCIENTISTS have assured us that Man is the most adaptable of all warm-blooded creatures. Whether or not this statement is correct, I do not know, but that there is some truth in it I discovered upon settling down to living out in the open, regardless of the diversity of climatic conditions. A strong constitution helped me resist heat and cold, but, in the case of the many different human beings with whom I forcibly came into contact, it was entirely due to the attitude I took towards them that, here and there, serious trouble was avoided. I am convinced that my previous dealings with so many peculiar people, and the experience derived from such associations, now stood me in good stead. Somehow I was at my ease wherever I went, and, strange to relate, as on former occasions, every now and again a strange feeling overcame me that I was familiar with certain places. Perhaps these vague sensations or "hunches" were due to the fact that, sub-consciously, I remembered descriptive passages out of books I had read. Often, when I was thinking of nothing in particular, certain sounds or smells brought back to my memory incidents and places which had been completely out of my mind for many years. Again, uncommon types of human voices, facial expressions or mannerisms, made me remember people I had forgotten, in several cases since the days of my early childhood.

Whilst living among primitive Indians, I always felt that they were, if not my superiors, at least my equals, and therefore I treated them with due honour and respect. It always struck me that they, like animals, birds and even insects, know things which are beyond white man's comprehension, and consequently such primitive people fascinated and intrigued me greatly.

· · · · ·

At the cold, windswept and barren border between the Argentine and Bolivia, where the international railway line crosses from one country to the other, I happened to be at the small wooden station (La Quiaca) when the bi-weekly train from La Paz arrived. I was talking to several miners and prospectors, when a number of tired and dusty passengers alighted to stretch their legs. One of them, a tall skeleton-like man with long, black hair and a short, pointed beard and moustache, was so peculiarly dressed that I wondered if he had been to a fancy-dress dance. By means of an elastic ribbon, a kind of miniature Tyrolese hat was fastened to one side of his head, and he wore a threadbare, tight-fitting jacket, the sleeves of which only reached halfway down his thin, sunburnt forearms. The legs of his trousers were equally short, showing a pair of thick, pink woollen socks. In striking contrast with these garments, this veritable clown wore enormous narrow shoes, almost the size of small canoes.

Having descended from the train, the man turned towards Bolivia, and, standing on tiptoe, waving his arms and shaking his fists, in several languages bellowed curses in the direction of the country he had just left.

Observing my bewilderment, an American mining engineer with whom I was conversing told me that the grotesque apparition was a Swiss geologist whose name was famous among miners and prospectors throughout Bolivia. My companion went on to inform me that this wizard in geological matters had been in the employ of the Bolivian Government for many years, and that he knew more about rocks, strata, minerals and other matters connected with the earth's crust than anyone else in those parts of the world. My companion also told me that, for months on end, the geologist disappeared into the Andes, later to return to headquarters with valuable data, but that every two or three years he left Bolivia in a fit of temper, swearing that never again would he return. Apparently, however, after having spent a few weeks in Buenos Aires, he always changed his mind, and once more turned up in Bolivia in order to set out into the rocky wilderness.

When the Swiss came to the end of his thunderous monologue, I was introduced to him, whereafter for a while the two of us had

M

an interesting chat. Upon hearing that I was about to cross the whole
of Bolivia on horseback, and that it was my intention to ride right
up to the U.S.A., without saying a word the geologist turned, and
quickly jumped on the train. Presently, as it began to move, he
thrust his clown-like head out of a window, and, staring at me,
shouted, "*Adieu, espèce de fou!*"

Some ten thousand feet above sea-level, in a remote valley among
bleak mountains, in the heart of a region inhabited by primitive
Aymara Indians, I came to a few low stone huts, one of which was
so large that it might almost have been called a house. There was
a neatness about it which is to be found nowhere among Aymara
dwellings, the very aspect of which is as unfriendly as the sulky
and sullen people who live in them. To my surprise, I noticed that
a well-built little canal irrigated a small garden, in which grew
vegetables and even flowers—things I had not seen for some weeks.
The tiny house, with creepers growing up its crude stone walls,
looked most inviting, so I rode up to have a closer look at it.

A few Indians who squatted on the ground, and were busy spinning thread, cast furtive glances in my direction, but their aquiline
faces remained completely expressionless. The men wore knitted
caps with long ear-flaps hanging down, which gave them sphinx-
like appearances. All were dressed in loose-fitting blouses made of
coarse llama wool, and short trousers which barely reached down to
the knees. There was something of the Stone Age about these people,
and had it not been for the garden I saw, the scene would have been
as prehistoric as it had been in other similar settlements which lie
hidden away in some of those remote Andean valleys.

Upon reaching the low, one-storied house, with its roughly
thatched roof, to my amazement a bearded white man appeared at
the door, immediately to be followed by a beautiful girl who must
have been about eighteen years of age. Like the man, she was
fairly tall, and had a remarkably fine figure. Her Madonna eyes,
with beautifully shaped eyebrows, long black hair, which was
parted in the middle, delicately moulded features and rosy cheeks,
would have been a fine subject for a Rafael.

As during the two or three previous weeks I had only seen

Indians and half-castes, the unexpected apparition of two white people gave me such a surprise that, for a few moments, I remained staring at them, unable to utter a word.

"*Parlez-vous français?*" the man asked, and when, in the same language, I replied in the affirmative, the two came towards me to greet me in a most friendly manner. Immediately I was asked to unsaddle my horses, and to make myself at home. Later, when I strolled about with my host, he informed me that he was a widower, and that the girl was his only daughter, but beyond this—what had brought the two to this remote part, to live among such primitive Indians, and how they contrived to exist in this wild region—I was told nothing; and, of course, I did not ask.

The Aymara language is very guttural, and by far the most grating to the ear I have ever heard spoken. Some of the sounds seem to come up from the stomach, and give one the impression that the speaker is in pain. Therefore, it can be imagined what a shock I had when the Frenchman's daughter had a violent row with an Indian woman, and, losing her temper, cursed her up hill and down dale in the language of the region. Whilst the volcanic erruption lasted, the formerly Madonna-like French girl reminded me of the snake-haired goddess from Tartarus, and I was glad not to be the target of her fury.

For various reasons I was led to suspect that this mysterious Frenchman had chosen to live among those sometimes dangerous Indians because he wanted to gain their confidence. His provisions were brought from far away, over snow-clad mountains and through wild valleys, by Indians who drove pack llamas before them. How and where he found the money wherewith to defray these costs still puzzles me, but I venture to guess that he lived on capital, hoping some day to find a hidden treasure, of which a number are waiting to be discovered in various parts of South America.

During my travels I met several such adventurers, and later, especially after some of my books and a series of newspaper articles were published, a number of letters concerning treasures reached me. Invariably my correspondents referred to ancient historical documents they had found, or to accounts written by more modern travellers, some of whom even left rough maps showing where such treasures are supposed to be buried.

No doubt, at different times, ever since the *conquistadores* set foot on the continent, vast quantities of gold, silver and precious stones were hidden, but even if a few Indians know where such treasures lie, they will never divulge the secret to anyone, save, perhaps, to a trusted son. Natives—particularly those whose forefathers were ruled by Incas—still believe that, some day, their empire will once more be restored to its former glory. Therefore, objects out of old temples and palaces, which may have been hidden during the Spanish conquest, are held as sacred.

If my suspicions concerning the mysterious Frenchman are correct, I imagine that he felt sure he knew the place where a treasure lay buried, or, perhaps, that he had discovered gold. Therefore he "squatted" in that remote region, hoping that, in the not so very distant future, a road would be constructed through it. This, of course, would bring in its wake white man's protection, and then it would be fairly safe to get at whatever he had his eye on.

·   ·   ·   ·   ·

In a miserable Bolivian Indian village I was surprised to meet an elderly, thin and sun-parched American, who told me that for some twenty years he had been on various treasure hunts. With him he had two small, patched-up and battered leather trunks, most of the contents of which consisted of tattered and frayed maps, sketches and documents, all soiled and stained with use and age. For hours on end the old man told me fascinating stories about different treasures he had been trying to find during all those years. Whenever I showed signs of doubt as to the clues on which he worked, with the help of his documents he endeavoured to convince me that he was not on a wild-goose chase. My enthusiastic new friend had travelled through many practically unknown regions, and for long spells had lived among different tribes of Indians, whose languages he spoke fairly well. What interested me more than the treasures he was determined to find were the amazing stories of high adventure he had to tell.

Years before I met him, he had been a successful prospector, and it was during his travels through Peru and Bolivia that he accidentally found the first clue as to the whereabouts of a certain hidden treasure. With the passing of time, this discovery—on paper—led to others, and thus, by degrees, the treasure fever gripped him. He told me that a considerable sum of money he had saved in the past had kept him going all those years, and he optimistically assured me that, in due time, his heavy expenses, and the hardships he had endured, would prove to have been a sound investment. He explained that age was beginning to tell on him, and said that a good companion would greatly facilitate his task; and therefore I was not in the least surprised when he invited me to join him. Naturally, I did not accept his offer, but replied that, if instead of continuing his researches, he returned to the U.S.A., and there set his unique experiences on paper, or lectured on them, he might easily earn quite a lot of money. However, he flatly refused even to consider my suggestion, and when I saddled up to depart, the grizzled old treasure-hunter told me that he was determined to continue his quest, even if it meant meeting his death somewhere in the wilds. As I shook his leathery hand and looked into his clear steel-blue eyes, set deep under bushy eyebrows, I realised that his last words were not merely an idle boast.

·　　·　　·　　·　　·

In one of those innumerable hidden valleys in the high Andes, I was surprised to meet another lone white man. It was evident to me that my arrival filled him with more than ordinary curiosity, for ever since I had come into his view, he had been standing outside a hut, watching me intently.

"*Buenas tardes, senor*" ("Good afternoon, sir"), he greeted me. I had hardly returned his salutation, when, in a peculiar tone of voice, he asked, "And what brings you to these inhospitable parts?"

Whilst replying to this somewhat blunt question, I had a good look at my questioner, who was a tall, fine-looking man, some thirty years of age. I noticed that in a holster he carried a revolver of heavy calibre, and that, near him, placed against the wall, was a rifle. This, as well as his inquisitiveness, led me to think that perhaps he was a policeman dressed in civilian clothes.

As usual, I carried my ·45 Smith and Wesson on my hip, and on the pack saddle, wrapped up in a waterproof sheet, were my rifle and shot-gun, on which sometimes I had to rely for getting my food.

Before I had finished introducing myself to the man, he warmly shook my extended hand, and at the same time exclaimed, "Oh, so you are the *caballero* who is trying to ride from Buenos Aires to Nueva York. I'm very pleased to meet you! Only a few dags ago, some friends and I were talking about you. In a newspaper we read that it was believed you had disappeared somewhere in the Andes. Of course, as you and I know, this is quite easy, but, fortunately, there is a great difference between disappearing and coming to grief."

For some time the two of us laughed and joked about the report concerning me, and then the stranger helped me unsaddle the horses, and carry my belongings into the hut, which evidently had been left uninhabited for some time. Having piled up my pack and saddles, we went to attend to the horses, and when, thanks to my new friend's assistance, an old Indian sold me a few bundles of dried maize leaves, and the animals began to munch them, we sat down on the doorstep to converse.

A touch of malaria and an acute pain in the kidneys made me feel so bad that, when the time came to share a stew of dried llama meat and barley, I preferred to lie down and try to sleep. My companion, who was genuinely worried about my health, prepared a hot beverage with herbs, and made me drink a canful. He assured me that my kidney trouble was caused by the manner in which I wore my heavy revolver, and advised me in future to loosen my belt a few holes, and thus to allow it to slip down to my groins, and consequently to leave the kidney region free of pressure. Next, he demonstrated to me how, especially whilst riding, I should carry my revolver. This he did by fastening to the muzzle end of the holster two leather thongs. These, when tied below the knee, prevent the weapon from bumping up and down. My expert instructor went on to explain to me that this manner of securing a revolver had the further advantage of making it possible to draw it from the holster with speed.

Feeling seedy, I stayed in the Indian settlement for two days, during which my friend did everything possible to make me and my horses comfortable. On the third morning, when I decided to leave, despite my protests he insisted on guiding me towards the nearest town. Accordingly, he mounted on his goat-like mountain pony, and led the way over hardly visible Indian foot tracks. Towards evening he found a suitable camping place, where a spring and patches of grass provided our animals with water and sufficient fodder to give them a fill. On the fourth day, upon reaching the top of a high pass, on a table-land below us we had our first view of the little town. Dismounting to give the horses a rest, we stood for a while, beholding the vast panorama.

Presently, my companion broke the silence, "Friend," he said, "this is where I must leave you, and turn back; but, before we part, I want to tell you something."

Pointing in the direction of the town, with a wry smile he informed me that, having had "*un pequeño contratiempo con la ley*" (a little reverse with the law), it was necessary for him to keep at a distance, until the storm should blow over, whereafter he would return to civilised parts, in another region where he had friends.

When we shook hands, and I finished thanking him for all his kindness, for the first time he told me his name.

"Most likely you will be hearing stories about me. If you do, please tell no one that you have met me, let alone where." With this he swung, into the saddle, and with an "*Adios, amigo, y buena suerte*" ("Goodbye, friend, and good luck"), at a fast amble made off in the direction whence we had come.

A few hours later, in a guest-house I heard a great deal about the bandit and killer who had been so kind to me, but although it was with keen interest that I listened to stories about his latest exploits, I told no one about my recent experiences in the mountains. On the following day, when I was ready to resume my journey, and bystanders warned me to be on the look-out for the ruthless bandit,

I thanked them for their advice, and as I jogged away, it was only with difficulty that I repressed an inward chuckle which tickled my throat.

.   .   .   .   .

In a certain Andean town, the military authorities very kindly put loose-boxes and fodder at the disposal of my two horses, and from local potentates down to the humblest folk, everybody was exceedingly kind to me.

In the one and only more or less decent hotel were several American and European guests; among the latter a pleasant-looking young man and his attractive wife, who was a doctor. The three of us soon became friendly, and often strolled about together, seeing what sights the quaint old Spanish colonial town had to offer. One night, when I was in bed, reading, someone knocked at the door, and presently the lady doctor's husband came into my room, evidently worried about something. After a few preambles, he frankly told me that he was a trafficker in drugs, and that he had reason to fear that the authorities were on his tracks. Unwrapping a parcel, he produced two square tin boxes, the sliding lids of which were secured with adhesive tape. Having opened one of the tins for my inspection, the nocturnal caller informed me that the white stuff which it contained was cocaine, and he implored me to take charge of the two tins. My visitor worked himself into a great state of agitation, and in a faltering voice whispered that if the cocaine were found in his possession, besides being ruined, he and his wife would inevitably land in jail.

"For God's sake," the young man pleaded, "put these tins into your pack. No one will ever suspect you, and when you get down to the Pacific coast, I shall be waiting for you. Please take great care of this valuable stuff, for, upon delivering it to me, the reward I shall pay you will be handsome."

Before I had time to refuse to take a hand in this ticklish affair, my visitor tiptoed out of the room, and gently closed the door behind him.

About a month later, when, after having crossed high mountain ranges, I arrived at Lima, near the coast, the two drug traffickers called at my hotel, and when I told them that after the cocaine had been handed over to me, I had emptied the stuff into the lavatory, the pair listened to me with tears in their eyes.

Pointing to the door, I told them to get out of my sight as quickly as possible, lest I denounce them to the authorities. Of course, I should have done this a month before; but, fearing to become involved in a long and tedious legal entanglement, I had decided to act as related.

Thus I let the pernicious couple depart, whither, or on what future business tours, I did not care one iota.

Whilst in the same city, an American called on me. He was about thirty-five years of age, of medium height and build, and wore a light Palm Beach suit. Having read in the local newspapers that I had arrived from Buenos Aires on horseback, the caller merely wanted to introduce himself to me, and have a friendly chat.

As it turned out, my visitor was a globe-trotter who had spent many years tramping through the interior of China, as far as Afghanistan, and even far into parts of Siberia, Kasakstan and Turkistan. Now, for a change, he had come to have a look at South America. In order to defray his costs, he was busy roping in commercial firms to put advertisements into a kind of glorified calendar he intended to produce. Being a well-educated and jolly kind of person, his conversation was both interesting and entertaining, and therefore, whenever there was nothing else for me to do, I wandered about the city with my new acquaintance. Thanks to the fact that he spoke several Eastern languages and dialects, he was a great favourite among Chinese merchants and *restaurateurs*, of whom there were many in Lima.

Besides introducing me to rare and savoury Chinese dishes, my companion also took me to opium dens, where I satisfied my curiosity by smoking some of the drug. In my book, *Tschiffely's Ride*, my reactions to "hop" are fully described, so here I will only add that the effect the drug had on me was so unpleasant that I have no desire to make any further experiments with it.

Having seen enough of South America, my friend the globe-trotter gradually worked his way back to the U.S.A., mostly in small coasting vessels, and shortly after having reached New York he was given an excellent job in a well-known American insurance company. On my way north, I received two or three letters from him, and I was pleased to learn that he was doing exceedingly well. About a year and a half later, upon reaching New York, I went to call on him at his office, only to be informed by one of the directors, that, tired of conventional life, the man I sought had given up his job in order to resume his tramping through the interior of China.

.   .   .   .   .

On the shores of the Pacific Ocean, whilst conversing with a group of Americans who were doing constructional work in one of the republics, I heard about a certain countryman of theirs who was said to have gone "native" or "tropical." I was told that, formerly, he had been a clever engineer, and that he had done great things in many parts of the world. Upon retiring from business, to his friends' disgust, he married an elderly coal-black "mammy" who was the mother of several illegitimate children, from a grown-up son down to piccaninnies, with whom, my informants told me, he had settled down in a village through which I would have to pass on my way north.

About a week later, upon coming out of a region covered with dense forests and jungles, I reached open country, soon after to arrive at the village in which lived the ostracised American engineer. A half-caste Indian guided me towards a well-built, one-storied house, outside which I dismounted. Several half-naked black children played in the sand, and from a nearby garden a young, tall and muscular Negro watched me, leaning on a spade with which he had been digging. Presently, out of the front door came a man whose general appearance immediately brought to my mind Buffalo Bill, as depicted on coloured covers of old Wild West thrillers. With his long iron-grey hair falling down to the shoulders, pointed beard, flowing moustaches and bushy eyebrows, he looked every inch the hero of my early boyhood days.

"Good afternoon. Are you Mister So-and-So?" I said.

"I am. And who may you be, stranger? And what brings you here?" the bearded man asked in a friendly tone of voice.

I introduced myself and answered his question, whereupon he invited me to unsaddle. The expert manner in which he assisted me showed that he was an old hand with horses, packs and saddles. When these had been placed in a nearby shed, and my animals had been turned loose in a small field, the two of us went into the house, where I was shown into a spotlessly clean and comfortable bedroom, which was to be mine for as long as I wished to stay with my host.

Until after sundown he and I sat in the garden, conversing, and later, in a well-stocked library, discussed books. After an excellent dinner, when my host began to talk about himself, he informed me why he had chosen to live as he did. He explained that for many years he had worked hard in many parts of the world, and that upon beginning to feel that he deserved to enjoy the fruits of his labours in the way he liked best—by living quietly, and eating the kind of food he fancied—there was one big snag: housekeepers and cooks came and went, and most of them were not worthy of their hire.

"I'm sure," he said, "some of my countrymen must have told you about my having married a black?"

Feeling uncomfortable, and not knowing what to say in reply, I slightly nodded my head, whereupon the speaker continued: "Oh, I know they're disgusted with me for that; but, let 'em be. I don't care a hoot for what they think and say. My marriage is *my* business. And let me tell you right now that when I hooked up with the old Negress, I knew exactly what I was doing. You may be shocked to hear the truth; but, since you're here, I might just as well tell it to you. Now, to begin with, I'm sure that you'll agree with me that the dinner we've eaten to-night is the best you've had for a long time. If you stay with me for two or three days, as I hope you will, I shall show you what *I* call food fit for the gods. Yes, friend, the Negress who prepared our meal is the best cook I've ever come across, and therefore, in order to make sure that she shouldn't leave me, I damned well married her."

My host went on explaining to me that his wife and all her children lived in a bungalow, situated at the back of his house, and that the hefty young Negro I had seen working in the garden was her eldest son, who, besides being a good mechanic and chauffeur, did odd jobs for him. Two of her daughters acted as housemaids, and a boy of about fifteen made himself generally useful. The "cook"—as the speaker now referred to his wife—and all her dusky offspring had their meals in the kitchen, and at night the boss of this extraordinary family remained alone in the house, two Newfoundland dogs being his companions and guardians.

As I was to realise soon, in telling me that he would give me "food fit for the gods," my host was right, for some of the dishes served during the time I stayed with him were as good as the best I have ever tasted. Apart from the excellent food, and the perfect manner in which the two "maids" served it, the long conversations I held with this intelligent and widely travelled man were so intensely interesting that I was sorry when the time came to move on.

As I rode away, the reincarnation of Buffalo Bill stood in front of his house, waving me goodbye, whilst the fat, ugly, coal-black cook and some of her children did the same from outside the kitchen door.

Chapter XIV

De luxe explorers.—Jim the anthropoid and Jim the Monkey.—An American seeks happiness among primitive Indians.—Professor Max Uhle.—"El Lobo" meets his death.—Eavesdropping on political intriguers, and the sequel.—Two kinds of duel.

HERE and there, sometimes in the most unexpected places, I came across lone wanderers of different nationalities. Some of these men were orchid or fern collectors, prospectors, or treasure hunters, whilst others merely tramped for the sake of tramping.

In striking contrast with such nomads, upon jogging out of a jungle, soon after to reach a hilly region where the temperature was delightfully cool, there, to my surprise, I saw several snow-white tents of various sizes. Presently I discovered that this luxury camp had been pitched by an expedition, all the members of which gave me a reception as if I had arrived from the planet Mars. Young doctors, botanists, mineralogists, zoologists, ornithologists, ethnologists and other "ists" wanted to know about the region I had just traversed, and when I told them that the best thing they could do was to go and look at them with their own eyes, their frank reply was that they had not come to "rough" it, but to have a good time.

Though the camp was pitched in a relatively little-known region, it was not far from the coast, whence the expedition—with the assistance of native porters and mules—had come in four easy stages, winding their way through what these stout-hearted "explorers" called "dense jungle, hitherto untrodden by human foot." When I compared my limited equipment with the luxuries these glorified Boy Scouts had at their disposal, I felt like a half-starved, nomadic Indian. However, this did not deter me from continuing my lonely travels on the following day, heading for a distant mountain range which I would have to cross before reaching regions which, I hoped, would be pleasanter than those through which I had struggled recently.

·   ·   ·   ·   ·

In a tropical port, I was told not to miss going to a certain "dive" in which I would see something unique.

A retired geologist who, besides having gone "native," was also far "gone" with drink, was a regular tippler in this primitive "booze joint," in which the greasy half-caste Indian boss kept his client's formerly inseparable companion, a big ugly black monkey. The few English-speaking people—mostly mining engineers, who periodically came down to the coast—always referred to the degenerate but jovial "booze hound" as "Jim"; but in order to differentiate between him and his old pet, the latter was called "Jim the Monkey."

During several years, twice per day these inseparable companions had visited the saloon, where, sitting at the bar, perched on high stools, they drank until both were inebriated. One day, the monkey —who evidently was the more practical of the two—decided that it would be much more convenient to make his home in the place. Formerly, rolling back to Jim's bungalow had been most difficult and sometimes even dangerous, so when a large shelf behind the bar was placed at the disposal of Jim the Monkey, he took advantage of it. Whenever his owner arrived to seat himself at the bar, the monkey climbed down to take his place alongside him. Then the pair sat, drinking and often quarrelling violently, until, unable to swallow another drop, the monkey made his way back to the shelf. As excess of alcohol began to show its ill effects, invariably the intoxicated animal held its head in both hands, and at the same time wailed and moaned like one of Dante's damned.

The two Jims were of such interest to me that I made several visits to the "dive." On one occasion when I entered, I had hardly seated myself at the counter when Jim the Monkey descended from his shelf, to squat on the stool next to mine. Having dug me in the ribs with an elbow, with the flat of his hand he struck the top of the counter, and when a small glass of rum was placed before him, he quickly picked it up and drank its contents in one gulp. Having deposited the glass before him, the monkey again dug me in the ribs, and several times struck the counter as before. There was something so weird and uncanny about the ugly animal's actions and looks that I was glad when Jim appeared to take my place, thus enabling me to watch the amazing pair from a respectful distance.

The two sat together, drinking glass after glass of rum, and when this began to take effect, the monkey suddenly jumped on the counter, shot out his lips, and furiously jabbered at his owner. The amazing quarrel lasted until the boss of the "dive" intervened with a broom, whereafter the monkey struggled up to his shelf, where he acted as already described until he fell into a drunken sleep.

All this time, Jim, with his legs crossed, and slowly moving a foot to and fro, sat at the bar, drinking and staring at the tip of one of his rope-soled slippers, and when he, too, got drunk, staggered out, to make his tortuous way home.

Many a time, since having witnessed this amazing and disgusting sight, its memory has haunted me, and I often wonder what was the end of that almost incredible pair, Jim the anthropoid and Jim the Monkey.

.   .   .   .   .

In romantic Quito, the capital of Ecuador, situated high up in delightfully cool regions near imposing snow-clad peaks, I met an American gentleman, about whose subsequent life and adventures also I frequently wonder. He was about forty years of age, and was a graduate of one of America's foremost institutes of technology.

Whilst resting my horses in that quaint old Spanish colonial town, in his company I visited Indian markets, monasteries, churches, and other places of interest, and sometimes we sat on a bench in the main *plaza*, conversing and enjoying the sunshine. My friend told me that, some four years previously, he had held an important position in a vast industrial enterprise in the U.S.A., and that, when overwork caused a nervous breakdown, he went to Ecuador in order to recuperate. Being an active and adventurous-minded person, upon regaining his health and strength, he made a one-man expedition into the far interior, eventually to reach a practically unknown region, somewhere near the upper reaches of the Amazon. There he made friends with the primitive Indians, with whom he hunted and fished, and generally had such a pleasant and interesting time that, upon returning to the U.S.A., he found it difficult to settle down. For about two years he carried on with his job, and when the wilds called him, he decided to hand over his private affairs to a lawyer, and to return to his Indian friends, among whom to spend the rest of his life.

He explained to me that it was his intention to enjoy himself according to his own tastes and inclinations, and that, as far as he was concerned, no money in the world could buy what the region of his choice offered. Should he ever be in need of medical assistance, or wish to have a change, he could always return to civilisation for a while, or even go on a visit to his homeland. For this reason he had made arrangements to leave most of his clothes and belongings in Quito, as well as adequate funds, on which, if necessary, to be able to draw.

At first I listened to my friend, thinking that he was not serious, but merely trying to lead me up the garden path, but when he showed me the luggage and equipment he had brought with him, I realised that he was in dead earnest.

Among many other things he had brought with him, were two fair-sized wooden boxes filled with fish-hooks of different sizes, masses of old safety razor blades, and dozens of knives, and in several long boxes were packed steel bows and machine-made arrows. My friend explained that these articles were invaluable to the Indians, who preferred them to the crude wooden type they made, and that the bows and arrows he had brought with him would make excellent presents for some of his old friends.

Often, primitive dwellers of the little-known interior of the continent came to Quito, bringing with them marmosets, parrots, beautiful feathers, skins of different wild beasts, and even reduced human heads, with which to barter for articles they needed. My American friend was awaiting the arrival of such a party, the members of which would guide him towards the interior, and carry his supplies for him.

Looking at my well-groomed and neatly dressed friend, who was about to become a kind of Robinson Crusoe, I admired him for his convictions regarding happiness. Whilst listening to what he said, I could not help comparing him with long-haired Raymond

Duncan and Company, who, as we have seen, took good care to do their preaching in cities, and I could not help wondering what they would have said if my companion had asked them to join him on his return to the Eldorado of his choice.

In Quito I made friends with another remarkable man, who belonged to a very different category. This, to me, almost legendary figure was the great scholar, Professor Max Uhle, undoubtedly one of the greatest archæologists of modern times.

It was with hesitation that I pulled the heavy wrought-iron handle of an old-fashioned door-bell, and when the wires squeaked, and a tinkling sound from within the Spanish colonial house reached my ears, I waited with bated breath. After a while, an old bare-footed half-caste Indian woman opened the door, and when I handed her a none-too-clean letter of introduction I had carried in my pack for many hundreds of miles, she asked me to step inside and wait. Presently, a white-haired, bespectacled old gentleman came to greet me, and soon after the two of us sat in his book-lined study, talking six to the dozen. When I thought it was high time to leave the professor to his work, he insisted on my staying to have dinner with him, and after this had been served, and the table was cleared, we chatted over glasses of wine. Every time I rose to leave, my host persuaded me to remain a little while longer, just to discuss one more point on ancient South American history, of which, in comparison with this great scholar, I knew nothing. When it was 3 a.m. he said that old men, such as he, could very well do without sleep, and he suggested that, unless I felt tired and bored, we might just as well carry on our conversation until breakfast-time, where-after he would have to go to the university, where he was busy sorting out old records and doing research work in the archæo-logical section of the library.

Accordingly, I remained, and in the evening, when we met again to continue our conversation, the seemingly tireless pro-fessor held me spellbound until midnight.

Trouble was brewing when I arrived at a camp where con-structional work was being carried out. The supervisor—a small,

N

insignificant, though wiry man—informed me that the presence of a newly-arrived foreman was a source of great worry to him. He had been given the job at the headquarters in a distant town, where, evidently, they did not know about his activities in the past. Ever since his arrival, the new foreman had "thrown his weight about" in a most unpleasant manner, thus causing discontent and apprehension among the workers, who soon discovered that he was an outlaw, known as "El Lobo" (The Wolf).

In the evening, when I happened to be sitting in the large mess tent, chatting with the supervisor, the feared man swaggered in. Seeing a boy cleaning a revolver, with the heavy handle of his whip he knocked the weapon out of the youngster's hand, saying, "In this camp no one but myself is allowed to carry a revolver."

"I beg your pardon," my companion said, rising from the packing-case on which he had been seated, "*I* am the boss here. If you don't like it, clear out!"

"El Lobo's" eyes flashed fire, as with a rapid movement he drew his revolver; but before he had time to raise it, the supervisor whipped out his gun, and with amazing speed fired several shots which caused his antagonist to lurch forward and slump to the ground, which he hit with a dull thud, whereafter there was dead silence in the tent.

"Take him away," the Supervisor said, turning to a group of his men who stood staring at the corpse, and whilst his order was being carried out, he calmly seated himself beside me and began to clean his revolver as if nothing had happened.

.   .   .   .   .

In Bolivia, an Indian uprising and a revolution made things lively for me in a very different way, and when I reached Central America, the political situation there was unpleasantly volcanic. Along my trail, at different times I met revolutionary chiefs of both sides, as well as adventurous foreigners who tried to cash in on those troubles, supplying with armaments and ammunition whichever side offered the best odds.

An American, whose acquaintance I made in San Salvador, openly bragged that he was a gun-runner for Sandino—who, at the time, made things most uncomfortable for the American marines who occupied parts of Nicaragua. Shortly before I met the gun-runner, one of Uncle Sam's warships had chased the small coasting vessel in which he carried his "goods" into a shallow bay, where he managed to slip away among a number of sand-banks and small islands, though with the loss of three men killed.

My hotel in Salvador City was a favourite meeting place for revolutionary intriguers from neighbouring republics. Most of these men were jovial happy-go-lucky adventurers and soldiers of fortune, who made no secret about their ambitions, plans and activities. For hours on end they sat in the hall, exchanging yarns, and discussing prospects for the future. One shifty-looking, middle-aged Englishman claimed to be the official correspondent of the London *Times*, and told the assembly that he had come down from Mexico City in order to report on happenings in Nicaragua. For various reasons, I suspected that the man was a mountebank, and when, one night, he disappeared, leaving behind him a mass of debts, my suspicions proved to have been well-founded.

Some weeks later, when I happened to be sitting in the hall of my hotel in Guatemala City, to my astonishment the same man arrived, now looking like a tramp. His clothes and shoes were in a sorry state, and since our last meeting he had grown a stubbly beard. Evidently he had travelled afoot, and was tired, but despite his ragged appearance he was immediately given a room, to which he went without seeing me.

That night, as I lay in bed, making efforts to doze off, through a partition door I heard voices. Not being interested in other people's conversations, I pulled the blankets over my head, and inwardly cursed the jabberers next door. By degrees, their conversation became louder and louder, and I was about to give a knock of protest on the partition door, when I distinctly heard my name being mentioned. Yes, there was no doubt, the person who spoke was the self-styled *Times* correspondent.

"Don't talk nonsense," he shouted, "I assure you that the man whom you suspect of being an American agent is Tschiffely who has come on horseback from the Argentine. I saw quite a lot of him in San Salvador."

What I heard was so intriguing that, for the first time since my childhood, I did some eavesdropping. Propping myself up comfortably against my pillow, I listened to the animated conversation next door. It did not take me long to come to the conclusion that the mystery man had no connection whatever with the *Times*, but that he was a political intriguer and informer, and that the two men who interviewed him were well-known Central American revolutionary leaders who hoped to get into power.

I heard that the pseudo-newspaper correspondent actually had come down from Mexico, where he had left his wife and daughter, and I was not in the least surprised to discover that his interests were focused on something much more exciting—and possibly lucrative —than journalism.

Several months later, upon reaching Mexico City, I made enquiries regarding the mysterious Englishman, and it did not come as a shock to me to learn that he was a shady character, or a *mula* (mule), as a certain type of political intriguer is called in Central America.

Having obtained his wife's address, I went to call on her. She lived in a crowded tenement building, and when I introduced myself to the thin, poorly dressed woman, she became pitifully nervous. However, she calmed down considerably when I told her that I had merely come to tell her that I had met her husband during my travels, and that he was in the best of health. Her daughter—who must have been about eighteen years of age—was very suspicious of me when she arrived to see me talking to her mother, but after a while the two women began to converse freely, and the tale of woe I heard from them made me regret that I had called merely to satisfy my curiosity.

.   .   .   .   .

Riding through countries in which revolutionary armies are on the war-path, or across wild regions where, at any moment, a traveller may be attacked by bandits, is apt to bring out of him whatever of the fatalist is within him. Thus, in one republic through which I had to pass, after a time I just rode along, taking next to no notice of anything but the trail and the scenery. After a long day thus spent, towards evening I was glad to dismount in a village situated among picturesque *sierras*. I had hardly done so when some-one informed me that a few hours before my arrival, a detachment of soldiers who were stationed there had succeeded in capturing two redoubtable bandits. Shortly after having been told this bit of exciting news, when I went to introduce myself to the commanding officer, I found him busy interrogating the two prisoners. Both pleaded innocence, but when witnesses came forward, and their evidence could leave one in no doubt that the captives were guilty, they began to accuse each other in no uncertain terms. Gradually, the argument between the two desperados became so heated that one defied the other to settle this "matter of honour" by fighting a duel. The challenge was immediately accepted, and when I heard how the duel was to be fought, I could hardly believe my ears.

Without further ado, the prisoners were led to a filthy den, where their feet were put into stocks. This having been done, a double guard was placed near the two wretches, whose flashing glances at each other conveyed more than words could have done.

The commandant did everything within his power to make me comfortable; my horses having been put into a nearby enclosure, they were given a liberal allowance of dried maize leaves, and when a corner of the mud-floored guard-room was more or less swept clean by a dusky soldier, there I deposited my pack and saddles, and spread out my blankets in readiness for the night. After a frugal meal, we sat round a small fire, talking about things in general, and it must have been close on midnight when the commandant rose and lit a lantern.

"Bring out the prisoners!" he ordered gruffly.

This having been done, he took the lantern, and led the way towards the entrance of a large square corral, surrounded by high adobe walls. Followed by the two prisoners and their armed guard, a number of soldiers and myself, the leader of this solemn procession halted in the middle of the corral. Turning round so as to face the two desperados, he asked them if they were still determined to fight the duel.

The light of the lantern flung grotesque shadows on the adobe walls, and the inky sky seemed to have descended as a roof to the corral. Both prisoners having replied that they wished to fight to the death, the officer ordered them to take off their jackets and shirts, and when both were stripped to the waist, they were handed a dagger apiece.

"As you will see, both are exactly the same," the commandant said, and after a pause continued, "And now, after we have retired, and the corral gate has been closed, you may begin the duel, using whatever methods or ruses you wish. This afternoon both of you accused each other of being guilty of murder and other crimes; so now, if one of you is less despicable than the other, may he escape with his life."

Having said this, the speaker ordered his men to place the duellists in opposite corners, whereafter all of us witnesses withdrew, closing the large wooden corral gate behind us.

For some time, not a sound reached my ears, but, presently, the almost unbearable silence was broken by a series of hisses, curses, grunts, and the noise of scuffling. Then, after a while, a grunt-like noise, followed by moans, suggested to us listeners outside that a blade had struck a vital spot.

Following the commandant, who carried the lantern, we hurried into the corral, where a gruesome sight awaited us.

One of the desperados was lying, face down, evidently dead, and the other staggered about, breathing stertorously, with blood flowing from several horrible deep gashes. Presently, he sank to his knees, and with a great effort placed himself in a sitting position. Weakened by the rapid loss of blood, he swayed to and fro, his head drooped, and then he fell backwards, his glassy eyes staring up into the blackness of night.

"They have handed out their own justice," the commander said, and then, turning to some of his men, ordered them to bury the corpses at once. With this, in grim silence he led the way back to the military quarters where, smoking black cigarettes, we sat for a while, discussing recent events.

In striking contrast with this horrible duel, here I cannot refrain from giving a literal translation of the account of a totally different kind of passage of arms, as published in a well-known South American newspaper.

Out of profound respect and consideration for the heroic gentlemen involved in this affair of honour, I will call the actors by different names, though retaining their military and naval ranks and academic degrees.

Printed in large thick type, and splashed across a whole page, the sensational account of this *recontre* begins:

"TO-DAY GENERAL PANZA GORDA FOUGHT DR. TEMERÓN.
"THE ENCOUNTER OF HONOUR TOOK PLACE IN MIEDO.
"DUEL WAS FOUGHT WITH PISTOLS. NO ONE HURT."

The masterpiece of high-class journalism and descriptive writing reads as follows:

"Great expectancy reigned over the agreement during the early hours of to-day to bring into effect the gentlemanly encounter with arms between General Panza Gorda and Dr. Temerón. The rift between the two was caused by differences of opinion which arose in consequence of a letter, couched in violent terms, the last-named sent to the former.

"The fact that, ever since arrangements for the duel were in process of being made, there existed a doubt as to its realisation greatly accentuated the tense expectancy, and even more so owing to the intervention of the police, who took energetic preventative measures, watching movements of seconds and duellists.

"Last night the duel was definitely arranged, and it was agreed that it be fought under severe conditions, but, as stated, the decision of the police to watch all roads leading out of the city, and, if possible, to arrest the actors and other participants in this affair of honour, obliged these to resort to an artifice in order to evade the vigilance.

"By Train to Miedo

"Thus, in a train which left the capital at 9.35, the duellists, their respective seconds and doctors, travelled to Miedo, where they

alighted. Near the station, two cars awaited them. General
Panza Gorda, together with his seconds, installed himself in one
of the vehicles, and Dr. Temerón did likewise in the other car.
Immediately, both vehicles left in the direction of the estate
owned by Admiral Terra Firma.

"*The Duelling Site*

"After a few minutes the cars arrived at the said estate. The
first to reach the field in which the duel was to take place was
General Panza Gorda, who was accompanied by his seconds,
Generals Polvorín, Colonel Cabaretti and his doctor. Moments
later, Dr. Temerón's car drew up, and from it descended his
doctor, and seconds, Colonel Retintin de Retirada, and a gentleman whom our reporter did not recognize.

"*The Duel Takes Place*

"The usual formalities gone through, the duellists faced each
other. Dr. Temerón, who won the toss, chose the south side. It
was exactly 11 a.m. when Admiral Terra Firma, who acted in
the capacity of director of the duel, ordered the commencement
of the same, which was carried out with pistols at a distance of
twenty-five paces. Dr. Temerón took aim and fired the first shot
without consequences, whereas General Panza Gorda fired into
the air. Both made a second discharge into the air. Therefore,
uninjured, the duellists were invited to make a reconciliation,
which both refused. With this ended the gentlemanly affair."

The foregoing goes to prove that chivalry is still with us, and
that there are different ways of settling affairs of honour. In one or
two Latin-American countries I know well, duels are serious matters,
so unless a prospective combatant is prepared to take an even chance
of being either the star turn at a funeral or the victorious hero, he
had better not recklessly throw about challenges.

Chapter XV

Portrait under a black veil.—A wise mule.—Mexican revolutions.—
General Aspirina.—Echoes from Pancho Villa's hectic days, and an
anecdote connected with the famous outlaw.—An eventful bullfight.—
"If these are roses . . ." A Bohemian *médico*.—Dipsomania and song.—
Archduke Maximilian's coffin.

AMONG the many adventures I had during my wanderings
through the Americas is one I am not likely to forget.

Long before the sun was due to rise over southern Mexico, I
rolled up my blankets and brewed myself some black coffee, and
even when my horses were groomed and saddled up, the Sierra
Madre was still wrapped in inky blackness. I was glad when the last
rope and strap were fastened, for my fingers were rendered almost
useless by the penetrating chill; so as I rode out into the night, it
felt good to press them against my mount's warm neck.

Here and there, the trail led through low shrubbery, or past
clusters of gigantic octopus-like cactus plants, the black shapes of
which were eerie. Occasionally, when some fleeing wild animal ran
across our path, or rustled through the bushes, my horses shied or
snorted nervously. When the first violet and purple tints over the
jagged peaks announced the arrival of another day, I had already
ridden a number of miles. Gradually, the indescribable display of
colours over the mountains became brighter, and, like a flag being
unfurled slowly spread over the sky, until, finally, the first glittering
rays of the rising sun shot over the peaks in the east. Soon after,
resembling liquid tar, the shadows of night began to recede down the
mountain-sides, and presently the imposing golden vastness of the
Mexican *meseta* (table-land) spread before our eyes.

As the hours passed, and league after league was left behind us,
the rays of the sun became hotter and hotter, until the heat rose from
the sandy ground in shimmering waves. Towards evening we
reached an *hacienda* (ranch), and as I approached one of the low

mud-built out-houses, a group of *peones* (workers) watched me with curiosity from under their huge sombreros.

"Good evening," I greeted them. "Is this the Montezuma Ranch?"

"*Si, señor*; and if you wish to see the boss, you will find him in his house over there," one of the bystanders said, pointing towards a large gate.

Passing through it, I rode into a spacious courtyard, and as I did so, a tall lithe man, dressed in the picturesque costume of a *charro* (Mexican cowboy) appeared under the massive stone arches which ran along the whole length of the house. Opening my saddle-bags, I took out of them a letter of introduction a friend had given me, and handed it to the owner of the ranch who, after having read its contents, gave me and my horses a hearty welcome.

After dinner, the two of us sat under a tall spreading tree in the courtyard, talking about recent events connected with the revolution. The moon had risen over the high adobe walls which surrounded the house, and a soft breeze made the leaves rustle mysteriously. When there was a pause in our conversation, I listened to the hardly audible "ee-ee" of bats crazily darting in and out under the arcades, and every now and again I heard the mournful "oo-hoo" of an owl. As the air became chilly, we rose, and, candles having been lit, my host showed me the way to a bedroom, where he left me with a cheery "good night."

Alone, I stood for a while, looking round the room. Above the bed hung a large crucifix, made of hand-beaten silver, and on a dressing-table I noticed a number of toilet articles, which suggested that the room had been occupied by a woman. Above this piece of furniture hung a frame, covered over with a black veil. Curious to ascertain what was beneath it, I raised a corner of the flimsy material, and held up the candle in order better to see. To my surprise, I discovered an oil painting of a beautiful, dark-eyed girl, who seemed to smile down at me.

Since entering the room, I had noticed a peculiar musty smell which now seemed to become stronger, and, after a while it dawned on me that what I was smelling was the faint odour of stale incense.

My curiosity satisfied, I undressed, climbed into the large Spanish colonial bed that was overhung with a brocaded canopy, and soon fell asleep.

Early next morning I was awakened by the song of birds, and upon going to the stable to see how my horses were getting on, I met my good host, who had already gone there for the same purpose. Having eaten a hearty breakfast, consisting of coffee, maize pancakes (*tortillas*), stewed black beans (*frijoles*) and fried eggs, I made ready to depart.

For some strange reason, the picture under the black veil had been on my mind ever since I had had a final look at it before leaving my bedroom, and so, prior to departing, I asked my host who was the beautiful subject of the portrait.

In a choking voice and with tear-filled eyes, he replied that recently a great sorrow had befallen him, his beloved wife and daughter having departed, never to return.

Embarrassed by having inadvertently asked so painful a question, I continued to saddle up in silence, but, after a pause, my host again spoke.

"It was in the room in which you slept last night that my beloved daughter died," he said huskily, "and, ten days ago, my dear wife followed her to a better world. . . . The bubonic plague knows no mercy. . . ."

Having shaken the broken-hearted man's hand, and thanked him for his hospitality, I quickly mounted, and with a final "*Adios y muchas gracias,*" trotted out of the courtyard.

During the next three or four weeks I kept a watchful eye on my health, and often, whilst haunted by the memory of a beautiful girl smiling at me from under a black veil, I imagined to be smelling the faint odour of stale incense.

.   .   .   .   .

Among these random recollections of my ride through Mexico, I must relate an extraordinary experience I had in a southern section of that fascinating land. In those mountainous parts there are a number of deep, narrow canyons, through which flow exceedingly turbulent rivers, some of which can be forded during the dry season.

Where such chasms are spanned by railway bridges, these are constructed in a manner which makes it impossible for cattle and horses to cross them. Railway sleepers being laid cross-ways under the rails, and no floored space being provided for treading upon, riders and their beasts are obliged to make détours, and to cross such canyons wherever Nature provides a suitable place.

Upon reaching one of these tantalising railway bridges, I made the descent by cautiously leading my horses down a break-neck trail which led to the river below, and after having forded it, we began the tortuous and exhausting ascent of the opposite wall. Having successfully reached its top, I was glad to put up for the night in a small kind of wayside inn.

Several peasants and *vaqueros* were there, making merry over *tequila* and *pulque* (two potent drinks), and late at night, when one of the revellers made ready to depart on his mule, he was so drunk that he had to be helped into the saddle. Despite his friends' advice to remain with them until the morrow, he stubbornly insisted on going home, and, accordingly, set out in the bright moonlight. Shortly after he had gone, a man came rushing into the inn, and excitedly told us to hurry outside, where something terrible was happening.

There, in the middle of the giddy bridge, we saw the mule, slowly and cautiously stepping from sleeper to sleeper, with its rider fast asleep on its back. Evidently, the knowing animal had decided to make a short cut for home, and in so doing avoid the fatiguing descent and ascent of the deep canyon. It had almost reached the far side of the bridge, when the rider raised himself in the saddle, and for a brief moment had a look round. Upon realising his position, he got such a fright that, with a violent jerk at the bit, to our horror he caused the mule to lose its footing, and to fall, its body coming to rest on the sleepers, with the legs dangling down between them. Whilst we hurried to give what assistance we could, the drunken peasant frantically clung to anything within his grasp, all the while calling on all the saints to save his life.

It was fairly easy to assist the man to safety, but in the case of the mule it was a very different matter. Though frightened, the animal was wise enough not to allow itself to be thrown into a panic, and therefore, ropes having been brought, after some difficulty, with our assistance it managed to rise, and to regain its foothold on the sleepers. This ticklish feat accomplished, the mule gingerly proceeded until it reached safety, whereupon its now amazingly sobered-up owner threw his arms around its neck and showered kisses upon it.

A little later, whilst duly celebrating our successful rescue work, we all agreed that it was a pity the peasant had woken up before his mule had carried him home, for otherwise, if, later, anybody had told him about his animal's tight-rope-walking act, he would never have believed it.

. . . . .

Two generals, Gomez and Serrano, led an insurrection against the Government, but by the time I reached Mexico City, most of their troops had surrendered to the "Loyalists," and the two revolutionary leaders were taken prisoner. After a short trial, both were executed by a firing squad, later to be given a State funeral in the capital. As the country's guest of honour, I met most of the high officials, among whom I particularly remember those who were great and daring riders. Besides being a fine horseman, General Palomera Lopez—the Chief of the Mounted Police—was also an expert aviator. During one reunion of *charros*, after having ridden a buck-jumper to a standstill, he went up in his Curtis biplane to do a number of stunts, some of which he performed so near the ground that the slightest misjudgment would have meant certain death. The Chief of Police, General Roberto Cruz, and other officials, showed me what they could do on horseback, so with these new friends I spent several exciting and happy days. In a subsequent revolution most of them had the misfortune to be on the losing side, and therefore those who could not flee to neighbouring republics were "provisionally" shot.

I shall always remember a fine-looking young general, who jokingly gave me his definition of "provisional" executions. He said that foreigners found it difficult to understand the Mexicans' mental attitude regarding such "liquidations," which, according to him, in his country are carried out without the least ill-feeling on either side.

It was after a banquet in a beautiful old estate, situated far out of the capital, that this same general gave me an interesting glimpse of his attitude towards life. Leading the way through a magnificent garden, our host was showing us his property, which, once upon a time, had been a monastery. My friend, the lively and amusing young general, looked superb in his *charro* costume, adorned with silver and gold, and his hat, which was studded with precious stones, must have cost a small fortune.

Slipping an arm through one of mine, my companion took me along a narrow garden path, away from the rest of the sightseers, and when we were out of earshot, he halted, turned round so as to face me, and said, "Friend, no doubt this is a beautiful place; but how I would hate to own it! Just imagine, if this were the case, how depressing it would be to think of having to die some day. Just look at me; here I stand, and all I possess in the world are a few *pesos*, the costume I wear, and my excellent horse, on which to ride wherever fancy leads me. These passports to the world are sufficient for me, and whenever things get dull, a revolution makes a nice change. Even if, some day, I should have to go the way many other rebels have done before me, well . . . *paciencia*. But to be the owner of such an estate—no, friend, a thousands times no! Give me my horse and the wide open spaces, and I envy no man."

.   .   .   .   .

Like most human calamities, revolutions have their humorous side, and therefore Mexicans, being an extremely witty people, tell countless jokes connected with such upheavals. The chief causes of most large-scale wars are of a commercial nature, but if one boils down the simple pot-pourri of what leads to most Latin American revolutions, it will be found that only two main factors are responsible for them. The first of these is very simple. The "Outs" try to get into power, and the members of the "In" party do their utmost to keep the others out. The second cause, though easy to perceive, is a little more difficult to explain in so-called "diplomatic" words.

Having no desire to beat about the bush, I will be frank, and accordingly state that foreign instigation and, in some cases, even open support of one party or the other have been behind a number of revolutions. Of course, the Latin-American soil being fertile for such intrigues, seeds that are sown, and at an opportune time nursed with a golden watering-can, will sprout and thrive amazingly.

Among the countless friends I made in Mexico were a number of military leaders who, during different revolutions, had fought on opposite sides. That such trifles are soon forgotten was proved to me when, on several occasions, my friends humoured one another, or referred to amusing happenings during previous campaigns.

One of these redoubtable scrappers was known as General Aspirina (Aspirin), and when I inquired why he was given such a peculiar nickname, the explanation was as follows:

One day, the general was making merry with a friend, and late that night, as the two were sitting in a tavern, upon being brought the "umpteenth" drink, the latter complained that he had a splitting headache, and told his generous friend that all he longed for was aspirin wherewith to alleviate his pain. The general—who was very drunk—insisted on his suffering companion having another drink, and when he repeated that all he could possibly swallow was aspirin and a little water, the general drew his revolver from his holster, and shouting, "Well, if you really want an aspirin, take this!" fired a shot through his friend's head, killing him instantly.

And so, ever since that friendly interlude, the drastic Samaritan bore the nickname of "General Aspirina."

Whilst in Mexico, I met a number of men who had fought with Pancho Villa. From all first-hand accounts I heard about this famous outlaw, he must have been a remarkably astute, brave and daring man, as also were many of his officers and their subordinates. No doubt, Pancho Villa and his followers were a murderous gang, but, in a peculiar sense, they were fanatical patriots. Among his officers, a certain General Fierro was by far the most sadistic and bloodthirsty. His very name, Fierro, meaning "Iron," suited this monster, who sometimes took a fiendish delight in killing for the mere sake of satisfying his blood-lust.

Once, when some three hundred prisoners were rounded up in a yard, surrounded by high adobe walls, he seated himself on a post some twenty yards from one side of the gate and, as armed soldiers let out the captives one by one, Fierro shot them as they tried to run the gauntlet. He was such a deadly marksman that not one of the prisoners escaped with his life.

This ruthless killer and formidable fighter, who would take no orders or advice from anyone save Pancho Villa, eventually, died true to type. One dark and stormy night, whilst riding towards his temporary camp, in order to shorten the distance, he began to wade through the shallow arm of a lagoon. One of his men, who knew the region, warned Fierro that the bottom of the lagoon was treacherous, and advised his leader to make a détour. Annoyed by this suggestion, Fierro thundered that he needed no advice, that his mind was made up, and that he would cross the lagoon in the very middle. Knowing their commander, the men watched in silence as he spurred on his horse. Soon Fierro reached deep water, and the last seen of him was when he and his faithful horse swam out into the inky and turbulent darkness.

Like General Fierro, Pancho Villa also died true to type. Some time after he had retired to a more passive life, hired assassins attacked the car in which he was being driven. Though mortally wounded, before collapsing he killed two of his assailants with his unerring revolver.

Here I cannot resist setting down on paper one of the many humourous anecdotes Mexican friends told me about Pancho Villa.

A *gringo*,[1] as Americans are often called in Mexico, arrived in a town, where he put up in a hotel. He had retired to his room, and was about to go to bed, when someone knocked at his door. Upon opening it, the American saw a *charro* who, having looked about him in a most furtive manner, whispered, "*Señor*, you buy curiosity?"

"Wal, it depends on what you have for sale," the other replied.

"Sssh!" the *charro* warned, at the same time raising his *sarape* (cloak), to show a human skull. "Pancho Villa," he whispered,

[1] In the Argentine and in Uruguay, Italians are often called *gringos*.

pointing at it. "Just dug out of the grave. Take it. Only fifty dollars; very cheap, unique souvenir."

Though not too sure that this was the genuine article, the American replied, "Fifty dollars? Do you think I'm Rockefeller? Take twenty, and it's a deal."

"Done!" the Mexican whispered. "It's yours, but mind you tell no one about it, or they'll kill me."

Having received the twenty dollars, the Mexican made his way towards the nearest tavern, there to celebrate his success.

Wondering how and where he had made so much money, his friends asked him to explain, but it was only when alcohol loosened his tongue that the *nouveau riche* divulged the source of his wealth. Amid roars of laughter, he let his listeners into the secret of how he had dug out the skull in the local graveyard, and later sold it to the *gringo* as Pancho Villa's.

This information, and a few more drinks, gave one of the carousers an idea. Without saying a word to anyone, he disappeared, soon after to sneak into the cemetery to dig out a skull.

The American was fast asleep when someone tapped at his door. Upon rising to see who the caller might be, he was confronted with an inebriated *charro*, who, after a warning "Sssh!" lifted his cloak to show a human skull. "Pancho Villa's!" the caller whispered, "I have just dug it out of the grave. Buy it. Very cheap; unique souvenir."

"You won't kid me that easy," the American replied, going into his room, to fetch the skull he had bought a few hours before. Then, tapping it with a finger, with a superior smile he told the tippler, "This is Pancho Villa's. Just have a look at yours. It's a baby's. Can't you see?"

Having studied the object on which his fondest hopes depended, after a little thinking, the *charro* babbled, "You're quite right, *señor*, but for this very reason my skull is much more remarkable and valuable than yours; mine is Pancho Villa's when he was a baby."

.　　.　　.　　.　　.

In Mexico I met a number of bullfighters, who invited me to go and see them perform, but the entertainments I enjoyed most were

o

jaripeos, or "rodeos," as cowboy competitions are very wrongly called in English. (In Spanish the word *rodeo* means a round-up of cattle.)

Usually such roping and bronco-riding displays were followed by amateur bullfights and picturesque folk dances. No horses were used in such bullfights, and in most cases the bulls came to much less harm than some of the young bloods who tried to emulate great masters of this difficult and dangerous art.

In an old town situated on the main tableland of Mexico, such a *jaripeo* was given in my honour. During the display of daring and skill, two things happened which caused thunderous laughter, such as I have rarely heard. Roping and buck-jumping having come to an end, a drunken *charro* staggered into the arena. Facing the balcony in which I sat in the company of the Governor, a few ladies and several generals, he took off his huge sombrero, and with a great flourish declared that he would ride a fighting bull. Loud cheers greeted this announcement, and soon after, when a trap-door was opened, a nasty-looking black bull dashed into the ring. Presently he halted and began to scratch the ground with a foreleg, and to throw sand over his back. This was an unmistakable sign that the beast meant business, and I was pleased to think that it was not up to me to ride the beast.

Next, three mounted *charros* rode into the arena, and when the bull charged one of them, the others threw their lassos with such good aim that within a few seconds he was brought to the ground. This done, the drunken man was called, and when he was ready, the ropes were unfastened, whereupon the bull struggled to his feet, with the rider sitting on his back. Immediately the infuriated animal began to buck-jump, twist and turn in every direction, and at the same time even trying to dig its horns into the rider's legs. Amazed to see how the inebriated *charro* managed to stick on, the crowd cheered wildly. Soon, however, the inevitable happened; the rider lost his balance, and, with the next buck, was unseated. If ever a drunken man sobered up quickly, it was that *charro*; for within a second he was on his feet, and before the bull had turned round, began to run towards the wooden barrier which surrounds

all bull rings. Chased by the beast, he fled with the speed of a champion hundred-yards sprinter, and when the horns were almost
touching him, headfirst he dived over the boundary boards, into
which the bull crashed, whilst the man knocked himself unconscious
against the foot of the stands. All the while, the mass of onlookers
fairly howled with delight, hats were thrown into the air, women
screamed, and there was general pandemonium. Upon recovering
his senses, the unfortunate *charro* staggered to a seat, where, after
someone had thrown a bucket of water over his head, he remained
meekly watching the rest of the show.

Following this incident, a number of would-be bullfighters were
busy showing off in the arena when one of my companions in the
balcony whispered to me to rise and follow him. Leading the way,
he made for the back of the stands, where, in a small corral, rested
several formidable looking imported Spanish fighting bulls, which
were to be used in a professional show billed to take place on the
following Sunday. The beasts with which the amateur bullfighters
amused themselves and the spectators were relatively small, and had
been provided by a local rancher, but the ones I saw in that corral
behind the grandstand were the real articles.

Taking a long pole, my companion prodded one of them until
it entered a chute with an iron trap-door at either end, the far one
leading into the arena. Having shut in the bull, the practical joker
waited until the moment arrived to let another into the arena.
Presently, he turned a handle, thus raising the trap-door. When the
terrifying Spanish bull tore into the ring, snorting like an over-
heated steam engine, there was a wild scramble for safety, all the
local smarties bolting like so many rabbits. Thus ended the amateur
bullfight, but even when I left the hospitable town, whenever one
of those heroes walked down a street, bystanders teased him unmercifully.

Mexicans are very proud of their women's beauty; and, in a great
many cases, quite rightly so. Often, when I reached some town or
village, new acquaintances would tell me, "Just wait until our next
fiesta, that's when you'll see our *señoritas* at their best." This reminds
me of an anecdote of which I am very fond.

A visitor was told by a friend that in his town all the *señoritas* were like roses, so it was with great pleasure that he accepted an invitation to a dance. In due time, upon entering the hall where all the members of the local élite were assembled, the would-be Don Juan suffered a rude disillusionment, all the girls there being very much on the plain side.

Turning to his proudly smiling host, the disappointed visitor said, "My dear friend, if these are roses, I never want to see another spring."

·   ·   ·   ·   ·

In the pleasant company of newly-made friends, I sat in the porch of a picturesque, old-fashioned Mexican hotel in which I was staying. Whilst sipping a cup of black coffee and listening to the animated conversation, I noticed a haggard woman peeping in through the door. When she had gone, one of my companions—who was the local doctor—informed me that the poor creature was not a beggar, as I had thought, but that she was mentally deranged. He told me that, some years before, her husband, who was a confirmed drunkard, had died, and that ever since then every night the woman went from tavern to tavern looking for him.

The doctor who told me this pathetic story was an extraordinary man who had seen much of the world and who had done many strange things. Born and educated in Mexico, upon qualifying as a *médico*, he went to Vienna, in order to study music, but by the time he got his second doctor's degree, it struck him that the life of a common sailor was the most attractive. He happened to be in Genoa, waiting for a ship to take him home to Mexico, when a sudden impulse made him apply for a job as deck-hand in a cargo boat. Instead, he was made a cook's assistant, his chief duties being to keep the galley clean, peel potatoes and wash up plates, dishes and sauce-pans. Thus, for nearly two years he happily sailed all over the world, later, in turns, to become the medical officer to an expedition into then unknown parts of southern Mexico, conductor of a symphony orchestra, active participant in a revolution, rancher, and, finally, to settle down where I met him.

Whilst we sat in the hotel porch, talking over our coffee, an

unkempt, podgy and unshaven loafer happened to slouch past in
the street, and when the doctor saw him, he quickly rose and ran
after him. Meanwhile, one of the group of men with whom I sat
told me that the tramp-like individual I had seen pass had a wonderful voice, and that, until dipsomania gripped him, he had been a
great success on concert platforms in various parts of the world, but
that all he did now was to go from tavern to tavern, hoping that
someone would give him a drink.

Soon after having left us, the doctor returned, bringing with him
the subject of our conversation, and when a guitar was produced,
and the unkempt newcomer had swallowed a large glass of *mescal*
in one gulp, he was ready to sing. (*Mescal* is a potent liquor made of
the agave plant, in Mexico called *"maguey."*) Having strummed the
guitar for a while, the podgy man cleared his throat, and then began
to sing most beautifully. As he worked himself into a state of
exaltation, and was carried away by his art, he held me so spellbound that I no longer noticed his exterior appearance. Song after
song this amazing tenor sang, and as his recital continued, the porch
filled with people, whilst many others listened from the street.

It was fascinating to see how the singer and his audience reacted
to the various songs, the last of which, *"Donde estas corazón"* ("Where
art thou, my heart?"), a great favourite in Mexico at the time, made
tears run down the artist's unshaven face. Well after midnight, when
he rose to depart, some of his admirers embraced him, and after having
accepted money from them, he slouched away to spend it on drink.

The Gomez-Serrano revolution was fizzling out when I reached
the old town of Queretaro, situated on the main *meseta* (tableland)
of Mexico. It was there that, in 1866, Ferdinand Joseph Maximilian,
Archduke of Austria, was shot. Three years previously, in 1863, he
had been proclaimed Emporor of Mexico by the invading French
troops, who had captured the city of Puebla. This execution was the
result of various intrigues and interests at stake; on the one hand,
America's determination to enforce the Monroe Doctrine and, on
the other, the Mexicans' resolve to remain a free and independent
republic. To make things even more complicated, Bazaine, the
ambitious commander of the French troops, tried to supersede

Maximilian, so when the recently proclaimed Emperor arrived, he was arrested and, after a trial, executed outside the town of Quere-taro. To-day, a small and simply-built chapel marks the place where the hapless Emperor fell.

Shortly before I arrived, revolutionary troops had attempted to occupy the town. During a lively shoot-up, the old municipal build-ing was the target of the main attack, which, however, was repulsed.

In a small museum on the first floor of the building are kept a number of interesting relics, among them the crudely-made deal coffin in which Maximilian's body was brought into the town after the execution. When the local *alcalde* (mayor) took me to see the relics, we discovered that during the recent skirmish one of the defenders had been killed in the museum, and that the historic coffin had been badly ripped by one or two bullets. Examining it closely, I noticed that it had been roughly painted over with some dull black substance, and that, on the bottom of its interior—which was unpainted—besides several significant smudges and stains, one of the Emperor's bloody hands had left a remarkably clear imprint in the soft wood.

Seeing the badly damaged coffin, my guide asked me to accept a piece of it, and when I politely explained that if I took away such a souvenir this would amount to vandalism, he saw my point, and there and then decided to have the coffin restored.

The man who was killed in that room, met his death in a curious way. Only one bullet had struck him, about two inches above his nose, right in the middle of the forehead. From there, without penetrating through the skull, it had travelled to the top of the head, tearing out a narrow strip of scalp and wiry black hair, thus making what looked like a perfect parting. Small tufts of hair were stuck to the ceiling in a straight line, a freak which interested my companion much more than any of the exhibits in the museum.

Before leaving Mexico, I again wish to make it clear to the reader that in these random reminiscences connected with that beautiful and fascinating country, I chiefly write about some of the more unconventional characters I met there. And with this I say "*A Dios*" to the land of the *charros*.

Chapter XVI

Laredo, Texas: a fright and a successful plot with a master-brewer.—
Smuggling egret feathers.—Texas Rangers.—My horse fails to appreciate Will Roger's sense of humour.—Mayor "Jimmy" Walker, and a
few yarns about prohibition.—My first attempts at writing and lecturing.
—Flash-back regarding the sinking of the *Vestris*.—Return to the
Argentine, and a cheap passage back to the U.S.A.—The Odyssey of an
oft-rejected manuscript.—London once more.

IN the days about which I am writing, the vast majority of
travellers obtained their first view of America when the ships
in which they sailed approached New York Harbour. If this city
of towering steel and concrete can be described as the porchway or
main entrance to "God's own country," I rode into it through one
of its back doors, my out-of-date means of locomotion being two
Patagonian mustangs. However, despite this and my weather-
beaten appearance, the American authorities in Laredo accorded me
a cordial reception, and the many excellent friends I made there, did
everything to make me feel at home.

The day before I crossed the Rio Grande—which was done by
jogging over the international bridge which connects Nueva Laredo
(Mexico) with Laredo, Texas—I happened to be talking to my kind
host, the Governor of the state of Tamaulipas, when a messenger
arrived to inform him that a delegation of American bankers had
crossed the border, and that the train in which they travelled was
standing in the station.

At the time, Ambassador Morrow was endeavouring to bring
about a rapprochement between the U.S.A. and Mexico, and it was
for the first time in many years that American bankers had officially
visited their southern neighbours.

The stout and jovial Governor of Tamaulipas spoke no English,
so he asked me to do him the favour of going to call on the American
delegation, and to inform its members that there would be no
Customs inspection, and that, if there was anything he could do to
assist them in any way, he would be delighted to do so.

Mounting my pinto, I galloped over to the station, and presently entered the restaurant car in which most of the bankers were assembled. It was only when I saw the surprise that was written on several faces that it dawned on me how peculiarly dressed I was for acting in the capacity of semi-official messenger. On my head was a large Mexican sombrero, round my neck I wore a bright red scarf, from my bullet-studded belt dangled a big ·45 six-shooter, my sun-burnt face was the colour of a boiled lobster, and my hands and bare arms were covered with a mass of freckles.

Having apologised for my appearance, I duly delivered the Governor's message. Besides asking me to reciprocate his greetings and to thank him for facilities accorded and assistance kindly offered, the visitors had no other news for me to communicate. I was about to retire when one of them offered me a cigar, and asked me where I had learnt my English. I had hardly begun to explain what had brought me to those parts when several of the travellers rose from their seats, and came to shake hands with me. They had read about the progress of my ride from Buenos Aires, and therefore were delighted to meet me on the eve of my entry into their country. Months later, when, according to their invitation, I visited some of them in their headquarters in Wall Street, they hardly recognised me in my "civilised" clothes, and they admitted that when I had entered the restaurant car in Laredo, for a moment they thought I was a *bandolero* about to do business.

On the Texas side of the Rio Grande my first delightful host was Colonel Robert Foy, the Commanding Officer of Fort Myer. During a military parade—at which I was accorded the honour of taking the salute—I recognised an old sergeant who formerly had been stationed in Panama, where he had reconditioned my pack and saddles. He was a grand fellow, and what he did not know about handling mules and horses was not worth knowing. But, as I discovered shortly after the parade, he was also an expert in another line—namely, in the art of brewing beer. In view of the fact that prohibition was in force at that time, the sergeant's skill as a brewer was a godsend to his intimate associates, who had turned into a brewery a disused Army shed, situated in a secluded place behind the barracks. The duties of a sergeant being manifold, my old friend from Panama complained bitterly that he had but little time to dedicate to the manufacture of "home-brew." Going into a huddle with him, after some hard thinking we devised a plot which, should it be successful, would suit both of us admirably.

The colonel had already invited me on the morrow to accompany him during a lay-out inspection, so the wily sergeant pointed out to me the spot near which I would find him.

Early in the morning, when I was sleeping like a marmot, a terrific bang shook the house, making me jump out of bed as if released by a steel spring. Under the impression that I was still somewhere in Mexico, and that a good old revolution had broken out, I rushed to the window. To my surprise, and relief, I saw American soldiers lined up on the parade ground, whilst, to the accompaniment of bugle calls, the Stars and Stripes were being hoisted up a tall, snow-white flag-pole. During breakfast the colonel told me that every morning at sunrise, and again at sunset, this ceremony was held in all American Army posts, and that it was customary, prior to raising or lowering the flag, to fire a cannon shot. This having been done almost under my window, no wonder I was shaken out of my peaceful slumbers.

When, together with the commanding officer, I rode along the files of soldiers, upon approaching a certain section of the parade ground, I looked for my friend, the burly old sergeant. Sure enough, there he was, looking as innocent as a prize-winner in a Sunday School.

"Good morning, Sergeant Simpkins," I exclaimed, stopping my horse. "What a pleasure to meet you again!"

Surprised at this recognition, the colonel turned to me and asked how I came to know the sergeant. I explained that, whilst resting in the Panama Canal Zone, and waiting for the dry season to set in in those parts, the sergeant had looked after my horses, and that, besides having done the job marvellously well, he had very kindly reconditioned all my equipment. Hearing this, the good colonel asked me if I would like the sergeant again to take charge of my animals, and when I replied that if this were not asking too much,

I should be delighted, he ordered my co-plotter to take them in hand, and instructed his company commander to release him from all other duties.

Needless to say, my horses were almost pampered, and the sergeant's spare time was very usefully employed in the "brewery" behind the barracks. In due time, when during a specially arranged tour of inspection, I was shown over it, and the master-brewer explained to me certain intricacies of his art, frothy glasses were raised to the success of our plot.

During the most pleasant fortnight spent as Colonel Foy's guest, I went back to Mexico several times, crossing the bridge across the Rio Grande on foot. During one of those visits, when the train from Mexico City arrived at the station and I happened to be on the platform, talking to several friends, a voice hailed me from the train. Turning round, I recognised two elderly Americans whom, months before, I had met in San José, the capital of Costa Rica, where they had gone to spend a holiday. Boarding the train, I went to greet them, and to exchange news about our respective travels. Before I left, one of my old friends told me that with him he had a bunch of beautiful egret feathers. Having explained to me that, according to American law, no feathers were allowed to be taken into the U.S.A., he asked me if I would be good enough to smuggle his in for him. Being on friendly terms with the Customs house officials, I took charge of the feathers, and, before crossing the bridge, carefully tucked them inside my trousers.

Seeing me approach, several of the American border officials asked me to go into their office for a smoke and a chat, and whilst we were joking and laughing, the sharp prickly feathers began to dig into my skin, making it itch as if red ants were biting me. The irritation grew from bad to worse, and, at last, when under some pretext I asked to be excused, and hurriedly made for the Baker Hotel in which I was to deliver the feathers, the discomfort became almost unbearable.

Upon reaching the room in which my friends waited for me, I made such haste to get rid of that bunch of feathers that the two onlookers wondered if I was subject to fits. Soon, however, I explained what had happened, and when the three of us finished laughing, I made a vow never again to smuggle egret feathers for anyone.

Besides my ride from the Mexican border to Washington, D.C., during two subsequent visits to the U.S.A. I met innumerable people, but here I will only mention a few of various types and callings with whom conventional travellers, had they been in my place, probably would not have come into personal contact.

Bootleggers, smugglers, cowboys, preachers of various denominations, coast-to-coast stunt-mongers, pole-sitters, spiritualists, revivalists, Texas Rangers, politicians, film stars, confidence-trick men, professional gamblers, and even gangsters I met during my travels through that land of startling contrasts. In most cases this happened without intention on my part, Fate bringing us together like pieces of driftwood on the watery main.

In Texas, I saw much of the Rangers, a fine body of men, who took me under their wing. Among them, Captain Tom Hickman, a charming, but, when necessary, extremely tough "guy," became one of my best friends.

.   .   .   .   .

The first time I met Will Rogers, the inimitable American "wisecracker," was at Meadow Brook, where my friend, Jack Nelson, the famous Argentine polo-player, introduced us to each other. Will was anxious to see the Patagonian pinto pony which had carried me all the way from the Argentine to the U.S.A., so I took my new acquaintance to the loose-box in which my pet was kept.

Here I must explain that Mancha (in English meaning "Spot") was essentially a "one-man" horse. Born among the Tehuelche Indians, he was still unpleasantly wild when I set out from Buenos Aires, but, by degrees, he tamed down, and later became very attached to me. Travelling through the wilds had made him distrustful of strangers, and if ever anyone approached him too closely or, worse, attempted to touch him, he strongly disapproved. Usually he frightened people away who tried to be too familiar with him, by laying back his ears and by pretending that he was making ready to bite. When thoroughly annoyed, he swung round to lift a threatening hind-hoof, and sometimes he even lashed out good and hard. However, all these antics were sheer bluff, for during all the years I handled the animal he never hurt anyone, and if an intruder was bold enough to ignore his threats, he immediately changed his tune and became more friendly.

So many strangers had upset Mancha's temper before Will Rogers and I visited him that he was in a particularly standoffish mood when we appeared. Keen to have a close look at the horse, Will was about to step into the loose-box when I warned him to be careful.

"You just leave the pinto to me. I know how to handle a horse," Will said, advancing confidently. But, before he had time to beat a hasty retreat, with a wicked mulish look, Mancha dashed towards him, quickly spun round, and let fly with both hind-legs. Had Will stood perfectly still, the kick would have missed him by a yard, but, being unfamiliar with such Patagonian horse-play, Will jumped back so hurriedly that he tripped up and sat down very hard indeed.

"Do you know what's wrong with my horse?" I asked poor Will when he recovered from his fright.

"No," he replied, brushing dust and straw off the seat of his pants.

"Evidently he doesn't appreciate your sense of humour," I said.

At this, a number of bystanders laughed so uproariously that Will walked away in a temper—an attitude which surprised me. Subsequently, for several days he avoided me whenever possible, and it was not until some time later that he once more became friendly; but the little episode in the loose-box, though not forgotten, was taboo when we met.

Another delightful "wise-cracker" I met in the U.S.A. was Mayor James J. Walker of New York, better known as "Jimmy" Walker. In September, 1928, on behalf of the Mayor's Committee, he did me the honour of presenting me with the magnificent New York City Medal, which, later, together with other trophies, I handed over to the Colonial Museum of Lujan, near Buenos Aires. As I am writing this, these things are on view beside the stuffed and mounted effigies of my two faithful horses, Mancha and Gato.

(Gato died in 1944, aged thirty-four, and Mancha in December, 1947, after having reached the ripe age of nearly forty.)

James Walker was a real Bohemian, bubbling over with life and wit, but, despite his light-hearted exterior, he was eminently aware of how many beans make five. Some years after having made his acquaintance in New York, I was delighted to meet him again in England where, according to him, he was on a "kind of prolonged vacation." He loved to hear some of my yarns, but the one he enjoyed most was connected with prohibition, which he had always detested and openly flouted, as once I saw him do during a banquet of the National Horse Show Association in the Biltmore Hotel in New York.

On that occasion, he and my friend, the late Mr. McEntee Bowman, the famous hotel magnate and a keen horseman, were in charge of proceedings, which went with a swing.

Before hundreds of guests entered into the main banqueting hall, in an ante-room, out of veritable crystal aquariums cocktails were served, and when the assembly was about to sit down to eat, after a short and witty speech, "Jimmy" Walker drew the guests' attention to the fact that beside every cover there were two bottles of Apollinaris. The one with the cap on, he explained, contained table water, but the other, with its cap off, was filled with authentic Scottish "Apollinaris," which, he guaranteed, had come straight from a ship to the hotel.

But to come to my prohibition story which he so greatly enjoyed.

In a wooded part of a certain State, big business was being done by clandestine distillers of "moonshine" liquor. Among these American Robin Hoods, I had several acquaintances, who let me into some of the secrets of their trade, about which, having ridden all the way up to those parts from the Mexican border, I had already learnt a thing or two. As it happened, I was staying in a glorified log hut belonging to a friend of mine when one of the bootleggers dropped in for a chat. Knowing that I was "on the level," the visitor spoke freely about his particular line of business, and, before departing, told me on no account to miss going to see the "show" which was to take place in his distillery on the morrow. For various good reasons, I was not keen on accepting the invitation, but when my visitor assured me that there was no earthly chance of my getting involved in anything unpleasant, I promised to go over and see him.

Accordingly, next morning I followed a footpath through the woods until I came to a clearing in which stood several wooden huts, and two fairly large sheds. Seeing me approach, the bootleggers came to greet me, whereafter we smoked and chatted for some time. When we were beginning to wonder if anything had happened to the people whose arrival we expected so eagerly, the burring of motors reached our ears, and soon after three cars and a truck drove up.

Most of the men who emerged from these vehicles were in uniform, and evidently the chief of the contingent was well-known to my host, who greeted him as an old friend. Glasses and a jug filled with liquor having been handed to the uniformed men—who had driven a long distance—a few of us strolled about, and when certain things had been unloaded from the truck, everybody got busy making preparations for the show to begin.

A "movie" camera having been carefully set up on an appropriate spot, and the act having been thoroughly rehearsed, the camera-man shouted, "O.K. Let's go!" whereafter the uniformed men rushed hither and thither before the camera, and presently rolled out a number of kegs which they proceeded to smash up with axes, making the precious liquid flow ankle-deep. As a grand finale, with admirable histrionic determination and zest, sticks of dynamite were placed under a still, which, presently, was blown sky-high. This done, the commanding officer gravely inspected the *débris*, whereafter the operator ceased turning the handle of his camera. The one-act drama having been duly recorded on celluloid, on the morrow, in news-reel theatres, the ever-gullible public would see how thoroughly prohibition was being enforced. However, audiences would never guess that the kegs I watched being smashed up by strong arms swinging law-enforcing axes were leaky with age and filled with water, and that the still which was blown heavenwards was completely worn-out, and therefore had been condemned as unserviceable. Not only this, but had the camera been swung round 180 degrees, a shed in which was a brand-new still would have come into the picture, besides rows of perfectly sound kegs, and several smiling faces, including the bootleggers' and mine.

After an excellent meal of cold chicken, delicious Virginia ham and other savoury foods, the heroes of this perfectly acted drama departed, taking with them bottles filled with liquor, with which our host presented them as tokens of admiration and friendship. As they drove away, the jovial bootlegger shouted after them that he hoped oceans of "hooch" would be dispatched from his place before the new still would deteriorate and other "props" would be available for the shooting of another documentary film dealing with the systematic and ruthless stamping-out of the social scourge—alcohol.

.   .   .   .   .

Among newspaper men, particularly in New York, I met several full-blooded Bohemians, and also among actors, artists, rodeo cowboys and members of the sporting set.

Thanks to newspaper men with whom I had made friends, I had another experience connected with prohibition.

Having arranged to dine together, and later to go to a show, we foregathered in a certain editor's office, whence we proceeded to a "speak-easy" where my friends were regular clients. The door—which was level with a busy street—was wide open, and only a swing door, backed by a screen, hid the interior of the bar from the view of passers-by without. Having obtained our drinks at the counter, we sat down at a round table in a corner near the entrance. Patrons came and went, no one taking any notice of them. Quite casually, I observed two well-dressed men, who, upon entering, appeared to hold a confidential conversation across the counter with the owner of the place. Both newcomers held folded papers under one arm, which made me think they must be Press-men. They had hardly left the "speak-easy" when the boss called one of my companions, and calmly told him that, whilst we had been sitting there, talking, he had been held up and forced to hand over all his cash.

Apparently, inside the folded-up papers, the two gangsters had held a revolver apiece, and, covering the proprietor of the place

and his barman, had demanded the money which, no wonder, had
been handed over to them without a murmur of protest.

Whilst taking part in the international horse show in the Madison
Square Gardens, I had a different kind of experience with "speak-
easies."

A policeman—who kept an eye on my horses, as well as on
peculiar-minded souvenir-hunters who cut hair off their tails—
noticed that I was looking ill. When I explained that it was malaria
I was suffering from, and that a glass of whisky and quinine was the
only remedy I fancied, he suggested that I go up to the "Millionaires'
Club," which had a bar in the building. Being in no mood to do
much talking, I told my sympathetic informant that I would go
back to the Army and Navy Club—where I was staying—and try
to sleep.

"If you want a shot of good whisky," the policeman said, "just
go out of the door over there, cross the road to No. so-and-so,
press the bell button, and when a kind of peep-hole opens, and
you're asked what you want, say Pat So-and-So, the cop sent you.
It will be O.K.; they'll give you what you want. And take it from
me, the stuff they sell over there is real Scotch."

I followed these instructions, and everything happened exactly
as the good Samaritan had told me, and therefore, before going to
bed, I was able to drink the medicine of my fancy.

As mentioned in an early chapter, if, when I was in my teens,
anyone had told me that I would become a schoolmaster, so seemingly absurd a prediction would have made me laugh. However,
as the reader knows, it happened. Many years later, when I jogged
into Washington, D.C., Dame Fortune had another surprise in
store for me.

During my long ride, I often wrote letters to friends in Buenos
Aires, never suspecting that some of my hurriedly scribbled messages would be printed in newspapers, let alone that they were
worded sufficiently well to appeal to a wide reading public.

Unless memory plays me false, it was when I arrived in Indian-
apolis that one of the editors of the *National Geographic Magazine*
put a long-distance telephone call through to me from Washington,

D.C., inviting me on arrival in the capital to visit the Society's headquarters. In due time, I was delighted to do so, and to make the acquaintance of a number of charming people whose friendship I have treasured ever since. Here, in particular, I must mention Dr. John Oliver La Gorce, the Vice-President of the Society, who, indirectly, is responsible for the fact that, instead of continuing to enjoy an open-air life—as was my intention—I have settled down to the sedentary occupation of writing.

Apparently, the editorial staff of the Society's magazine had followed the progress of my ride, stage by stage, and they had read some of my letters, which had been published in leading Argentine newspapers. When Dr. La Gorce urged me to write an article for his magazine, the very suggestion frightened me, but after some argument I gave in, with the result that, in 1929, a condensed story about my ride was printed in the said world-famous publication. Also, to my consternation, I was invited to deliver the opening lecture of the season. After some hesitation, I agreed to make the attempt, and so, a few days later, found myself on the platform in the City Auditorium in Washington, addressing five thousand members of the National Geographical Society, a severe ordeal out of which, somehow, I managed to come without adverse criticism.

A few days after my arrival in New York, I intended to sail back to Buenos Aires, taking my two horses with me. However, when the lecture in Washington was arranged, I cancelled my passage, and in so doing possibly saved my life, and certainly my animals'; for a few days after the *Vestris* sailed, she sank, with the loss of one hundred and ten lives. Later, through the courtesy of the owners of the Munson Line, accommodation was made available for Mancha and Gato on the liner *Pan-American*, and three weeks later, after a most enjoyable voyage, the three of us safely landed in the Argentine.

The reception given to us was such that I felt like fleeing out to the wilds, and subsequently there were so many banquets and *fiestas*—with their inevitable speeches—that it was with a deep sigh of relief that I boarded a train, on which, together with my horses, to return to the pampa. There, for some time, I enjoyed a delightful rest, until, one day there arrived a letter which put an end to this.

P

An old friend—the Headmaster of the Buenos Aires English
High School—wrote, informing me that he wished to visit his
aged parents in England, and that, being unable to find anyone
to take his place, he wondered if I would be good enough to help
him out of his difficulty. In a weak moment, I promised to do so, with
the result that for several months I felt like a caged bird. After the life
I had led in the wilds, sitting in a classroom, trying to teach pupils
what I had forgotten long ago (or never known at all), was purgatory,
but somehow I (and my pupils) managed to survive the ordeal.

At about that time, the article I had written for the *National
Geographic Magazine* appeared in print. To my surprise, it proved to
be a success, so when my friend returned from England and once
more took over the headmastership of the school, I made a bee-line
for a ranch in the pampa, and there set to work, writing what I
hoped some day would be turned into a book. Soon I discovered
that writing articles is one thing, but that the turning-out of a
lengthy manuscript is quite another proposition, the former being
comparable to a sprint, whereas the latter is an endurance test.
Sitting for hours on end, trying to put thoughts into words, shaping
and re-shaping obstinate sentences, was torture, but, nevertheless,
gradually pages began to pile up. After lunch, when everybody
retired to sleep a *siesta*, I usually went to a veranda to work.
During the summer months, often the heat was such that I fairly
dripped with perspiration, and I had difficulty in keeping my eyes
open, but early afternoon being the only time when I was left
undisturbed, wearily I carried on whilst *chicharras* (cicadas, large
winged and shrill-chirruping insects) serenaded me with their ear-
piercing notes, and near me lay my inseparable companions, the
dogs, sleeping so peacefully that I envied them.

Having refused to accept substantial cash prizes which were
offered to me for my ride across the Americas, and as my funds were
sinking ominously low, somehow I had to earn money, and so,
instead of returning to school life I became a journalist and
wrote a series of articles for *La Nación*, one of Argentina's leading
newspapers, as well as for several magazines and periodicals.

One evening whilst in Buenos Aires, I was waiting for a friend in a restaurant, known as "The London Grill." In order to pass away time, I ordered a dry Martini (in the Argentine called *San Martín seco*), and whilst I was sipping it, a sun-tanned gentleman— who also stood at the counter—turned to me and asked if I would like to shake dice with him for another cocktail. Delighted, I agreed, and thus it came about that I made the acquaintance of a sea captain whose cargo boat was due to sail back to her home port within two days, and that, when she steamed down the River Plate towards the South Atlantic, I was on board, with my bulky manuscript tucked away among the luggage in my cabin. On our way north we called at various small Brazilian ports, to which I had never been, and after having seen Devil's Island in the distance, merrily sailed through the Caribbean Sea, after forty days of Paradise to arrive at New Orleans, whence a long and hot voyage by train once more took me to Washington and New York.

The little anecdote about shaking dice with a complete stranger goes to prove that, if casual acquaintances are made with a little judgment, they can lead to most desirable new friendships, and, in this case, to a practically free cruise of several thousand miles.

Quite apart from this, to me, important consideration, I have always found that by far the most pleasant and interesting way to travel by sea is in cargo boats. In these there is no formality, no dressing for dinner, no boring deck games, no pushing on the clock by dancing or playing cards, and, above all, no necessity to make conversation with passengers who do not know how to mind their own business. In cargo boats I have always eaten food that was more than good enough for me, my cabins have been roomy and spotlessly clean, and everybody, from the skipper down to greasers in the engine-room, I have found to be excellent company. What with being up on the bridge—perhaps trying to learn something about navigation—yarning in the mess-room or wherever someone happens to be off duty and glad to converse, reading, writing, or giving a helping hand where a job is being done, days seem short.

Upon arrival in New York, I took my manuscript to a famous firm of publishers, but after having kept me waiting for a considerable time, it was returned to me, accompanied by a short note thanking me for having allowed the directors to read it. More or less the same thing happened when I submitted my story to the consideration of other publishers, all of whom informed me that my story lacked adventure and drama, and one rather more enterprising gentleman even suggested that I hire a "ghost-writer" to put "pep" into my "lifeless" stuff. He even went so far as to propose that a literary genius of his acquaintance should submit to me the first chapter of *my* book, as *he* intended to write it, for a consideration of $1,000, cash down in advance, plus 50 per cent. of the net profits on the sales later.

Although I had no intention of letting anyone turn an authentic story, told in simple language, into highly-spiced "tripe," out of sheer devilment and curiosity I asked the "ghost" to write his first chapter as a kind of sample. A few days later, whilst reading the stuff, I all but fainted. The story opened in a pampa brothel, and, in rapid succession, came a knife-fight, a terrific thunderstorm, during which a friend of mine was struck and killed by lightning, and I vomited whilst galloping away at full speed. The artistic and technical touch to the last incident was masterfully provided by that genius of the pen and imagination, who wrote that years of experience and practice had taught me "always to vomit with the wind, never against it!"

Out of pity and inverted admiration, I stood that amazing man of letters an excellent dinner, during which I politely told him that, even if my manuscript were to be rejected by every publisher, I did not want any alterations made to it, and that I would keep it as a souvenir of months wasted on a literary effort.

As it happened, a few days later I received a long letter from an old friend who is a well-known American author and traveller. He wrote to me from Florida (November 17th, 1931), and among other items stated:

". . . *The panic has almost everything stopped for the time being.*[1] *Down here they are using sweet potatoes for money. One beauty of this state is that the cost of living is almost nil.*

[1] The writer refers to the panic caused by the trade depression.

"*Re your MS., I wouldn't change a damn word of it to suit anybody.
That's an old dodge of most American publisher's readers. They want you
to change this, and rewrite that, and fix this and sort of change the other
around. I have met an even hundred of them personally, and wouldn't risk
rewriting one paragraph on anything they suggested. The truth of the matter
is that I doubt if you can sell that MS. here in the States, but I am 100 per
cent. sure you can sell it to an English house. . . . I would suggest Messrs.
X, but there are also a couple or three other good ones. Look up the
publisher of "XXX," and any of the several excellent travel books
American publishers would not undertake unless Roosevelt, Hoover,
Bill Hearst, or some other notable made one of those trips, exploring the
Panama Zone! . . .*

"*About ghost writers: There are many of them in the fiction game, and
quite a number who ghost for famous illiterates, such as XXX, XXX,
XXX, etc. I know several of these fiction ghosts personally, but they are
worthless on fact books and articles. Some of our best-known fiction
writers haven't written a word for years, and a gang of ghosts keep their
stuff going. . . . As I said before, let your MS. stand as it is, and to hell
with what anybody says. . . . It's real, anyhow. . . .*"

If ever anyone gave me good and sound advice, it was the friend
who wrote the above letter. Long before receiving it, I had noticed
that, at the time, a regular "Explorers' Racket" was thriving in
America. The recently published book, *Trader Horn*, had made
such a hit that many adventurers who looked for easy money became "explorers." Thus, to give just one or two examples, jungle
films were faked on Long Island, near New York, where tropical
vegetation was cleverly imitated in strongly-wired enclosures in
which caged wild beasts were turned loose, to be photographed
fighting and devouring each other, or to be shot by "daring"
hunters. Other heroes hurried to certain big game reservations,
where, from their cars, on good roads, they took motion pictures
of awe-inspiring lions and other wild beasts, later to be shown to
the gullible public for dollars. Yes, it was a grand game while it
lasted.

My funds were dwindling rapidly, so after having taken serious council with myself, I decided to gamble all for all. Accordingly, I packed up my manuscript, boarded a cargo boat, and soon was on my way to London, where I had not been for many years. Not unlike a cork being slowly carried round the outer rim of a gigantic vortex, the big circle of my wanderings was about to take me back to the city in which my Bohemian life had begun. However, many surprises and adventures were yet in store for me, and despite my many-sided "education," soon I was to realise that there remained a great deal for me to learn about this difficult, though sometimes entertaining world, in which the majority of human beings spend their existence, making frantic endeavours to amass as much as possible of what no less an authority than Job assures us "also is vanity."

Chapter XVII

Two schoolmasters, among them the Reverend Crimpus Jilt, M.A., are
mentioned in "dispatches."—Revisiting old haunts.—Visions of the
past, and an incongruous apparition.—Happy reunions with old Cockney
friends.—Visit to a colony of circus artists.—How I came to meet Cunninghame Graham, and what this meeting led to.

AND so, with the manuscript in my trunk, after a pleasant
crossing of the North Atlantic, I stepped ashore in England.
Prior to the 1914-18 War, passports were not necessary, but since
those happy-go-lucky days—before almost invisible pink silk
threads began their transformation which has turned them into a
mass of sticky red tape—things have changed almost everywhere
in the world. That good old England had joined the ranks of "self-
protectionist" nations was proved to me when, upon being handed
back my passport, I found that the Immigration Officer[1] had put
the following stamp on it: *Leave to land granted on condition that the
holder does not enter any employment, paid or unpaid, while in the
United Kingdom.* Nevertheless, Immigration and Customs officials
were quite civil, which is more than I can say about similar public
servants who boss travellers about in different parts of the world.

My first Sunday in London was memorable for three main
reasons. The first two surprises awaited me in the columns of a
certain newspaper, and the other when I went to re-visit old haunts,
which, though many years had passed since I had left them, were as
fresh in my mind as if I had been there only on the previous day;
fresh because places and persons can only be as distant from us as
our hearts allow them to be.

Reading through a certain Sunday newspaper, my eye fell on a
name I remembered very well indeed—Crimpus Jilt!

Well, well. So he was still alive, but . . . what? There it was, in

---

[1] Nowadays it is the fashion to call many officials "officers." Yes, we even
have "rodent officers," formerly called "rat-catchers."

print, and in English Courts of Justice they usually get their facts right, and newspapers have to be careful about libel. Crimpus Jilt, now the Rector of a certain parish, had been up to some of his old tricks; nothing very serious this time, but he had been found out. How true to type—just like our Crimpie of old!

On another page of the same newspaper, several names seemed to stick out above all others: "St. George's College, Buenos Aires," "Captain So-and-So." . . . Now what could this be?

As I read, my eyes and facial expression must have been a rare study to passengers in the Underground train in which I was travelling at the time. According to the report, a woman who had believed herself to be the captain's legal wife had put in a claim for life insurance, due to her on account of her husband's death, some-where in South America. However, upon investigating the case, the insurance company discovered that, after having been dismissed from St. George's College, Captain So-and-So had last been heard of in Brazil. And, even worse for the "bereaved" wife, the man, whom she had thought to be her legal husband, had married her bigamously.

Humming to myself the tune of "St. George for Merrie England," I folded up my newspaper, left the Underground, and walked towards a street corner where, outside a certain "pub," I hoped to find the old one-legged Irish newspaper vendor, Denny. Sure enough, there he was, looking very well, though considerably older.

"I bet you don't remember me," I said, halting before him.

After having had a good look at me, Denny quickly rose from the wooden box on which he had been sitting, and, stretching out a hand, exclaimed, "Well, I'll be damned if it ain't Mister Shiff, the schoolmaster!"

This recognition called for a drink, so soon after the two of us were inside the "pub," whilst newspapers were left outside to sell themselves. Denny—who had heard about my wanderings through South America—fairly bombarded me with questions, and when, at last, I managed to get him to reply to one of mine, and I heard that the Gristins had moved to another place, their old lodging-houses having been sold and condemned to demolition, this piece of news was a great disappointment to me, for I had hoped to find the *Maison Gristin* still flourishing, and, with a bit of luck, that one or two of the old "steadies" had survived. Having chatted for some time, I left Denny, promising to call upon him again in the evening, and presently I strolled towards my old "digs."

On my way, I passed the fire station, which had been considerably renovated and modernised. The big red doors being open, I stood for a while, looking at the motorised fire engines and other modern appliances. The horses and men who, many years before, so often had thrilled me were there no longer; but such is progress—and everything in this world is fleeting.

With vivid pictures of stalwart fire-fighters of old flashing through my mind, I slowly wandered on.

The row of houses I had come to visit was still there, but with the passing of years the bricks of the outer walls had turned considerably blacker. The iron railings which fenced in what, for lack of another name, we had called "front gardens," were more dilapidated than ever, and it was only due to a miracle of equilibrium that they remained standing. Broken or missing windows gave the low, square-built houses the appearance of fantastic skulls, with their black, hollow-eyed sockets staring into space.

Having seen enough from the outside, I pushed open the street door of one of the old "annexes" in which—it now seemed to have been in another life—I had often occupied the first-floor room which faced the street. Squeaking and groaning as if in agony, the unlocked front door opened, and upon stepping into the narrow entrance passage, I recognised a peculiar faint smell I had forgotten. Everything was silent as a tomb, and the floor was littered with rubbish. As I advanced, some of the loose boards on which I trod creaked, the noise reverberating through the empty house. Going upstairs, I noticed that the wooden banisters had been torn away, and that pieces of worn-out linoleum were still nailed to the steps. Here and there, wallpaper had peeled off, and hung down in wide strips, showing patches of damp, rotting brickwork. Upon peeping into my former abode, I saw that, like huge black cobwebs, torn and sooty imitation lace curtains were still hanging at the windows, and that, in a corner lay what, many years before, had been a mattress.

Continuing my sentimental explorations through this veritable graveyard of memories, I went to have a look at the Gristins' old kitchen. As I entered, a dirty stray cat made a hurried exit, spitting at me as it scrambled past my legs. Everything had gone: only refuse remained. Here and there loose boards had been wrenched off, gas fittings and even the grating of the old fireplace had been removed. I was about to leave this depressing scene of desolation when I remembered the back-yard, which formerly had been the storage site for Bill Gristin's amazing collection of salvaged building materials, as well as, occasionally, our recreation and sports ground.

The notion of revisiting that back-yard led to the third surprise I was to experience that day, as well as, subsequently, to bring me into contact with interesting Bohemians of a type which was entirely new to me.

Leaving the empty shell which formerly had been a cosy kitchen, upon rounding the corner of the old wash-house, which faced the back-yard, I suddenly stopped, wondering if I was suffering from hallucinations. Was this a ghost, or just a mad prank of my imagination, caused by the many memories which, for the past half-hour or so, had whirled through my brain like wind devils dancing across a desert?

As it was about midday and the sun was shining brightly, surely no sane ghost would possibly venture out into the middle of the filthy back-yard, let alone do so dressed as a cowboy, and perform tricks with a lasso, as was the man of flesh and blood whom I watched jumping in and out of fast-spinning loops.

Amazed, I slowly approached the performer, and seated myself on a corroded water tank, whence to watch him practise his tricks. After a while, upon becoming aware of my presence, the cowboy ceased his activities, and whilst wiping the perspiration off his forehead with the back of one hand, he greeted me with a cheery "Good morning. Lovely day, ain't it?"

The last words, apart from the manner in which the speaker pronounced them, left me in no doubt that he was not an American, as I had thought, but a Cockney; for where else in the world, but in

Britain, do people constantly tell one the obvious concerning prevailing weather conditions?

"Yes; it's a grand day; just right for a gallop over the prairies," I replied, my last remark being intended to pave the way for a question I fairly itched to ask the cowboy.

Having offered him a cigarette and a light, whilst he took a few puffs, I continued: "You seem to be an expert with the rope. Have you ever worked on a ranch, or taken part in a rodeo?"

With a ten-gallon hat placed at a saucy angle on his head, coiled-up rope held in one hand, and the thumb of the other stuck into the waist-strap of his chaps, and cigarette dangling from one corner of his mouth, the young man looked eminently prairie-worthy.

"No, sir, I've never been on a ranch. As a matter of fact, I've never been outside England. The little I know about American and Mexican cowboys I've learnt as a spectator when Tex Austin brought his first rodeo show over 'ere, an' other bits I got out of books and from performin' blokes on the stage. I'm only a 'Brixton cowboy.' "

"Brixton cowboy? . . . What do you mean?" I asked.

"Oh, just blokes like meself; rope-spinners, fancy-ropers, knife-throwers, trick-shooters an' others what earns their livin' workin' on the variety stage or in circuses, doin' their stuff, dressed up as cowboys. Nearly all of 'em 'as their 'eadquarters on the other side of the river, in Brixton where there's an 'ole blinkin' colony of 'em, as well as lots of other variety artists and circus people. As a matter of fact, by profession I'm a cabinet-maker, but when I was a kid, the cowboy bug bit me, so I practised ropin'. And now, every now and again, when I want a change, I take a job in some circus where, for a few weeks, I earn easy money an' 'ave a good time."

"How very interesting," I replied, "But don't let me interrupt you, so please go on practising. If you don't object, I'll sit here and watch you."

Opening a dilapidated suitcase, my new acquaintance proceeded to take out of it different kinds of lassos, and to explain to me their various uses. Besides the usual easy-spinning hemp ropes (generally used by "drug-store" cowboys and rodeo performers), he had real

Mexican *reatas*, made of the tough *ixtle* and *maguey* fibre; and when he began to show me what he could do with them, I all but rubbed my eyes.

I had seen several so-called "world champion" ropers perform in different rodeo shows, but what this modest Cockney now did with his ropes and lassos, not only spinning them in every imaginable way, but, for the lack of a horse, even trick-lassoing an old chimney-pot, equalled the best performances of this kind I had ever had the good fortune to witness.

The young man told me that, when practising, he usually wore the full cowboy costume—huge hat, chaps and high-heeled boots—not to please himself, but in order not to lose the knack of spinning the rope without getting it entangled in his garments, particularly so in the flaps of the chaps.

After an interesting conversation, before parting we arranged to meet another day, and to make an excursion to Brixton, there to visit some of his friends in the "profession."

Denny, the Irish newspaper-vendor, had given me the Gristins' new address, so upon leaving the Cockney cowboy I took a 'bus, hoping to find Bill and Ivy in their new home, situated in a semi-slummy part of London. Luck was with me, for when I knocked at the door of a house—which had seen better days at least a century before—Ivy came to see who was calling.

It was a grand reunion, and soon afterwards my old friends' three daughters—all married and with children—came rushing in to greet me. Bill was still in the building and decorating trade, but Ivy, since there was only room for two lodgers in the house, as a little sideline had started a second-hand business, which, she told me, was flourishing, and provided her with a lot of fun. Bill's curly hair had turned snow white, and, owing to his war wound, he walked with a limp. However, in every other respect he was still the same old lovable rascal, and his alert eyes had lost none of their merry twinkle, but Ivy—who formerly had been thin and wiry—had put on so much weight that her scarlet blouse threatened to burst whenever she laughed.

After a gargantuan tea-party, during which three generations of the Gristin tribe tucked away staggering quantities of bread and butter, jam, buns, cakes, shrimps, and a huge bowl filled with winkles, Chief Bill and his wife "dolled up" in order to accompany me, "doin' the rounds," and, on the way, to call on old Denny, the newspaper-vendor.

Everything worked out according to plan, but the one-legged Irishman so frequently and enthusiastically toasted my return that when we bundled him into a taxi to send him home, and someone prematurely slammed the door of the cab, his wooden leg was broken. A few days later, a collection having been made among a number of his friends, a beautiful artificial leg was presented to him, but somehow this gift changed its wearer's appearance to such an extent that he lost much of his former character. Fortunately, however, a little accident intervened.

Having received a particularly big commission for services rendered to a street bookmaker, Denny over-celebrated the windfall, with the result that, whilst in his home, sleeping in an armchair in front of the fire, he put his cork foot into it. Although we offered to replace the badly damaged artificial limb, he preferred to go back to an ordinary wooden stump, which, he said, had many advantages over the "posh" contraption, one of them being that, at times, the former was very convenient for poking the fire.

Whilst publishers dallied over my manuscript (probably pushing it on to hack readers to report on its merits, or otherwise, for the princely remuneration of £2), I wrote a great deal, and employed my spare time in looking up old friends or wandering about wonderful old London.

After my chance meeting with the rope-spinner in the back-yard of the condemned *Maison Gristin*, one evening, as arranged, my new friend took me out to Brixton to introduce me to some of his colleagues.

On our way, whilst, seated in a bus we were passing a park, my companion told me that when he was younger, whenever weather conditions permitted, every morning, winter and summer, he used to go there at five o'clock in the morning to practise with his ropes. He related how difficult it had been to learn in the dark, and how, in order to make things a little easier, he used a white rope, which, however, often became wet with dew, and therefore heavy and stiff. Early one morning when it was still dark, and he was about to enter the park, a suspicious policeman stopped the boy, who had great difficulty in explaining that the ropes were not intended to be used for anything but spinning practice. After such early morning outings, the youngster usually returned home to sleep for another hour, whereafter he had breakfast, and then went to his work.

Yarning thus, the two of us crossed the Thames as night was descending on London, and a fine drizzle began to fall, making the pavements shine and umbrellas look like huge animated mushrooms. Finally, we descended from the bus, and presently entered a dimly lit side street. Upon reaching a large wooden gate, my companion pushed it open, in so doing causing several dogs to bark furiously. My eyes having become accustomed to the darkness, I realised that before me lay a vacant lot, and as we slowly advanced I distinguished several shapes of what seemed to be caravan wagons, such as are used by travelling circuses. Obviously, some were inhabited, for quaint little windows threw out feeble beams of light, and as the two of us approached this hamlet on wheels, walking over planks which had been laid across particularly wet or muddy patches, I noticed that smoke curled out of several small tin chimneys above the arched roofs of some vehicles.

Satisfied that our intrusion was friendly, the dogs, having cautiously sniffed our legs, with a few final growls retreated to their respective shelters beneath their owners' dwellings.

Presently, the silhouette of a stooping figure appeared in the frame of the small door of a wagon.

"Good evening, Jack. It's only me," my guide shouted. "I've brought the gentleman I told you about on the postcard I sent you a couple of days ago."

"That's fine," came the reply.

Having been introduced to the inmate of the caravan, he invited me to enter.

"Look out for the steps. They're wet and slippery. And mind you don't knock your head against the top of the door," he warned.

As I stepped into the warm and cosy interior, my host, grandly waving a hand, as if to show me a vast panorama, exclaimed, "Here you have it all, sir: Prosperity Mansion; good cold water at a tap some fifty yards away, fresh air and mud thrown in free of charge." Then, turning to a young man who was reclining on a kind of bunk, reading a magazine, with assumed anger and indignation, he shouted, "Rise, lazy knave! Why didn't you answer the bell and announce the gentleman? Do you think I keep a flunkey only to have him lie here, looking at photographs of platinum blondes, whilst I, the lord and master of this castle, have to show in visitors, watch the kettle come to the boil, and sully my hands by opening a tin of condensed milk for our tea? Up, useless lout. Help the gentlemen take off their coats, and show them the way to my reception-room!"

The pleasant-looking, red-haired young fellow who was being spoken to put aside the magazine, took his feet off the shelf on which he had been resting them, and rose to greet me with a smile. Two wooden boxes having been brought in, to be used as extra chairs, we seated ourselves, and, having lit cigarettes, began to chat.

In the wagon were two bunks, and its interior was illuminated by an oil lamp suspended from the low ceiling. At one end of this romantic, though terribly untidy habitation were piled up saddles, lassos, whips, battered brass trumpets, sheep-skin chaps and similar things, and on its walls hung cowboy hats, head-gear such as used by clowns, wigs, bright scarves, and two quiver-like containers filled with ornate knives, evidently used for throwing. All round a cracked mirror were stuck photographs of girls, cowboys, clowns acrobats and jugglers, and under it, on a little shelf, were none-too-clean hair brushes, combs with some of their teeth missing, grease-paints, and other theatrical make-up materials.

Attracted by an elaborate Texan saddle, I asked for permission to examine it closely.

"By all means," said my host, going to pull it out from under the pile of things that were stacked up on it. "A fine stock saddle, as you see," he remarked, placing the object of my curiosity on a bunk. "Off and on, in the course of years, it has been owned by

almost every Brixton cowboy. You know, when a chap is broke,
he either sells it to Parkers', the saddlers and harness-makers in
Upper St. Martin's Lane, or another Brixton cowboy buys it off
him. This saddle has changed hands dozens of times, and if all its
previous owners' names were punched into the leather, you'd have
pretty well the complete register of us Brixton cowboys, past and
present."

And so, over cups of tea, we joked and chatted, and during the
course of conversation I was told that, besides doing cowboy stuff,
my two new acquaintances also acted as clowns, knife-throwers and
tumblers, and that, if things really came to a pinch, they could also
do a trick shooting act. When, after about an hour, I realised that
there was nothing to eat in the wagon, and my companions
could do with a square meal, I invited them to accompany me
to some nearby restaurant they might know, there to have
dinner with me.

Delighted with my proposal, they immediately got busy putting
on coats and hats; the oil light was extinguished, and after short
calls at two other caravans, we wended our way towards a fairly
well-lit street, where we entered a kind of superior coffee-stall.
My guides explained to me that this was their club, and that, even
if they had no money, they often went there for warmth, and to
meet fellow artists.

The aromatic smell of coffee and the appetising odour of sausages,
onions and eggs being fried greeted my nostrils, and whilst shaking
my wet raincoat, I had a quick look at my immediate surroundings
and the people congregated there.

Standing at a small counter, or sitting on two long benches
placed alongside a narrow table, were a number of men: taxi-drivers,
labourers, carters, as well as three or four nondescripts, all sipping
tea or eating. The atmosphere was thick with tobacco smoke, and
when one of the two men behind the counter saw my companions,
he greeted them with a merry, "Good evenin', 'Ow are the cowboys
to-night?"

"As usual, hungry as wolves, so make it four lots of sausage,
mash and onions, and a cup of tea apiece." Then, turning to me, the

speaker whispered, "I hope you don't mind my cheek, ordering what you're going to pay for. I only did it to save time, and to avoid the frills of formality."

Whilst we were eating, several other variety artists strolled into their "Club," and when I asked them to join us at one end of the long narrow table, they gladly accepted my invitation. Sausages, bacon, eggs, cold veal-and-ham pies, buns, slices of bread and butter, and cakes were tucked away as fast as the two men behind the counter could serve them, and when appetites were satisfied, we sat talking over cups of tea or coffee. It was both amusing and interesting to hear everybody and everything in the profession being discussed: lion- and tiger-trainers, trick-cyclists, trapeze artists, tumblers, rope-spinners, high-school riders, acrobats, jugglers, clowns, trainers of liberty horses, dogs, pigeons, seals and other performing animals, conjurors, trick-riders, knife-throwers, whip-crackers, in short, all who formed this miscellany of artistes.

I was sorry when the time came to return home, but before departing I promised my new friends that this would not be my last visit. When I asked for the bill, to my astonishment it amounted to no more than a dinner for one person would have cost in a good West End restaurant.

Longing for a little fresh air and exercise, together with the rope-spinner whom I had met in the Gristins' old back-yard, I started to walk towards my distant "digs." As we passed over Westminster Bridge, rows of lights in the jagged outline of the Houses of Parliament suggested that the House was in session, and, owing to the prevailing drizzle and haze, the illuminated dials of Big Ben resembled moons. When, in Parliament Square, I hailed a taxi to drive my companion to his modest home, the familiar bell boomed midnight.

.   .   .   .   .

Several weeks passed, and at long last a firm of publishers, to the consideration of which I had submitted my manuscript, returned it to me, together with a short note informing me that the director regretted being unable to publish my story—of which, most likely,

Q

friendships sprang up in my path, and the cheerful sun of companionship broke through the dismal clouds of memories of the irretrievable past.

Whilst in London, I met many artists, actors and writers, as well as talkative dilletantes whose chief ambition in life seems to be to pose as expert connoisseurs. At cocktail parties, and after dinners given by prosperous lion-hunters, such gabblers are in their element, constantly interspersing their weighty statements with fashionable words, such as "frightfully," "dreadfully," "definitely" and "actually"—the last, for better effect, being pronounced "ayctually." In a way, such dilletantes and "intellectuals" amused me immensely, and often, whilst listening to their harangues on painters, musicians, poets, or on social reform, I could not help thinking that in one respect the tongues of such babblers are like racehorses, because the less weight they carry, the faster they move.

Fortunately, all parties were not of this type, and certainly not those given by my friend Mrs. Dummett, who lived in No. 17 Walton Place, near Harrods Stores. For many years her drawing-room had been the meeting place of famous men of letters, and artists of all nationalities. There, on different occasions, I met Sir Max Beerbohm, H. G. Wells, Dr. Axel Munthe, Compton Mackenzie, Dr. Cronin, Ramón Perez de Ayala, General Rafael de Nogales, Segovia, the world-famous guitarist, Sir John Lavery, Lady Benson, Maude Allan and a host of others, as well as that last of the highlights of the Edwardian period, that often startingly dressed and delightful veteran, Lady Alexander. But no matter who happened to be in Mrs. Dummett's *salon*, whenever Cunninghame Graham was present he overshadowed the company, not only with his hidalgo appearance and manners, but also with his inimitable wit and grand sense of humour.

This also happened when G. B. Shaw and his wife entertained the two of us in their flat in Whitehall Court. On that occasion, with no gallery to which to play, I found Mr. Shaw to be an extremely modest and likeable man. As he knows but little about horses and open-air life, and I rather less about the theatre, the two of us got on splendidly, whilst, from lunchtime until after tea, Mrs. Shaw he had not read one single word. Some time later, after my pile of, by now, tattered paper had been in the hands of another firm—and with the final result to which I was beginning to get accustomed—I reluctantly came to the conclusion that, as far as my literary effort was concerned, I had wasted my time and money, and that, in having attempted to dabble in literature, I had only got what I asked for. Tired of kicking my heels in London, and apprehensive at seeing my funds dwindle away, I decided that it was high time to get a move on. But whither? Though I longed to re-visit certain parts of Europe, particularly Switzerland—where I had not been since my youth—the idea of going there as a kind of tourist was so distasteful to me that I decided on returning to South America, where, if I wanted a job on a ranch, it would be mine for the asking.

As mentioned at the beginning of this chapter, when I arrived at Southampton from the U.S.A., I was granted leave to land only on condition that I did not enter any employment, paid or unpaid, while in the United Kingdom; so even jobs such as shining shoes, taking blind lap-dogs for walks, or working as a groom were officially taboo, as far as I was concerned. Yes, the First World War had made things difficult for drifters such as I had become. However, having fought my way out of many tight corners, single-handed, and sometimes when I was far away from human help, I was far from down-hearted; in fact, bearing in mind that wisdom's best school is adversity, I almost enjoyed what seemed to be a serious predicament.

Whilst making preparations for my departure, I called at the Argentine Embassy, in order to take leave of my friend, the late Dr. Manuel Malbran, who at the time was Ambassador to the Court of St. James. After a conversation with him, I was about to leave the Embassy when a Scotsman—Mr. Colin Paterson, who, true to type, was in charge of the finance department—came to introduce himself to me. Upon hearing that I was about to book a passage for Buenos Aires, he told me that it would be a great pity if I left London without having met a famous countryman of his, Mr. R. B. Cunninghame Graham. Of course, I had read a number of this famous author's books, and therefore, in a sense, he was no stranger to me. Having explained to Mr. Paterson that I preferred not to bother Cunninghame Graham, I departed.

Great was my surprise and joy when, that very evening, I received a telegram from the latter, who invited me to have lunch with him at Martinez's Spanish Restaurant in Swallow Street, near Piccadilly Circus.

My meeting with him and his friend, Mrs. Dummett (*née* Miéville), the exquisite horsewoman, having been described in another book of mine, all I will say here is that from the moment the three of us met, things happened with lightning speed. When asked if I had written anything about my ride through the Americas, I told my host all about my "boomerang" manuscript, and offered to send it to him as a gift. Upon returning to my lodgings, I dispatched my bundle of agony by special messenger, and on the following morning received another invitation to have lunch with Mr. Cunninghame Graham. When I returned to Martinez's restaurant, there he was, and also Mrs. Dummett, and, on a vacant chair beside the table at which they sat, reposed my blessed manuscript, the very sight of which I hated by that time.

"I have spent the entire night reading this," my host said after having greeted me, and then continued: "This must, and will be published. In fact, I have already made an appointment for us to meet my publishers after lunch."

I will not attempt to repeat the flattering things my new friend said regarding my story, nor what, a week later, the publisher told me about it. Suffice to say that the stuff was accepted, and that Cunninghame Graham wrote a beautiful Preface to it. When I informed him that I was about to leave for the Argentine, he urged me not to do so, but, if possible, to postpone my departure until after the publication of my book. Despite my arguments in favour of carrying out my intention, Cunninghame Graham— or "Don Roberto," as I called him by that time—won the verbal tussle, and so I cancelled the passage which had already been booked.

My meeting with this Scottish *hidalgo* was to lead to many unexpected happenings. Formerly, in turn, he had been a gaucho, rider of wild horses, explorer, social reformer, for six years a trouble-some but respected Member of the British Parliament, author of many books, and modern Don Quixote—whom he strikingly resembled. From the time we sat together in that restaurant in Swallow Street, he and I got on like the proverbial house on fire, and hardly a day passed without our meeting, telephoning, or corresponding with each other. Once, when I asked him why he wasted his time on me, he told me that since his friend, W. H. Hudson, had died, until he met me, there had been no one with whom he could talk about gauchos and the pampa, which were Don Roberto's spiritual home.

Cunninghame Graham had followed me ever since—seven years before our first meeting—I had set out on my long ride from Buenos Aires. Taking his information from newspaper cuttings friends had sent to him from different parts of the world, he had written a story about me. The manuscript was completed before its author met me, and was included in a book of short stories entitled *Writ in Sand*. Little did I dream at the time that, some years later, I would be writing my new friend's biography, and that, after his death, his closest friends and members of his family would carry on a similar friendship with me.

When, after many pros and cons—mostly cons on my part, though I refrained from divulging my financial standing—I gave in to Don Roberto, and decided to remain in London, the die was cast; an entirely new life was about to begin for me. Without my being aware of it, the current into which I had drifted, carried me towards a new sphere of activity.

Chapter XVIII

A strange coincidence connected with the house in which W. H. Hudson died.—After many years, again I call on "Professor" Andrew Newton.—Cocktail and other parties.—Circuses, theatres and life.—"Brixton cowboys" and variety artists.

THE oft-rejected and widely travelled manuscript having been accepted by a publisher, whilst it was being turned into book form, my time was fully occupied, writing and doing research work in the British Museum.

Owing to the trade depression, masses of workers were unemployed, and so it happened that the husband of one of the Gristins' daughters—a carpenter by trade—was also out of work, and, consequently, on the dole. Having two young children, the weekly relief they drew did not go far, so when it was suggested that I should take lodgings with the needy family, I made my temporary home with this off-shoot of the Gristin tribe. Their three-roomed flat was on the top floor of an old, semi-dilapidated, three-storied house, situated in the dismal neighbourhood of Westbourne Park, and in the middle of a long row of identically constructed ones. Having me as a lodger made a great difference to the couple's budget, and even more so because I had most of my meals with the family, often providing the food for the five of us. My little bedroom was sufficiently comfortable to satisfy my simple wants, and whenever I wished to read or write, a sitting-room was put at my sole disposal.

I saw a great deal of Cunninghame Graham, who took a great interest in my activities. One day, although I warned him that my lodgings were extremely modest, and that three long flights of steep stairs had to be negotiated before reaching my den, he insisted on visiting me.

Despite his advanced age, he fairly ran up the difficult stairs, and, upon recovering his breath, turned to me. Slowly shaking his white mane, in a serious and mystified tone of voice he said, "Strange . . . very strange."

"What is puzzling you?" I enquired, wondering what might be the cause of all this mystery.

Instead of replying, my visitor went to the window, where he stood for some time, gazing down the road, every now and again shaking his head and muttering something to himself. Then, suddenly, he turned round, at the same time passing a hand through his flowing hair, as if to brush away his thoughts.

"Strange things happen in life," he said in Spanish. "When we get outside, I shall show you something that will interest you."

After this we talked for some time, and, on his insistence, I called in my young landlord and his wife, as well as the two children, all of whom I duly introduced to my friend. Having drunk a cup of tea and eaten something, we were ready to depart. His car was waiting in the street, and when the chauffeur opened the door for us to take our seats, Cunninghame Graham told him that we would walk a short distance, to a place where he wanted to show me something.

"Please follow us. It's not far," he added. With this, slipping an arm through one of mine, he slowly led me up a nearby side street. Halting before a most unattractive house, whilst pointing at it with his walking stick, he said, "No. 40, as you see. . . . Yes, No. 40, St. Luke's Road; the house in which W. H. Hudson lived during his last years, and in which he died, in 1922."

"How interesting," I remarked, not knowing what else to say.

"Strange, very strange, I call it," my companion said, again shaking his head, as he had done whilst standing at the window in my room. "Years ago," he continued, "despite Hudson's warnings that he lived in a desert of macadam, mud and fog, I came here to visit him several times; and to-day, although you gave me a similar warning, I also called on you. It was only upon arriving at the door of your house that I realised that you are living within a stone's-throw of the place where Hudson died. In the Argentine, he and you lived in the same region, and often must have trodden the same ground; and then, after many wanderings, both he and you came to

London, and, of all things, to this part of the city. Strange, is it not?"

Yes, indeed it was strange, for not only had Hudson's and my trails crossed in South America, but also in the New Forest, where, when I taught in Park Hill School, occasionally I had seen the tall, bearded and bird-like naturalist wandering through the woods.

For some time Cunninghame Graham and I stood in St. Luke's Road, talking about Hudson, and before seating ourselves in the car, my companion tiptoed up the steps leading to the entrance of No. 40, and, having gently touched the door-knob, rejoined me.

One day, whilst out for a walk, I decided to go and see if Newton's Boxing Academy was still in existence. Great was my joy when, upon reaching No. 241 Marylebone Road, I read the old familiar sign, "Newton's School of Boxing," painted in large black letters on the wall. I rang the bell, and soon after, to my joy, the "Professor" himself appeared, wearing what seemed to be the same old white flannel trousers, rubber-soled shoes and a sweater. He bore his advancing years remarkably well, though I noticed that round his eyes tell-tale wrinkles had appeared, but in every other respect he was still the same old "Professor."

Without giving my name, I asked him if he was still giving boxing lessons, and could re-condition men who are well past the prime of life. To both my questions he answered in the affirmative, and after having looked me up and down with a clinical eye, went on to say that he guaranteed to make a new man of me within a couple of months. Leading the way, he took me to the gymnasium, which looked exactly as it had twenty years before; the punch-balls were in the same places, and everything had an eminently business-like look about it.

Going to a punch-ball, after a few preliminary taps at it, I proceeded to do some fancy punching. This so surprised the "Professor" that, after having called "Time!" and I ceased my activities, he asked me who I was. When I explained that, many years before, I had taken a few lessons from him, and that he had seen me boxing in various London rings, he suddenly remembered. Then, for some time, the

two of us yarned about the old days, and we discussed different
boxers, most of whom, to-day, are either dead or practically forgotten. When I asked my old friend how his boy, Andy, was
getting on, he sadly shook his head. I told him that, a long time ago,
I had heard that he had become a professional boxer, and that during
a fight with Len Harvey, he had lost the sight of his left eye.

"Yes, unfortunately, what you have been told is true," he replied,
and after a short pause, in a sad tone of voice, continued: "But even
worse has happened to my son since then. Only recently the other
eye had to be taken out, so now Andy is totally blind. Come along
and say a few words to him; he'll be very pleased." Having said
this, the old "Professor" led the way into a room in which, sitting in
an armchair, was the unfortunate young man whom I had not seen
since he was a boy.

Though he said that my voice seemed familiar to him, he did not
remember me, so after a short conversation with him I made ready
to depart. At the door I told the "Professor" that, time permitting,
twice per week I would place myself into his expert hands for
"re-conditioning"; but unfortunately, owing to various circumstances, I was prevented from carrying out my intention.

To-day the National Sporting Club, Wonderland Boxing Arena,
Blackfriars Ring and the West London Stadium are but memories
with some of us, and probably only a few members of the newer
generation have heard their fathers and grandfathers talk about
those romantic old places, all of which had an atmosphere not to
be found in any of the modern boxing arenas.

Among the many old haunts I revisited were my two preparatory
schools, both of which had ceased to exist. Park Hill, near Lyndhurst, has been transformed into a country residence, and the
"Priory" (Malvern) to-day is the theatre in which the annual
dramatic festival is held. Mr. Charles E. Ridout, after having gone
back to Eton College, died, but I had the great pleasure of again
meeting my other Headmaster, Mr. C. H. Giles.

Wherever I went, things had changed; some of my old friends
had vanished in the whirlpool of life, and others had passed on.
Gradually, like early spring flowers taking the place of snow, new

and Cunninghame Graham—both great horse-lovers—indulged in their favourite conversation.

At irregular intervals a group of writers, among them the veteran supernaturalist, Arthur Machen, Thomas Burke of *Limehouse Nights*, Charles Duff, the political writer (formerly of the Foreign Office) and linguist, Philip Lindsay, the Tudors' historian, Frederick Carter, and John Gawsworth, the lyric poet, and artists such as Augustus John and Nina Hamnett, foregathered in the wooden cubicles of Henekeys' Wine Bar in Holborn where, formerly, the poets Lionel Johnson and Ernest Dowson had sat long and argued.

Jokingly, we called ourselves the "Holborn Republic," for the iron-work grills on the façades of our "confession boxes" bore the initials "H.R."—which, of course, Lindsay liked to consider commemorated Henricus (Oxtavus) Rex!

We were a very mixed lot: Catholics, Protestants, Buddhists, Agnostics, Conservatives, Socialists and even red-hot Communists; and we exchanged views on every imaginable subject. Sometimes, for a change, delegates of the "Holborn Republic" quite unofficially assembled in the "Byron Club," situated in Greek Street in Soho. This ramshackle but nevertheless homely "joint" was run by a tough-looking but most delightful and kind-hearted Spaniard, known to all "Members" of his "Club" as Pedro. There I met many interesting people, among them the poet, Roy Campbell, who, in opposition to his friend, Pedro, and several Bryonites, always staunchly upheld the Franco *régime*. Strange to relate, at Pedro's assembled several Englishmen who had fought in the Spanish Civil War, on different sides, and two of them, including Campbell, were wounded in that sanguinary tragedy. However, within the precincts of the Bryon Club, old animosities, though far from forgotten, were never brought up with any personal ill-feeling towards "honourable" "Members."

After having been "blitzed out" of his premises in Greek Street, Pedro established himself in nearby Frith Street, where he carried on his business until the authorities made him close down for serving drinks out of hours, which he did quite openly, without even bothering to close the windows which faced the street.

When Pedro had to appear in the Police Court, several of the "Members" went to testify in his favour, and when one of the volunteer witnesses finished by reciting an imposing list of famous artists and writers who made the "Byron Club" their home from home, the magistrate humorously remarked, "It sounds like a kind of super-Athenæum Club to me." However, despite the witnesses' reports in favour of Pedro, he had to pay a heavy fine; and that, alas! was the end of the "Byron Club."

Having made contact with the Brixton cowboys and circus artists, every now and again I visited some of my new friends who belong to that extraordinary fraternity.

Being childish, and therefore, perhaps, a realist, I thoroughly enjoy sporting events and circuses in which, save rare exceptions, performers provide spectators with the genuine and unadulterated thing. By this I mean, for instance, that if an acrobat is billed to turn a double twist-somersault, or a trick-rider to do the same off a cantering horse, he either does it or ignominiously falls on to the sawdust; or, if a sprinter runs the hundred yards in nine seconds, his performance speaks for itself. There is something pathetic about any man who takes himself too seriously, especially if he happens to be an actor or an interpreter of music who thinks himself to be greater than the dramatist or composer whose genius provides the artist with his champagne and caviare, or stale bread and dripping, as the case may be. Far be it from me to belittle the talent and work without which no such artist can hope to reach the top of the long and difficult ladder. However, in modern times, clever publicity campaigns have brought many second-rate performers to the pinnacle of popular success.

In the case of circus artists, only very few of them can exploit other people's work. Always faced with the stern reality of advancing age, unless they make their hay whilst the sun of youth and perfect health shines, their prospects for the future are very bleak.

Life being a stage or circus, and we the temporary actors, human freaks and clowns, the comedies, farces, dramas and fancy stunts enacted by all of us are so varied that I rarely go to the inconvenience and expense of looking in a theatre for what daily life offers so abundantly, provided one takes the trouble to keep one's eyes and ears open.

My newly made friendships among the kaleidoscopic Brixton fraternity gave me an insight into many strange lives, and brought me in contact with interesting people, about whose activities the general public knows nothing. Curiously, in certain respects, Cunninghame Graham and I had similar tastes, and I fully shared most of his views. Horses being a passion with both of us, whenever a circus was anywhere near, or a horse show was being held, we never failed to go to them. For many years he had known almost every outstanding *haute école* rider in Europe, and among his innumerable friends were many circus performers, but it was from me that he heard about Brixton cowboys for the first time; a piece of "inside information" which greatly amused him, especially so because formerly he had been under the impression that all cowboys he had seen on the London stage, or in circuses, were either Mexicans or Americans.

One day, after having seen the performance of a troupe of particularly good Arab tumblers, Cunninghame Graham turned to me, and remarked that these wild-looking men and girls must be Arabs from the Sus. When I replied that I knew them very well, and that they came from Brixton, my companion laughed so heartily that everybody in the circus looked in our direction, wondering what the joke was about.

When I met the late Mr. Bertram Mills, the famous English circus proprietor, he surprised me by saying that he had a whole album filled with newspaper cuttings about my ride through the Americas. As in the case of Cunninghame Graham, friends had sent them to him from different countries, through which I had passed, and thus, by the time I reached my goal, his collection had become quite bulky. Evidently Mr. Mills took an interest in everything connected with horses.

In the Hackford Road, Brixton, for close on a century (until, in 1944, a German flying bomb wrecked the place) there was a remarkable establishment, originally run by two veterinary surgeons named Price and King. Besides three huge rehearsal rooms, there was stabling accommodation for a hundred horses, and often lions, tigers, and even elephants were housed in this mixture of a Noah's Ark and Babylon, which was known to circus and variety artists all over the globe. There, members of the fraternity spoke in many different tongues, and every imaginable kind of act was rehearsed.

Interested in the lives and activities of these delightful Bohemians, on several occasions I accompanied some of my friends among them when they went to their agents to see if any engagements were open to them. One such agency has its offices in an old house situated at the Trafalgar Square end of the Charing Cross Road, behind the National Gallery.

The first time I went there, it was in the company of a well-known Brixton cowboy, whose humorous anecdotes and reminiscences amused me immensely. Upon approaching the agency I noticed that, outside in the street, men and women stood in little groups, talking among themselves as if communicating important secrets. My companion explained to me that every branch of the profession has its unofficial pitch on the pavement outside that agency. Thus, at a corner of a narrow alley, all the cowboys met, and a group assembled a few yards from them consisted chiefly of acrobats and tumblers, whereas jugglers, trainers of performing animals, and so on, had their meeting places further along.

My companion introduced me to several cowboys who were strangers to me, and when they discovered that I was not in the profession, but that I had merely come to pass away time, they all but heaved sighs of relief; for competition was keen, times not too good, and therefore professional engagements few and far between. No one smoked, but when I produced a packet of cigarettes, immediately all eyes were glued on it, and when I asked if anyone wanted a smoke, eager fingers took what I offered.

One by one, after having fixed their ties, straightened their jackets and adjusted their hats, so as to give an air of the prairies to their wearers, the cowboys went indoors to interview the agent. When they reappeared at the door, even I could guess if they had had any luck, for the two or three who had signed contracts came out swaggering and smiling, as if the whole world belonged to them.

All the Brixton cowboys affected the mannerisms and speech of Hollywood Texans, that being a custom among them, as well as part of their trade.

"Struck oil, Buddy?" one of the envious onlookers asked when a beaming swaggerer rejoined the group.

"Yep. An' let me tell the lot of you guys that from now on I'm in the big-money class. No more chicken-feed for me, Oh, no, boys! When they offered me only a lousy twenty quid a week, I told 'em to make it forty, or go to hell. They daren't argue with me, so now I'm fixed up for the next three months. But I must be off, boys. *Adios*, I'll be seein' you."

As the boasting would-be Crœsus strutted away, one of my companions turned to me, and, talking through the corner of his mouth, softly growled, "Liar! I bet he's workin' for ten, or even less."

Where we stood, in the course of years, the various groups of artists have worn some of the large square pavement stones visibly hollow, for only a very few members of the profession are in a position to act like *prima donnas*, and make impresarios and agents run after them; it was the other way about with most of my new friends.

There was something pathetic about these groups of work-seekers. Prospects and everybody in the profession having been discussed, our little gathering broke up, to assemble again on the following day. Having nothing better to do, a few of the Brixton cowboys and I strolled up St. Martin's Lane to Parkers, the saddlers and harness-makers, there to inspect and discuss second-hand saddles of every type and description. Opposite this establishment was another great attraction, Aldridge's horse market, and a little further along, towards New Oxford Street, were a number of pet shops where an amazing variety of animals, caged birds, exotic fish and even reptiles were exhibited for sale.

Among my companions were several excellent riders, and two or three could stage a good sharp-shooting act. One of the trick-shooters

—who was a man of about fifty—told me that, a few months before I met him, he was so hard up that he joined a gang of bootleggers who smuggled whisky into the U.S.A. During one cruise from Newfoundland, the ship in which he "worked" (the *I'm Alone* by name) was intercepted by American coastguards—outside the three-mile limit, I believe. As some readers may remember, the confiscation of this ship, and the internment of its crew, caused quite a stir in diplomatic and Press circles. Despite all this international fuss, my acquaintance—the Brixtonian trick-shooter and temporary rum-runner—was clamped into an American jail, where he spent three months as one of Uncle Sam's unhonoured guests.

One day, after having been out of work for a considerable time, two of the cowboys decided to go "on the streets." One of the pair —whose chief interest in life was the study of history and economics —formerly had worked in rodeos and variety shows in the U.S.A., but in London he fell on such hard times that, to use his own expression, he was glad to take a job as "pearl-diver." When I asked him what he meant by this, he informed me that a "pearl-diver" was one who washed dishes and plates in hotels.

Beginning their grand tour in London, the two companions gradually worked their way up to the Midlands, cracking whips, playing a concertina, and spinning ropes. When, after an absence of some two or three months, they returned to their starting-point, and I asked them how they had fared, the amusing yarns they told me were many. Laughing like two merry schoolboys, they told me that semi-slummy districts were the best, people there being more generous than they are in "nobby" districts, in which policemen do not see eye to eye with street performers.

Having selected a suitable pitch, in order to attract attention, one of the two "cowboys" would begin the show by cracking an Australian stock-whip, in so doing invariably making dogs bark furiously, and causing people to rush to their windows, or out into the street, wondering if a gun battle was taking place. Having thus collected a crowd, the whip-cracker finished his turn, with the dangerous-looking lash extinguishing a cigarette, held out between the lips of his companion. After this trick, the whip-cracker would take the concertina, and whilst the other spun his rope, jumping in and out of loops, the musician played what might be called the "Brixton Cowboys' Anthem," this being Sousa's "Star-spangled Banner."

As it happened, both performers had a passion for roast duck and green peas. Therefore, sufficient money having been collected, they packed up their whips, concertina, ropes, and ten-gallen hats, and went in search of a small restaurant where their favourite dish was on the menu. After a most enjoyable tour, sun-tanned and fattened with duck and peas, they returned to London, hoping that the approaching Christmas season had good circus or pantomime jobs in store for them.

The father and unofficial "Big Chief" of the Brixton cowboys is a remarkable Mexican, with whom I made friends as soon as I met him.

Born in Mexico City, in the early days of his manhood Carlos Mier became a famous rider of wild horses and bullfighter of no mean ability. Soon his fame as a rider and roper spread across the border into the U.S.A., where, in those days, fancy roping was a practically unknown art. When the great publicist and showman, Bill Cody (better known as Buffalo Bill) toured America with his "Wild West" show, he ran Carlos to earth, and engaged him as a member of his troupe. The novelty of trick roping, as presented by the tall, elegant and falcon-faced Mexican, was a great success, but owing to friction which set in between Mexico and the U.S.A., soon, whenever he appeared wearing his magnificent *charro* costume, many of the spectators—who all but clamoured for war to be declared against the southern republic—gave him such unfriendly receptions that, when the Miller brothers (of the famous 101 Ranch) decided to try their luck with a "Wild West" show in England, Buffalo Bill thought it wiser to transfer Carlos and another great Mexican *charro* (Pablo Ramos by name) to the new venture. Thus the two arrived in England where they were a great success, until, with the outbreak of the First World War, the Miller "outfit" returned to America.

Being typical, happy-go-lucky Mexicans, Carlos and Pablo

remained in London, where they had a grand time, enjoying the fruits of their labours. This continued until, completely broke, they applied to the Mexican Consul for repatriation. Having been given the money for their fare and incidental expenses during the voyage, the two light-hearted *charros* were 'so pleased with life that, instead of booking their passages, they proceeded to spend the money. It was only when the last shilling of it had gone that they put on their thinking-caps, and began to have a look round for something to do.

The British Army authorities were not slow in making use of the two excellent riders and tamers of horses, so when troublesome beasts began to arrive, chiefly from the Argentine and Uruguay, any which buck-jumped too hard for the rough riders in different remount depots, were sent to Market Harborough, in Leicestershire, where Carlos and Pablo broke them in. As far as the two Mexicans were concerned, the 1914–18 War was the best they had ever heard of, for what with riding such rejects, lassoing, and good pay, they were in the seventh heaven.

Shortly after the armistice, Pablo returned to Mexico, but Carlos decided to stay in England, and to run a "Wild West" show of his own.

Among the few young men whom he trained to assist him in the art of breaking in buck-jumpers, two or three had become sufficiently good riders to be able to sit on "goat-jumpers"—that is to say, horses which have a fairly easy (though showy) wave-like way of bucking. By this time, a number of Carlos' pupils had acquired the knack of spinning soft and pliable hemp ropes, and a few of the more enterprising among them had even got as far as to perform in shows as "cowboys." Brixton being a kind of magnetic pole for all circus and variety artists, inevitably these new knights of the rope and saddle were attracted thither, and thus it came about that the "federation" of Brixton cowboys came into being, and that, in a sense, the Mexican *charro*, Carlos Mier, was its founder.

Having recruited a few such performers, and acquired suitable horses and costumes, Carlos and his *troupe* of men from wild and

R

woolly Brixton toured the provinces and parts of Ireland, sometimes as an independent rodeo show, and occasionally working in circuses. Naturally, the experienced Mexican was the star turn, especially so because by that time he had trained an exceptionally good horse to perform tricks, some of which were so difficult and intricate that no artist is ever likely to equal them. However, most of Carlos' feats were wasted on the spectators, who, knowing nothing about such things, did not realise that, for instance, when he sat on his horse, spinning a huge loop with his Mexican maguey *reata* (a thin lasso made of the tough fibre of a sub-tropical plant), and made the animal skip through the fast-revolving rope, this was an amazing feat of skill and synchronisation of movement between rider and horse.

On the whole, the "Rodeo" was not a success, but touring about provided the performers with many adventures and much fun, especially when, on one occasion, whilst working in a small circus in Ireland, the impresario had a bright idea.

Upon realising that Irish people are fond of music, he made Carlos and the Brixton cowboys learn a sentimental prairie song, of which they were to give a rendering at the end of their act. When, after much rehearsing, the impresario considered that the heavenly choir had reached the pitch of perfection, he instructed the songsters to entertain the public whilst the iron cage and nets for the lion act were being put up in the ring.

In a sense, the vocal novelty was a howling success, for when the tough *hombres* from the wilds of Brixton began their recital, the crowd, under the impression that what they saw and heard was a comic act, roared with laughter. However, upon realising that the noises they heard were supposed to be a song sung in harmony, the agonised listeners began to throw all manner of missiles in the direction of the vocalists, who, as they beat a hasty retreat, were thankful that, in the meantime, the protecting iron grids and net had been set up, prior to the lions being coaxed into the arena for the final act.

For several years after this "Rodeo" tour, Carlos performed on the variety stage and in different circuses, but, eventually, finding that the training and keeping of horses was too troublesome and expensive, he decided for ever to pack up his lassos and saddles, and to build up an original act with performing dogs and pigeons. No one in the circus profession being able to handle the horse which, with infinite patience, he had trained to perform the difficult rope-skipping trick, eventually he had to sell him to a greengrocer for £40. This made Carlos swear that never again would he become the owner of a horse.

As I am writing this, the great Mexican *charro* is still in England, happy as the proverbial sandboy. When, a few days ago, I visited him outside London, where he was in winter quarters, he surprised me by releasing some forty white pigeons to fly about in the open. My surprise changed to amazement, when, as he called out their names, one by one the birds alighted on his outstretched hand, or, obeying commands, performed all manner of tricks. To me, all the fantail pigeons looked exactly alike, but not so to their trainer, who assured me that every one of them was different, and had its individuality and even distinct mannerisms.

When my friend whistled a shrill note, immediately, like huge, animated snowflakes, the pigeons fluttered back into a small wire enclosure. There, on wooden shelves, made into little square compartments, all have their respective resting and nesting places.

At the country railway station, as the train left to take me back to London, and I watched Carlos standing on the platform, waving me goodbye, I saw him, not as the trainer of performing dogs and pigeons, but as Mier, the great Mexican *charro*. Despite the passing of many years and the vicissitudes of life, the stamp and figure of such still cling to him; for, as the old Spanish saying tells us, "Figure and character go with us to the grave."

In 1933, the publication of my first book (*Tschiffely's Ride*), and its favourable reception by critics and the public, drew me further into the literary, artistic and social vortex of London. Thus, I came into contact with famous men of letters, sculptors, painters, politicians and other well-known public figures, a number among whom I class as being delightful Bohemians. In "chatty" books, so much has been written about the most famous that here I prefer only to give a few glimpses of the less publicised or even totally unknown characters with whom I became acquainted.

Shortly after my first book appeared in print, when least expected, Dame Fate surprised me by playing another trump card she had been holding up her sleeve.

Chapter XIX

Going into double harness.—Hail and farewell, General Rafael de
Nogales.

ENCOURAGED by the success of my first book, and strongly advised by literary friends to remain in England, in order to dedicate my full time to writing, after a long debate with myself, eventually I decided to stay. However, before carrying out my plans, first of all it was necessary to obtain permission from the authorities for me to remain in England. Accordingly, I sent in an application, and upon finding myself getting entangled in a veritable jungle of red tape, Cunninghame Graham came to my rescue, and after an interview with the Home Secretary I was granted permission to stay in Great Britain without limitation of time, but still under the condition which prohibited me from entering any employment, paid or unpaid. After the free and easy life I had led during the past few years, it needs no great stretch of the imagination to realise how I felt about having to go through such tedious official formalities. Still, I was glad to remain where I was, and as a result, in the course of a few years I wrote several more books.

One day, at a party given by that charming hostess, the late Miss Louisa Miéville, Cunninghame Graham introduced me to Violet Hume, who had been a friend of his for some years. Born in Buenos Aires, of Scottish-French parents, she is a talented musician and linguist who, under the stage name of Violet Marquesita (given to her by her singing teacher, the famous Mme. Blanche Marchesi), she played the part of Lucy Lockit to Sir Nigel Playfair's original production of the *Beggar's Opera,* and later, ever since the early days of broadcasting from Savoy Hill, she has taken part in many broadcasts, both in English and Spanish.

Yes, ladies, if you have not already guessed it, a few months after Cunninghame Graham introduced me to Miss Marquesita, he and Admiral Sir Frederick Fisher (better known as "Uncle Bill") acted as witnesses at my wedding to her.

Among the many new friends I made in London was James McBey, the painter and etcher. One evening when I went to visit him, he introduced me to a certain film producer from Hollywood, who happened to be in London on business. In the course of conversation, McBey—who is a widely-travelled man—mentioned Don Quixote. Whilst the two of us discussed Cervantes' immortal character, the man from Filmland sat and listened, though evidently bored. Already, when I was introduced to him, it was obvious that he had been imbibing rather too freely, and now, whilst my host and I talked about Don Quixote, I noticed that the American, growing more and more impatient, helped himself to three or four stiff whiskies in quick succession. Then, suddenly, he struck the table-top with a fist, and at the same time bellowed, "Stop kiddin' me, you so-and-sos! I've had enough of your Don—whatever his name may be! Let me tell you, I've travelled all over this gosh-danged world, and I've met everybody what's worth meetin', but I've never heard nobody mention the guy. So shut up, and let's talk sense!"

Although all those who were present made great efforts to pacify the by that time "well-oiled" film producer, it was only when McBey fetched a beautiful volume of *Don Quixote*, on the wrapper of which was the reproduction of a remarkable drawing of the pathetic cavalier's head, that the man from Hollywood began to calm down. Having got the drawing into focus—or, perhaps, for all I know, when it ceased looping the loop—with a sneer of profound contempt he said, "Wal . . . hic . . . if that's the guy . . . hic . . . I don't think much of him. Come on . . . hic . . . let's have another Scotch, an' talk about somethin' more . . . hic . . . interestin'."

In about 1932, when literary affairs and a series of lectures took me back to the U.S.A., whilst in New York I received a letter from Cunninghame Graham, who told me on no account to miss meeting a friend of his, who, as it happened, was staying in the same hotel as I.

Then and there I telephoned to the man's room, and was lucky enough to find him in. When I explained the reason for my call, in a cheerful tone of voice my interlocutor asked me to go and visit him without delay. The speaker explained that, as luck would have it, something good was waiting for me; not the kind of stuff supplied by the hotel bootlegger, but by a certain embassy in Washington. This sounded excellent, but what pleased me more than the prospect of a safe drink was the thought that, very soon, I would meet a man about whom I knew a great deal; for I had read two of his books, *Four Years Beneath the Crescent* and *Memoirs of a Soldier of Fortune*, their author being the redoubtable General Rafael de Nogales.

Whilst making my way towards his room, I wondered what this amazing person would look like in the flesh, and when I knocked at the door, to my surprise a short, stocky and extremely vivacious man, dressed in a smartly-tailored suit, appeared to greet me as if we had been intimate friends for years. Having hugged me, and at the same time slapped my back in typical Latin-American fashion, he linked an arm in one of mine, and led me into his room, presently to halt before a table on which were three bottles, one containing brandy and the other two champagne.

Whilst watching my host mix a champagne cocktail, I found it difficult to believe that this was the protagonist of so many stirring adventures, and that the jovial, debonair man before me was General Nogales, one of the greatest soldiers of fortune in modern times.

Born in the Venezuelan Andes, and having the blood of Spanish Conquistadores in his veins, when a child, his parents took him to Europe to be educated. In his early manhood, whilst studying in military academies in Germany, France and Belgium, he adopted as his motto, "When you see a good war, go to it." Accordingly, he fought in the Spanish-American War on the losing side, and after the Battle of Santiago in Cuba, realising that the "show" was as good as finished, Nogales called it a day. Subsequently he rushed to wherever a "good" war or revolution was being fought, or where political volcanoes threatened to break out in eruption. In the Russo-Japanese clash, at the opening of the Siege of Port Arthur, he was wounded, but, instead of deciding to take to a quieter and safer mode of living, soon after having recovered, longing for action, he attempted to overthrow the dictator, Gomez, and his hangers-on who held sway in Venezuela. After a number of fierce fights, most of which were fought in jungle regions where rivers teeming with alligators and *carribes* (as cannibal fish are called in those parts) had to be crossed by swimming, eventually Nogales found himself so hard pressed by his enemies that he was lucky to be able to slip away in a small fishing boat, in which he miraculously reached Haiti. Next, in turn, he fought in Morocco, took a hand in revolutions in South and Central America, looked for action in Persia and India, made another abortive attempt to rid Venezuela of Gomez, became a gun-runner, prospector in Alaska and Nevada, "rustled" cattle across the Mexican border, where he joined up with the redoubtable Pancho Villa, and generally made things lively wherever he went. In 1914, when this amazing adventurer was making preparations for another invasion of Venezuela, upon hearing that a far better war had started in Europe, he hurried across the Atlantic to offer his services, in turn, to Britain, France, Belgium, Montenegro and Serbia. However, in every case there was one hitch: though living in exile from his native land, Nogales refused to renounce his Venezuelan nationality, or to swear allegiance to any king. When offered a commission in the French Foreign Legion, he considered this to be beneath his dignity, so eventually he drifted to Turkey, where, after having distinguished himself in different theatres of war, he was promoted to the rank of general in command of a division— in which, by the way, he was the only Christian.

Though loyal to the Turks, and admiring them for their fighting qualities, Nogales fell out with his employers when he successfully intervened on behalf of British officers, who, after having surrendered at Kut, were about to be executed by their captors. After this intervention, whenever any desperate military operation was planned by the Turkish High Command, Nogales was ordered to carry it out. Thus, what with enemies in front, and others behind him, he had an uncomfortable time, to put it mildly. Despite being severely wounded (half his liver was shot out of him) the wily

Venezuelan survived the war, and later had the great satisfaction of having the following written about him in the Preface of his last book (*Silk Hat and Spurs*). The contributor is the late Field-Marshal Viscount Allenby, with whom, in London, on maps, the two often fought over again certain phases of their campaigns in the Near East:

"A brave enemy, Rafael de Nogales, now a trusty friend. . . . Wherever bullets whistle or swords clash, there he is to be found.

"And be this no rude filibuster. Love of arms, aptitude for war, blend with an unselfish patriotism and an altruistic chivalry.

"Rafael de Nogales tells us that 'Life is a joke and, occasionally, a very bad joke.'

"Truly reckless and gay—as befits a son of the Conquistadores —he has treated life as a joke; or, rather, as a joyous adventure. But, by his own showing, life has not—for him—been a bad joke.

" 'He has gambled boldly with fortune; and has won. May his luck endure.'

> (*Signed*) ALLENBY, F.M.
> "*London, 2.IX.33.*"

Could any man wish for a finer tribute, especially from an ex-enemy?

It was about 11 a.m. when I met Nogales in the hotel in New York. After having enjoyed several cocktails, we went for a stroll through the nearby Central Park, joking and laughing all the time. There being so much we had to talk about—people, countries, and places both of us knew, adventures we had had, and, above all, horses and more horses we had seen and ridden—time passed quickly. Both of us being free, after lunch we walked miles, and towards evening returned to my new friend's room there to eat sandwiches and drink excellent "diplomatic" wine, of which he had a good supply.

Shortly after this meeting I returned to London, soon to be followed by the restless man of action. Invariably, whilst recalling the occasion when, in a Fleet Street tavern, I introduced him to a group of well-known writers, I chuckle with mirth.

Most of the men who were assembled there knew the General by reputation, and therefore they were thrilled to meet him in the flesh. As it happened, upon being introduced to a certain famous poet, the delighted Nogales leapt forward to clutch him in a tight embrace, and at the same time to slap his back with both hands. Remembering the Venezuelan's reputation, whilst still being held tightly, the startled poet looked at me, and, stretching out his arms—as might a drowning man towards a log floating near him—gasped, "Is he safe?"

A few moments after this incident, Nogales settled down to joking, laughing and telling humorous stories against himself, thus keeping the assembly in fits of laughter.

If ever a man was what often is called "dynamite" it was that stocky, mercurial Venezuelan soldier of fortune. Though of low stature, he was so compact and bull-necked that if someone had knocked him down, one would have expected him to bounce up again, laughing all the while.

One day, when I visited him in the club in which he stayed, with a foot, from beneath his bed he pushed out a small leather attaché case, and then, kicking it towards me, said, "Open it, and have a look at my tin-works."

To my astonishment, the case contained a mass of medals and decorations, the history of which he proceeded to explain to me, making a joke of every one, and telling amusing anecdotes connected with what had led to his being awarded with the various distinctions.

Nogales was an excellent linguist, whose French, German and Spanish were perfect, but he spoke English with a slight American accent. In London I saw a great deal of him, and in his company went to many parties, where he always acted the clown to perfection.

Being a man of exceptional culture, his style of writing, though here and there somewhat disjointed, was vivid and in parts poetic. Sitting down to the slow and tedious task of writing was so against his grain that, in his hurry and impatience to set things on paper, he skipped over many interesting episodes in his life.

Unlike political plotters in other parts of the world, in the days about which I am writing, most Latin-American organisers of revolutions were quite open and outspoken about their intentions, especially so if, whilst living in exile, they were planning the over-throw of the "Ins" who temporarily ruled the roost in their respec-tive homelands.

In this respect Nogales did not differ from several such plotters whom I met at different times. Despite the fact that his previous incursions into Venezuela had failed, and that the dictator, Gomez, had placed a tempting prize on Nogales' head, this did not deter my friend from making preparations for another attempt to oust his pet enemy.

"Look at this old calabash," the General once said to me, pointing at his head and laughing heartily. "No one would think that it's worth such a lot of money. Every time I look at myself in a mirror, I feel highly flattered to think that on my shoulders I carry a potential fortune."

Whenever he met a person who looked like being adventurous-minded, and in a financial position to help him carry out his plan, his opening shot was of heavy calibre, and direct. On several occasions I heard him begin thus: "I want ten thousand rifles, a hundred machine-guns and a few aeroplanes. If you, or any of your friends supply me with these, and I become President of Venezuela, I shall see to it that your little loan pays handsome dividends."

Invariably, the General's direct method of attack so flabber-gasted the persons whom he addressed that either they thought he was joking, or they quickly looked for their hats.

One day, in Fleet Street, whilst talking with a number of journal-ists, Nogales expressed his disappointment at the lack of courage and enterprise shown by the people he had sounded regarding the private war loan he hoped to float. "Archie" MacDonnell, the author and playwright, suggested that Nogales should approach a certain well-known young man (a friend of mine who must remain anonymous), who was reputed to be one of the biggest shareholders in an important armament factory.

An extra glass of sherry having made me long for a little fun, I telephoned to my friend, who, upon hearing in whose company I was, immediately said that he would be delighted to make the acquaintance of the famous General. Accordingly, I arranged to take Nogales to the young man's office after lunch.

Good food and wine made the old warrior so enthusiastic that, when the time came to set out on our mission, he was in high spirits.

To put it briefly, this is what happened after we had been ushered into a luxuriously furnished waiting-room adjoining an office. When the young man—who, Nogales hoped, would become his Zaharoff—came in to greet us, my companion did not even wait for me to introduce him; but, instead, immediately proceeded to do this himself. Presently, after a vigorous handshake, without pre-amble he fired his usual opening shots.

"You have big interests in So-and-So Company, and I'm planning the overthrow of Gomez, the dictator of Venezuela. For this little campaign I need ten thousand rifles, a hundred machine-guns and a few aeroplanes. Can you procure them for me?"

Utterly bewildered, the young man shrank back, and for a while fingered his old school tie. After a few nervous coughs, with a forced smile he turned towards me, and asked, "Tschiffely, is the General serious about this?"

I nodded, and when Nogales finished rattling off a rough out-line of his plans, the now pale "candidate" stammered, "As a matter of fact . . . although I have . . . interests in the firm you mention . . . h'm . . . actually I am not directly connected with it . . . but . . ."

Raising a hand as if to say "That will do," Nogales interrupted: "If that's the case, perhaps you'll think it over, and let me know. I have another important appointment, and as I'm already late, I must be off. I'm very pleased to have met you. Here's my card. Hope to see you again. In the meantime, goodbye."

With this, taking his hat, and saying to me, "Let's go," he shook hands with the overwhelmed young man, and led the way out. When the door closed behind us, waving a hand in its direction, Nogales said, "No good; waste of time," and with this hurried along the heavily carpeted corridor, followed by me, feeling hot under my collar.

Nogales loved to tell some of his friends in London that, if he became President, he would charter the then recently completed luxury liner, the *Queen Mary*, to take the lot of us to Venezuela for a prolonged holiday, all expenses paid, of course. To Sir John Squire, the poet and critic, he would offer the position of Minister of Culture; MacDonnell he would make his Director of National Theatres; Charles Duff would become his chief adviser on international affairs, and I his Director of Land Development and Livestock Industry, and so on. With such prospects, perhaps it was better for our health that Nogales' ambitions were not fulfilled.

Generous-hearted, and fond of entertaining his friends, one day, when Nogales was in a particularly happy mood, he invited everybody he met to have lunch with him on the morrow. In the early evening, when I left him, his list of guests was truly imposing, and I could not help wondering how and where a banquet for so many could be arranged at such short notice.

I was fast asleep when the telephone rang, and my friend asked me for heaven's sake to help him get in touch with all the people he had invited, and to advise them that, for reasons beyond his control, the party could not take place. Early next morning, after much telephoning, between the two of us we succeeded in heading off most of the prospective guests, and therefore, when we sat down to lunch with those we had been unable to track down, there were only about fifteen of us.

On another occasion, when several of Nogales' friends, including myself, were dining in a West End restaurant, suddenly he jumped up. "Holy cats of Egypt! There enters one of my greatest Venezuelan enemies!" he exclaimed, and to our consternation rushed towards the newcomer, who was a man about fifty years of age. When we expected something terrible was about to happen, the two greeted each other with much hugging and slapping of backs.

Later in the evening, the "enemy" came to join us at our table. Over cups of black coffee and brandy, smilingly—but in all sincerity —he told us what he thought of Nogales, who thoroughly enjoyed the freely given censures as if they had been high praises.

"Just wait until I start my next campaign in Venezuela," the beaming General said. "If you fall into my hands, without ceremony I shall have you placed against a wall, and shot."

"Splendid," the other smilingly replied. "But, if things happen as I hope and pray they will, if you lead another insurrection, I shall not even waste bullets on you. Instead, I shall have you decapitated, and take good care to bury your body at least a league from your head, lest the two grow together again, and you resume your rebellious activities."

Thus the two joked, whilst the rest of us listened, sometimes wondering if our ears were deceiving us. Though many grievances were aired, for the time being Nogales and his compatriot were on the best of terms, but there was no doubt that, given the opportunity, their threats would be carried out.

It being a joy to yarn about old trails, people and animals one has known, and to relate adventures one has had, for hours on end Nogales and I discussed regions through which we had travelled at different times. Thus it came about that, whilst talking about a narrow, precipitous track which leads down to beautiful Lake Atitlan, in Guatemala, my friend said that the one and only time he had ridden along that break-neck trail, he had done it at a full gallop.

Having vivid recollections of that region, with its strong-smelling fir trees, volcanoes, and the picturesque Kachikel Indians who live there, but remembering particularly clearly the mountain trail we were discussing, I found it difficult to believe that anyone but a raving lunatic would ever attempt to gallop down it, let alone, after such a suicidal attempt, to survive to tell the tale.

"Before beginning that descent," I said, "I dismounted and, carefully leading my horses, went on foot."

"I should jolly well think so," Nogales replied, chuckling to himself. Presently, with a wry grin coming over his face, he added, "But then, you weren't fleeing for dear life, with the hounds hot on your heels."

When I asked him to be more explicit, he began telling me about Cabrera, a ruthless tyrant who, years ago, made himself boss of the republic of Guatemala. Always ready to defend the under-dog, and, having nothing better to do at the time, Nogales, determined to rid the country of its oppressor, made tracks for Guatemala City. Having rented a house facing one of the main streets, with great care and patience he and several confederates dug a small tunnel, and when this was completed, a heavy charge of explosive was placed at its end, which was under the middle of the street. It being Nogales' intention, not only to blow up Cabrera, but, if possible, at the same time also some of his chief henchmen, he waited for an opportunity when he might, as it were, kill several birds of prey with one stone.

At long last the moment arrived. No passers-by or spectators being within the danger zone, when the dictator and several of his closest associates drove over "zero" spot in a carriage, Nogales—who was watching from a window—pressed the button. Nothing happened, so once more the Venezuelan Guy Fawkes pressed frantically; but without result.

Suspecting that one of his co-plotters had betrayed him, he rushed down the stairs, and out into the back-yard, where a horse was waiting for him. Whilst vaulting into the saddle, he heard sounds of battering at the front door, and presently, as he galloped out into the night, several bullets whistled past him.

Heading in a north-westerly direction, the fugitive made for the Mexican border, and on the way raced down the giddy trail leading to Lake Atitlan. Some fifty miles further to the north-west, he descended from the mountainous regions, and crossed the then practically unguarded Mexican border into the state of Chiapas, and, though still hotly pursued, reached the Pacific coast during a dark and stormy night. A fisherman had left a small boat on the beach, and so, abandoning his horse, Nogales took possession of it, and rowed out into the turbulent sea. Fortunately, the storm soon subsided, and, thanks to the Humboldt Current, the boat was carried towards the isthmus of Tehuantepec, where its exhausted occupant made a safe landing.

When Nogales finished telling me this story, and I pointed out to him that it was not included in any of his books, he replied that, whilst writing, he must have forgotten all about it. "You see," he said, "I only remember some of my little adventures when I talk to

friends, and when something in the conversation brings them back
to my mind. Holy cats of Egypt! If I attempted to write about all
the fun I've had, there wouldn't be time to have any more. And,
anyway, I detest writing, even if it's only a letter."

Nogales' *The Looting of Nicaragua*—a rather disjointed and care-
lessly written book—raised, according to him, such a storm of
indignation in official circles in the U.S.A. that it looked as if the
State Department might sue him for libel.

Late one night, my door-bell rang as if someone wished to warn
me that the house was on fire, but upon opening the door, there I
found Nogales, smiling as usual.

"I've come to say goodbye," he said. "To-morrow I'm sailing for
New York, whence I shall go straight to Washington to see what all
the fuss is about. Incidentally, this will also give me a chance to look
round for someone who might be willing to supply me with the
arms I need for blowing Gomez off the face of the earth."

Astonished, I asked him if he was not afraid of running into
serious trouble with the American authorities. To this he laughingly
replied that he knew perfectly well what he was doing, and that,
anyway, life was unbearably dull in London. After a short conversation, we shook hands, and my nocturnal visitor departed with a
final joke.

In 1935, when Gomez (the Venezuelan dictator) died, Nogales,
after many years of living in exile, and experiencing hair-raising
adventures all over the globe, was able to return to his native land,
where he hoped to resume his military career. However, the new
authorities considered that to entrust a man of his type with
so dangerous a toy as an army would be asking for trouble; so,
instead, they gave him an appointment in the Customs. Though
very well paid for doing next to nothing, the dynamic ex-soldier
of fortune longed for action, or, at least, for something more exciting
and interesting to do than waiting for the monthly payments of his
salary. Again and again he sounded the Government regarding the
possibility of being put in command of the Army, but always with
the same result. Eventually, in order to get rid of Nogales without
too blatantly offending him, officially, for "health and climatic

reasons" he was given a roving commission to study police methods in the principal countries of the world. Whilst the ship in which he sailed lay at anchor off Panama, the remaining half of his liver gave him such serious trouble that he had to be taken ashore, where, upon examining the invalid, the doctors informed him that a very dangerous operation was his only hope of recovery. Unafraid, Nogales took this outside chance; but, alas! he died whilst the surgeons did their work.

Forgetting the past, and in token of admiration and respect for a great fighter, the American authorities in the Panama Canal Zone provided a magnificent coffin, in which his body was sent back to Venezuela. There, after having been stored, and forgotten, in the cellar of a Customs house, months later it was discovered by a faithful old friend. Despite the fact that former enemies continued to fear the very name of Nogales, his friend proceeded to take the necessary steps to convince them that honour must be given where such is due. The result was that, after much palaver and opposition, eventually the body was interred in the soil of the redoubtable warriors' native land. Despite the failings Nogales may have had, the very fact that, even after his death, some of his former enemies bore him a grudge, clearly proves that he was a far greater man than all of them put together.

As Field-Marshal Viscount Allenby said about him, "He was a brave enemy and a trusty friend, reckless and gay as befits a son of the Conquistadores, and one who treated life as a joyous adventure."

Vale, Nogales, Bohemian of the Toledoan blade!

S

Chapter XX

Lectures, amusing and otherwise.—Lord Lonsdale and his famous cigar.
—Another globe-trotter.—Biographical sketch of John Burns.—
Expedition through Patagonia and Tierra del Fuego.—E. Lucas Bridges,
one of the greatest pioneers of modern times.—Back to London, and
across Ireland on a gipsy tour.—The Second World War breaks out.—
Colin, the Alsatian dog.—Sophocles reappears in London.—Odd
recollections connected with the "blitzes."

IFE was far from being all fun and games for me; or, as some of
the vulgar and yet very delightful people of my acquaintance
prefer to put it, "all beer and skittles." True, I saw a great deal of my
friends, but work had to be done, and therefore most of my days
were spent in my study or in different libraries. Then, again,
especially during the winter months, the giving of lectures took me
all over the British Isles, often for charitable purposes. Shortly after
I had given a broadcast, the Governor of a certain prison wrote to
me, saying that if I could find time to lecture to his charges, this
would be greatly appreciated. I did as requested, and subsequently
gave so many "talks" in the same prison that I began to feel as if
I were an "Old Boy" of that institution, and therefore qualified to
wear its distinctive tie—that is to say, if such *esprit de corps* exists
among former pupils. One day, a friend of mine—a judge who
takes a great interest in prison welfare—came to listen to me.
Apparently the stories I told pleased him, for, shortly after, he asked
me to give the same lecture in a prison where inmates hardly ever
get any entertainment. Naturally, I was glad to be of assistance, so
it was arranged that I should get into touch with the prison chaplain.

Thinking that the ordeal of having to listen to me for one solid
hour would be too much for the old "lags"—who were in the
majority in this particular prison hardened cases—the idea struck
me that, in order to break the monotony, about halfway through
my "talk" it would be a nice change if I got my Brixton cowboy
friend (the clever rope-spinner whom I originally met in the Gristins'

old back-yard) to give a demonstration of his skill. Accordingly, I wrote to the chaplain, suggesting my idea, and in due time received his reply, part of which reads as follows:

". . . I think in view of the fact that we have 2 men here under sentence of death, it would be better *not* to bring the young man with the rope. . . ."

The "2" (for "two men") struck me particularly, but the best part of the joke is that the good chaplain could see nothing funny in what he had written.

In connection with prisons, here I must mention that, previously, I had visited a number of these in different parts of the Americas. Some of the veritable dungeons I saw in certain South American republics, reminded me of the Middle Ages, whereas a certain model prison I was shown over in the U.S.A. was so comfortable that I almost felt like putting my name down on the waiting-list for a cell. However, the electric chair did not look as inviting, nor did the switch-board for "shootin' the juice" which was concealed behind a black screen with a peep-hole cut in it; in fact, the general atmosphere in the bleak little "auditorium" was altogether too modern for my primitive tastes.

.   .   .   .   .

When another manuscript was completed, early in the summer of 1935 I decided to take a real holiday, and, incidentally, at the same time to collect material for another book.

Having found a suitable "cobby" type of horse, from the New Forest I set out to see the English countryside, and to meet the people living there. Riding north, after having passed through parts of Wales, the Lake District and the Scottish Border country, I finally unsaddled in Scotland.

Shortly before setting out, I received a letter from a man who was a perfect stranger to me. Though the sender's handwriting was somewhat clumsy, after having read a few lines, his simple poetic style began to impress me. He informed me that, previously, for many years he had been a globe-trotter, and that, having been in some parts of the Americas through which I had also travelled, he would very much like to meet me, if I happened to pass through the Lake District.

Although the late Lord Lonsdale—who had on several occasions entertained me in London—asked me to be sure to call on him at Lowther Castle, situated near Lake Ullswater, being in no mood to be "social," besides not carrying the necessary clothes for this, upon reaching those parts, instead of calling on Lonsdale, I went to look up the former globe-trotter.

As an aside, here I cannot refrain from making a short reference to Lord Lonsdale, that popular figure and *grand viveur*; the last survivor, on a grandiose scale, of the Victorian period. In some respects, he was an out-and-out Bohemian, and, as far as my experiences with him went, the nearest approach to a Baron Munchausen I have ever had the joy of listening to. No matter what a person had done or achieved in the sporting or athletic fields, Lonsdale always claimed to have gone, not one, but a hundred better. Being a perfect raconteur, when he was in a particularly boastful mood, it was most entertaining to listen to him. The white carnation he invariably wore, and the huge cigar without which he was never seen—let alone allowed himself to be photographed—were almost national institutions. Incidentally, I have a shrewd suspicion that it was only after Lonsdale died that Mr. Winston Churchill had the bright idea of adopting the ubiquitous cigar, Baldwin's pipe and Chamberlain's umbrella being someone else's "trade marks." Be this as it may, whilst Lonsdale was alive, he was the sole and undisputed owner of the big cigar's unofficial copyright. Had anyone attempted to infringe on this trade- or hall-mark, it would have amounted to sacrilege and moral suicide, in the same way as if, to-day, Mr. Attlee or one of his Cabinet Ministers adopted Churchill's famous stage "prop." Formerly, at race meetings, horse-shows, boxing matches, and public functions, there was only *one* cigar—Lonsdale's whopper. As far as the public, newspaper reporters, and Press photographers were concerned, there just was no other. And that was that.

But, from showmanship, back to earth, with its rocks, mud, sand

and dust, and to the old globe-trotter who wrote to me from the Lake District.

Upon reaching those parts, and having found my man—who lived in modest rooms above stables which had been converted into a garage—the two of us went to an old-fashioned country "pub," where, sitting in a corner, we yarned over pints of ale. My new acquaintance was well past middle age, but, despite the hardships often endured during his wanderings, he carried his years remarkably well. Grey-haired, the tropical sun had left its unmistakable wrinkles on his face and neck, but his keen eyes retained the lustre of youth.

Having discussed far-away regions we both knew, when I asked my companion to tell me what had made him take to globe-trotting, this is the story he told me.

Being the only child of a lion-tamer, as soon as he had grown big enough to be of assistance to his father, whenever the beasts needed exercise, he was assigned the duty of chasing them round the big performing cage with a broom, of which they were terrified. Though fierce-looking, in reality the lions were quite tame and harmless, and had it not been for such spells of forced activity, they would have been perfectly content to remain in their small travelling cages, sleeping and digesting their food.

One night, when the Bostock Circus happened to be under canvas in the outskirts of a little town in Wales, the boy—Walter by name—climbed up a nearby hill. Whilst the youngster gazed at the lights below and at the stars above, for the first time in his life he realised that the world in which he had lived for sixteen years was very big indeed.

For some time past he had been restless and dissatisfied with his lot in life, and now, as he stood on that hill, trying to peer beyond the dark horizon, he wished a pair of wings would enable him to fly away, to wherever fancy might lead him. Suddenly, seized by an impulse, he quickly descended from the hill, but, instead of returning to his parents' caravan, struck out in a different direction.

Some days later, with only a few coppers in his pocket, he arrived at Dover, where he stowed away on a cross-Channel steamer. Upon reaching Calais, the boy successfully stole ashore, and thus his wanderings through foreign countries began. Making himself useful on farms, but mostly living on his wits, he travelled through France, Spain, Italy, some of the Balkan States, Turkey, Syria, Arabia, Persia, India, and, after many years of tramping through various parts of the Far East, eventually reached China. In Arabia he spent several years among the bedouins, and with caravans crossed desert regions which, probably, until then, had never been trodden by any European's feet.

The hero of these adventures told me his stories so modestly, that his amazing travels might have been a mere Sunday-school outing, and as I listened to his fascinating tales, there was no doubt in my mind that every word he spoke was true. Interspersing his reminiscences with keen observations he had made during his travels, as well as excellent descriptions of people and places, the speaker made me feel as if, in his company, I were visiting many strange parts of the world through which his singular Odyssey had taken him in the course of some forty years.

In 1914, rumours about a great war having broken out in Europe reached the lone globe-trotter whilst he tramped through the interior of the Far East. Four years later, when he reached Shanghai, the fight for so-called World Freedom having been won, for the first time in his life he needed a passport. After a great deal of trouble and considerable expense, at long last the necessary document was handed over to him, whereafter he looked for a ship to take him across the Pacific Ocean, to any part of the Americas, North, Central or South; any would suit his purpose.

In the meantime, immigration regulations having been tightened up in the U.S.A., the globe-trotter did various odd jobs to earn his living. With practically no money at his disposal, his only hope of crossing the ocean was to find employment on some cargo boat, and, upon reaching the American continent, to "hop" his ship.

Whilst looking for such a vessel, he met two Chinese jugglers who were keen on performing in America. However, the entry of "coloured" people into the U.S.A. being to all intents and purposes forbidden, the artists could only make such a tour if they travelled with a white man as their manager. When the jugglers suggested to the globe-trotter that he pose as being their manager, and offered to pay all his travelling and other expenses if he did so, he seized the golden opportunity. And thus, in due time, together with the two Chinamen, he reached San Francisco.

Having toured most of the U.S.A., the trio parted the best of friends, the jugglers returning to their homeland, and their "manager," tired of city life, heading for Mexico, to resume his wanderings. Tramping south, sometimes avoiding bad jungle stretches by getting a lift in small coasting vessels, he reached South America, where, having passed through all the republics along the Pacific coast, eventually he reached Punta Arenas, on the Strait of Magellan. There, after a spell of waiting, he found a job on a cargo boat, and, a few weeks later, after an absence of almost half a century, once more stepped on his native soil in England.

For two whole days I listened to my new friend in the Lake District, and when I saddled up to resume my ride north, he insisted on presenting me with a beautiful *sarape de Saltillo* (coloured Mexican cape) which, as I am writing these lines, adorns the mantelpiece in my study.

On Christmas Day, 1935, in London, the postman delivered to me a heavy parcel, and when I opened it, to my surprise it contained two large, copiously illustrated volumes of Paul Marcoy's *A Journey through South America* (1873). Wondering who had sent me the books, I opened Volume I, and on the first page read the following inscription:

To A. F. Tschiffely.

A remembrance of the ending of one trail, and a reminder that others are to follow.

Sincerely,

(Here the ex-globe-trotter signed his name.)

Some time later, in his reply to my letter of thanks, among other things my friend wrote: "... *I feel like a caged eagle.* ... *It surely will happen one night, that when half awakening from a deep sleep, I shall stretch out a hand to switch on the electric light, and instead push over a smouldering log of my camp-fire beside a lonely trail. . . ."*

Since receiving that letter, I have heard no more from the old wayfaring man, which makes me wonder if . . .

.   .   .   .   .

When, after my delightful ride through England, Wales and parts of Scotland, I returned to London, an old literary friend asked me to do him a great personal favour.

The late Arnold Bennett's memoirs had been published, and as in the book appeared an insulting remark my friend was supposed (according to Bennett) to have made about Mr. Ramsay Mac-Donald, I was asked to go and explain the situation to the Prime Minister.

Upon arriving at No. 10 Downing Street, Mr. MacDonald received me in a most cordial manner, and when I brought up the subject which had caused me to call, he merely laughed, and said that he was glad I had come, and that he did not care one bit what Bennett had written, or what not, and went on to say that, anyway, Bennett "always had mud on his boots." With this the Prime Minister changed the subject, and then for an hour or so he asked me many questions about my travels through South America. Once, when I made a remark about politics, saying that I know about as much about them as the man in the moon, Mr. MacDonald astonished me by saying that probably I knew more about happenings in the world than he, and explained that the higher a person climbs up the wobbly political ladder, the less he knows, being, as it were, in a fog, or being carried along over an ocean, at the mercy of currents.

I found Mr. MacDonald to be a very modest and kindly person, and every now and again he amused me with little bits of "pawky" Scottish humour.

Some time after this meeting, I was surprised to receive a letter from the Prime Minister, who wrote to me from Lossiemouth:

"... I am planning to go away myself to some of those regions to which you have already brought me. I am planning to leave in the early days of November for Peru, where I shall go to Lima, Cuzco, Titicaca, then down to Chili, whence I either cross overland by the Lakes or go round by sea, and then up the eastern coast and thence home to London, getting back about the beginning of April.

"I would very much like to see you before I go, but I shall not be back in Town until nearly the middle of September. Are you to be in London then? Would you lunch with me one day, say at the Athenæum?"

As it happened, when this letter arrived I was about to leave for Scotland, and so it came about that a few days later I visited Mr. MacDonald at his cottage, "The Hillocks," in Lossiemouth, where I spent a most enjoyable day, talking about far-away regions I know well, and meeting some of my host's friends, among them a number of fishermen. I was most impressed by their knowledge of South America, where several of the humble men and women to whom I spoke had friends and relatives. It was evident that Mr. MacDonald's health left much to be desired, and that his eyesight was failing. Whilst we walked along, near the beach, close to "The Hillocks," with visible pride he pointed out to me a small humble fisherman's cottage in which he was born.

Later, from London, I sent Mr. MacDonald what information I could supply regarding South America and his proposed travels, and by return of post received the following reply:

"I am very glad that you have found your way back to London and that you have carried away good memories of your visit to Lossiemouth.

"I am most deeply obliged to you by the help you have given me by your map, your advice regarding places to visit and your suggestions of books which I should read. Everything you have sent me is most valuable, and will be carefully considered. . . . The idea of visiting a ranch is most attractive. . . ."

But, alas! it was not to be.

.   .   .   .   .

Among my Bohemian literary friends was one whom—although, as far as I know, he never wrote a book—I must place in this group. I am referring to that grand old man, the square-set, grizzly-bearded John Burns, whom I frequently visited in his house, 110 North Side, Clapham Common.

One Sunday morning, when he and I were sitting on a rustic bench in his garden, discussing books, I happened to mention Thomas More's *Utopia*.

"Strange you should mention that book," Burns said, looking at me through his bushy grey eyebrows. "If you wish, let us go up to my bedroom and I'll show you something I treasure greatly."

Accordingly, we went up to the first floor, where, in a bedroom that was filled with books, Burns went to the night-table beside his bed, and picked up a small, tattered volume of *Utopia*.

"This is the first book I bought in my life," he said, handing it to me; and after a pause continued: "In case you don't know, before telling you more about this little volume, I must tell you that I was born in poverty. My father died when I was very young, and as our family was large,[1] and many mouths had to be fed, my widowed mother kept the pot boiling by taking in washing. When I was about twelve years of age, one day, after having delivered washing, a lady gave me a tip of threepence. On my way home, passing a little second-hand bookstall, my eyes fell on this volume, and, as it only cost threepence, I bought it."

Burns went on telling me that after having read *Utopia* he made up his mind, if possible, to follow in Thomas More's footsteps.

Despite the poverty in which he was brought up and the barriers which this handicap placed in his path, young John faced the world bravely. After the acquisition of *Utopia*, books became a passion with him, but upon leaving school at an early age, and having to earn his living as best he could, he had not much time for reading, except at night.

Unfortunately, I do not remember everything my friend told me about his early activities and wanderings, but I hope that, some day

[1] If I remember correctly, Burns told me that he was the youngest of a family of thirteen, among whom were only two boys.

in the near future, a good and conscientious biographer will undertake the task of writing Burn's life. As far as I recall, at different times this remarkable man was a sailor, professional boxer, miner in South Africa—where he nearly died of black-water fever—pamphleteer, social reformer, and eventually Britain's first Socialist Cabinet Minister. This position—since he was opposed to war—he voluntarily resigned at the outbreak of war in 1914. But, above all things, later in life Burns became an inveterate and most knowledgeable bibliophile, and he never lost interest in *Utopia* and in Thomas More, its author. To give just a passing example of his enthusiasm for this work, suffice it for me to put on record that, in 1935, the British Museum owned eighty-four editions or translations of *Utopia*, whereas Burns' collection contained over a hundred, apart from exceptional copies. It lacked only the fifth and sixth Latin editions, but otherwise was complete up to the fiftieth, printed in 1631. Apart from this, he owned a document in vellum, signed by Thomas More. This he bought for £125. Most of his pension and every penny of a special annual grant from the Carnegie Trust he spent on books, for Burns never smoked or drank any beverage containing alcohol, and his personal requirements were of the most simple.

Among a mass of rare books, he owned two copies of the Second Folio of Shakespeare, printed in 1623, and also others of the Third and Fourth Folios, printed in 1632, 1664 and 1685 respectively. Another of Burns' favourite hobbies was the collection of books on London and town planning.

During all his long life, he never wore an overcoat, but, instead, no matter what the weather was like—hot, cold, dry or wet—he was always to be seen in a reefer jacket, into the two side-pockets of which, whilst walking, his hands were invariably thrust. When on a book-hunt, he always took with him a wad of bank notes, with which to pay, cash down, before hurrying home to enjoy his new acquisitions.

Whenever, after visiting his home, I made ready to depart, Burns, who was no churchgoer, told me the same little joke—namely that, as usual, on the following Sunday, his "chapel" would be open between 11 a.m. and noon, and then again between 6 and 7 p.m., and that, even if I refused to confess my manifold sins, a hearty welcome would be extended to me.

In 1936, after our mutual friend, Cunninghame Graham, had died whilst on a trip to the Argentine, and I settled down to writing my late friend's life, Burns took a great interest in what I was doing. During one of my usual Sunday visits, I told him that nothing would please me more than if he wrote a Preface to the book. I explained to him that, as he had known Cunninghame Graham for a great many years, and even had been imprisoned with him after the "Battle of Trafalgar Square" (or "Bloody Sunday," November 13th, 1887, when they fought for free speech) he was the obvious man to write the Preface.

Having promised to do as requested, Burns asked me to visit him again on the following Sunday, when he would give me his contribution to my biography.

A week later, when he read out what was pencilled on several sheets of foolscap paper, I was astonished at his fine style of writing, and the keen observations and witty asides with which his text was freely interspersed. Though Burns spoke with a strong Cockney accent, he held me spellbound until, suddenly, he interrupted his reading. Looking up at me, he said, "D'you know?—I'm beginning to like the stuff. You won't 'ave it; I'm going to add it to my collection."

And that was the end, as far as Burns' Preface to my book was concerned.

Off and on, even before Cunninghame Graham died, I worked at his biography for three years, and when the manuscript was completed, and I had handed it in to my publishers, I was so sick of a sedentary life that I decided it was high time I had a radical change. There were several parts of South America I wanted to visit, so after having thought over the matter, I decided to go and explore Patagonia and Tierra del Fuego, right down to the regions near Cape Horn. Hurried preparations having been made, after a delightful voyage in a cargo boat I landed in Buenos Aires, whence I travelled south, overland. This journey being described in my book, *This Way Southward*, here I will only mention one remarkable man I ran to earth after a tremendous chase.

At different times, in the course of many years, I had heard stories about an Englishman who was said to be a kind of white chief among the primitive Fuegian Indians, among whom he was born in 1874. To-day these savages have practically disappeared, and the few who survive are in the employ of sheep ranchers who have taken possession of the land.

Upon arriving in southern Tierra del Fuego, I was told that the man I sought was somewhere among the Andes in southern Chile, so when I had seen enough of Tierra del Fuego, I once more resumed my long man-hunt. This time luck was with me, for after having travelled hundreds of miles through wild regions of singular beauty, at last I met this veritable will-o'-the-wisp.

Tall, powerfully-built, E. Lucas Bridges was one of the most remarkable men I have had the good fortune to meet. When I started picking his brain, and in modest words he told me some of his stories, it did not take me long to realise that his knowledge of the Fuegian Indians was unique, and that if he wrote his memoirs, they would make a book for readers of every taste. When I suggested to my host that he take up my idea, he flatly refused, but subsequently, when we met again, he promised to make an attempt at what he called the "impossible." Now, after having worked hard and patiently for several years, his book (*Uttermost Part of the Earth*, Hodder and Stoughton, London, 1948) has been published, and our shelves have been enriched with a bulky volume which surely is destined to be read by many future generations.

About a year before *Uttermost Part of the Earth* saw daylight, when I wrote to my friend, Colonel Charles Wellington Furlong, the well-known American explorer and author, that Mr. Bridges' manuscript was ready to be submitted to the consideration of publishers, in his reply to my letter, among other things, the Colonel stated:

". . . I consider that Lucas Bridges is one of the greatest pioneer characters of our times. As far back as 1908 I realised that the story of Lucas Bridges, as well as that of his family, would be worth more than that of a dozen Balderwood's *Tales of the Australian Bush* or *Trader Horn*, plus those lesser advertised personalities of the past fifty years, all rolled into one. Lucas Bridges is one of the world's great characters, and if his MS. is one-half as colourful, romantic, dramatic and historically valuable as his life has been, I believe that anyone publishing it will be responsible for preserving one of the most outstanding annals of our day. . . ."

The reception given to *Uttermost Part of the Earth* by leading literary critics and the public alike has fully justified Colonel Wellington Furlong's opinion, and, if I may be boastful, my sense of "smelling" a book when, in the Chilian Andes I listened to Lucas Bridges tell me some of his unique and enthralling tales. Even if my trip right down to the regions near Cape Horn may have produced no other lasting results, I am both proud and highly satisfied that my one-man expedition to those uttermost parts of South America led to the publication of his memoirs, and that in those far-away regions I made the friendship of this extraordinary man whom I class as a super-Bohemian, the likes of whom never again this changing world will see. (In April, 1949, some six months after the publication of his book, Bridges died in Buenos Aires.)

After having travelled several thousand miles through Patagonia and Tierra del Fuego, I returned in a cargo boat to England, where I imprisoned myself in my study in Chelsea, in order to write another book. When this was finished, once more I began to feel restive, and so I packed up a few garments, and on the following day, in the company of a magnificent and well-trained Alsatian dog, arrived in Dublin, whence old friends drove me to their estate in County Wexford. Having found a two-wheeled vehicle (in Ireland known as a "governess trap") and an excellent light-grey Connemara pony to pull it, I set out on a kind of gipsy tour through rural Ireland.

Thus, followed by my wonderful companion, the dog (whose name was Colin), I slowly jogged along peaceful country lanes, going wherever fancy led me, meeting delightful people, and taking many photographs. Irishmen being very fond of animals, especially horses and dogs, wherever we went everybody made a great fuss of my pony and dog, which gave me many chances to talk to people who otherwise would have taken no notice of me. After having travelled for some two months, during which I saw many of Ireland's hidden beauties, I happened to be on the wild and rocky Aran Island off Galway, when the Second World War broke out. Upon returning to the mainland, I sent back the pony and trap by rail to the farmer from whom I had hired them. Some time later, he wrote me a letter of which I am as proud as I am of any testimonial that has ever been given to me. Among other flattering things, the farmer wrote: ". . . I also want to tell you I never saw the pony look better than when she arrived from Galway. You must have given her lots of oats. . . ."

Colin, the Alsatian dog, had been lent to me by a friend in England, so upon receiving a telegram, asking me if possible to leave the dog in Ireland, where he would be safe from the war, I took him with me on the next train which left Galway for Dublin.

Survivors of the *Athenia*—the first British ship to be torpedoed during the war—had been landed in Galway, so when I boarded the train, a batch of officers and members of the liner's crew travelled in a carriage in front of mine. The railway guard having given me permission to keep the dog with me, instead of putting him into the guard's van, he contentedly lay at my feet. Every time some of the sailors passed to go to the dining-car to have a drink, they could not resist patting Colin's beautiful head. This had been going on for some time, when a young officer, after having done the same, looked up at me, and after a short pause asked, "Excuse me, sir. Aren't you Mr. Tschiffely?"

As it turned out, a few years previously, when I travelled in a certain cargo boat, the young officer was one of her apprentices. Without further ado, I rose from my seat, and led the way to the dining-car to celebrate the young Sherlock Holmes' recognition.

As a result of the sinking of their ship, most of the sailors had lost their money, and as they were only given 10s. apiece to take them back to Glasgow, they had to go easy with their spending. When I offered to give money to the three or four whom I had treated to a round of beer, they flatly refused to accept it, so eventually we drew up a contract, according to which I made my companions a loan, to be paid back to me within a period of ninety-nine years, eleven months, thirty days, twenty-three hours and fifty-nine minutes from the time of signing the document. Names having been affixed to it, the loan was duly floated, whereafter, until the bar on the train ran out of beer, all signatories had a delightfully wet time.

Upon arrival in Dublin, I immediately got busy looking for a good home for the dog. Several people offered to take care of so fine and well-trained an animal as was Colin, so eventually I handed him over to the care of a nice-looking young man who was in the employ of the Eire Government. I felt sorry when the time came to part with my delightful canine companion, who howled dismally upon seeing me walk away with the suitcase he knew well. However, as he was to be taken out to a farm, I knew that there he would soon settle down to the kind of life he enjoyed, so I hurried away, feeling that under prevailing circumstances I had done my best for the dog.

In a ship that was packed with people who were in a hurry to return to their homes in England, I crossed the Irish Sea in a total black-out, and after a dismal and most uncomfortable voyage by rail, reached London, where I found everybody busy making preparations for aerial attacks.

Owing to the war, soon many of my friends were scattered far and wide, some joining the Forces, whilst others, who were too old for active service, gladly took any official job offered to them. As far as the less fortunate—such as I—were concerned, everything came to a standstill: authors slumped over their desks, publishers all but shut shop; and, worst of all for me, two verbal agreements I had—one in America and the other in England—for literary work, were cancelled. The bronco "War" had unseated me with his first buck. But, after all, even though the fall was a nasty one, there was nothing I could do about it but rise, shake myself, and look round for another mount. Used to hard knocks, and accustomed to paddling my own canoe, and bearing in mind that millions of people were far worse off than I, and that to-morrow is another day, I frequently went to the British Museum, where, despite the fact that almost everything of value had been removed, a section of the Library was carrying on as usual.

On several occasions, whilst I was busy with historical research work, German aircraft attacked London. Whenever the sirens sounded the alarm, one of the librarians announced that an air-raid shelter was available, and that those of the readers who wished to take cover were at liberty to make use of a deep cellar. Although, shortly after such announcements were made, sometimes gunfire and explosions shook the building, and windows rattled ominously, all the "book-worms" remained at their desks, and all that could be heard during quiet spells was the rustling of paper as leaves were being turned over.

When my friend who had lent me Colin (the Alsatian dog who had accompanied me during my tour through Ireland) expressed her wish to have him back, I wrote to the young man who had taken charge of him in Dublin. Time passed without a reply coming, so I wrote two or three other letters, all with the same result. When this silence was beginning to worry me, one day I received a note, in which the writer—evidently a young woman—sent me the following information:

"I have been asked by my friend, Mr. X, to write to you and explain that he has been incarcerated, and so was unable to make a move about the dog, which he was about to send to London. X regrets this terribly, but if you care to write to him his address is—

"Cell 13 B. (my number)
"Cork Gaol,
"Western Road,
"Cork.

"PS.—He is only allowed to write one letter a week, but may be able to get replying to you, so I hope I have made everything clear to you."

T

Upon receiving this startling bit of news, I wrote to the given address, and some time later received a charming letter from the prisoner's father. He did not mention his son, and when I wrote to Mr. X Senior, I took good care not to ask any questions about his son, who, I suspected, had been jailed either for political reasons or possibly because in making out accounts he had let the pen slip in his favour.

Owing to war conditions, it would have been difficult to transport the dog over to England, and therefore he had to remain where he was. For some time I corresponded with Mr. X Senior, who one day sent me a letter which, being typically Irish, gave me great pleasure. Here is an extract from it:

"Colin is now living on a farm owned by an uncle of mine. For a pal he has an old sheepdog, and between duties they strike a very successful partnership, very much to the concern of rabbits in the neighbourhood. It would interest you to see them at work! Old Billy (the sheepdog) nosing out the rabbits from the cover, and Colin well outside waiting to deliver the quietus. And useful work it is, as rabbits have become a pest in the area.

"I see him twice a week, and as he knows my arrival means an outing he gives me a hearty welcome, in his own bear-like fashion. We have done all kinds of poaching together. This no doubt will surprise you, but here in Ireland it's in our blood—not for any gain, but just for the thrill and adventure. You should see him after salmon in small streams during the spawning season. He plunges in the moment he sees one, usually to find that he is a split second late. Colin is a grand animal, and an ideal pal, and you may feel assured that he will be well cared for. . . ."

This letter came as a breath of fresh air to me, for what with dismal wintry weather, the black-out and similar trials, life had become miserable in London.

One evening, shortly after I had returned home from the British Museum, the telephone rang, and when the caller made himself known to me, my brain was thrown into a whirl, and I all but dropped the receiver. The man who spoke to me was . . . *Sophocles!*

More than a quarter of a century had passed since I had last heard his voice, and now, as I listened, memories flashed through my mind in rapid succession. I saw the speaker outside the Royal Exchange, dressed in immaculate City clothes, then in Grecian robes and sandals, eating vegetarian food in the old *Maison Gristin*. Again I remembered how he sat in the Doré Galleries, in Bond Street, listening to Raymond Duncan, and I recalled how hard he tried to make me become one of the pseudo-Greek's disciples. Then, in my mind's eye, I saw Sophocles depart to Russia, where some prince had engaged him as private tutor.

As related in an early chapter, when I was teaching in St. George's College in the Argentine, one day, from the blue, I received a letter from Sophocles, who informed me that when the Russian Revolution broke out, he managed to escape to the Far East, where, after having "made good," he enjoyed the luxuries that go hand-in-hand with wealth.

What could have brought this strange character back to London? When he expressed the wish to see me, I invited him to meet me in a tea-room in the West End. Remembering my Sophocles of old, that *par excellence* quick-change artist, I was fully prepared for any shock he might have in store for me.

In due time, when he appeared, anyone might have taken him for a Harley Street specialist about to make a professional call on some rich client, or perhaps his appearance might have suggested to some that he was a prosperous lawyer. His glossy black hair, though fairly long, was neatly cut and parted in the middle, but now he wore a toothbrush moustache which, though it suited him admirably, gave his mouth a somewhat sad expression. His large, dreamy black eyes were still those of a mystic, and, set in a pale face, reminded me of pictures painted by old Italian masters. As he was tall, and his bearing erect, his well-tailored morning coat, striped trousers and grey spats suited him admirably, and as I watched him approach, somehow I sensed that he had a "message" for me.

Having carefully placed his black hat on a chair, he halted in front of me, closed his eyes, and mumbled what I guessed was a prayer. Whilst observing him, I wondered if it was offered to God,

Allah, Mohammed, Buddha, Xuiteucli or Setebos; but soon Sophocles put me out of suspense by giving me the great news that, whilst out in the Far East, he had suddenly discovered the real Truth. Next he informed me that contentment being a gift of heaven, whereas wealth and luxury are its dangerous counterparts, he had cast his material possessions to the four cardinal winds, and returned to London, where God provided him with all his needs. Talking ceaselessly—excepting when he drank the tea and ate the cakes I ordered for him—he told me that the Christian Church was erring, and that, in consequence, as a warning, God directed both German and Allied bombs to destroy so many of our churches, which, according to Sophocles, in reality are nothing but material heathen temples. As had been the case a quarter of a century before our reunion, when the speaker wanted me to join the Duncanites, now he implored me to mend my ways, to cast aside vanity and riches (with which I have never been blessed), and with him to propagate the Gospel as God and Christ wish it to be done.

Realising that I was listening to a religious maniac, under some pretext I made ready to depart. A day or two later, the postman delivered to me a mass of pamphlets, chiefly pious verses and quotations from the Bible, and with them also a long epistle from old Sophocles. Despite the acute paper shortage caused by war conditions, his messages were written on luxurious, hand-made silk paper, which made me wonder who had provided the new apostle with such expensive stationery.

Remembering past experiences I had had with the writer when, in the Gristins' lodging-house, I had looked after him for some time, I took good care not to reply to his letter.

Time passed, and as I heard no more from the modern would-be St. Paul, he faded from my memory. One evening, whilst travelling in a bus in the company of an old friend of mine—who is a correspondent of *The Times*—to my consternation and embarrassment, Sophocles boarded our conveyance. The weather being cold, he wore a heavy black overcoat, and, hanging from his shoulder, suspended from a wide leather strap, he carried an enormous bag, stuffed full of printed matter. On his chest, in a glass frame, dangled a quotation from the Bible, for all the world making him look as if he wore some peculiar kind of bib. Upon recognising me, after some fumbling in his bag, Sophocles rose from his seat to present me with a handful of religious pamphlets.

Amazed by this singular apparition, my companion stared as if he were face to face with an armed hold-up man, and a little later, when the two of us got off the bus, and I explained who this pamphleteer was, my companion shuddered and exclaimed, "Phew, he gave me the creeps!"

.   .   .   .   .

In May, 1942, tired of being on air raid duty almost every night and trying to write in the daytime, I decided to take a day off. The weather being ideal, in the company of an old friend, I went out to Kew Gardens, and in the evening met a journalist of our acquaintance, with whom we drank a glass of sherry in the El Vino Tavern near Piccadilly Circus. From there we went to a restaurant to have dinner, and later I took my two companions to a most original kind of club, run by a delightful old Spaniard in Soho. Owing to the probability of a "blitz" starting at any moment, very few people were in the place, but congregated near the crude counter were several Latin Americans, including an elderly Minister of a certain South American republic.

We had not been there long, when, as fully expected, the sirens wailed, announcing that German aircraft were approaching London. Used to such alerts, no one took any notice, and when the Latin Americans started an argument about Simon Bolivar, the South American liberator, one of the vociferating patrons at the counter came to ask me to act as arbitrator. Having introduced my two guests to the debators, we were talking six to the dozen when the "blitz" started with thunderous anti-aircraft fire, and every now and again heavy thuds which were followed by ominous crunching sounds as bombs hit buildings, causing them to collapse.

Undeterred by such familiar sounds, our discussion continued uninterruptedly until, simultaneously, windows blew in, and a violent explosion shook the old house, on the first floor of which

we were assembled. With no windows and curtains left, and lights
having to be extinguished, we went downstairs, and out into the
street, all the while arguing about Bolivar. It was only upon reaching the open that we realised that the "show" was a big one, for
overhead planes seemed to be buzzing about like swarming bees,
gunfire was terrific, and bombs fell all around.

This being the first time I had missed being on voluntary air raid
duty in my street, together with my companions I groped my way
through the black-out towards Piccadilly Circus, where we hoped
to get a taxi. However, all traffic having come to a standstill, returning home was out of the question, and whilst we were in a huddle,
debating where we should go, a "whopper" came screaming and
whistling down, to explode with a terrific bang uncomfortably
near us, sending glass and débris flying in every direction. Things
were getting so hot that, after a short council of war, we decided
to go to the nearby Savage Club, of which the three of us are
members. Whilst on our way down towards Carlton House
Terrace, several bombs fell in our close vicinity, and upon reaching
our goal we were so pleased that we took the lift up to the third
floor to play billiards. We were just beginning to enjoy the game
when the windows and shutters blew in, fortunately without
injuring any of us. Several stranded members of the Club being
assembled in the cellar, we joined them in a game of poker, and
whilst we played, every now and again the house rocked and
trembled in a most unpleasant manner.

It was about 3 a.m. when things began to quieten down, and so
we made ready to walk home. Incidentally, without making use of
any of Bob Appin's (the card-sharper and gun-slinger I knew in
South America) methods, I pocketed most of the money. This my
expert opponents called "beginner's luck." Upon stepping out of
the door, countless conflagrations rendered the sky so bright-red
that one could easily have read the smallest print.

Having crossed St. James's Square, together with a friend (Tom
Greig, the antique and art expert), I walked down King Street,
where we discovered that Christie's famous auction rooms were
ablaze. When a solitary fire engine arrived, we gave the firemen a

helping hand with the hoses, only to find that, one of the mains having been hit by a bomb, there was no water.

Leaving Christie's premises to burn themselves out, we passed through the adjacent district, where a number of art and antique dealers have their shops. There I beheld one of the most extraordinary sights I saw during the many "blitzes," which sometimes had their humorous side.

In the middle of the street, seated on what appeared to be Chippendale chairs, were two stout, exceedingly prosperous-looking men, calmly smoking cigars whilst watching sparks fly into the house in which they had their shop. Thinking we might be of some use, Greig and I went to see if the place was burning, and upon discovering that a recently fallen spark had started a small fire on the wooden staircase, we stamped out the flames, and, in order to prevent further sparks from being blown in, closed all windows.

Instead of being pleased with our timely intervention, the two ringside spectators never budged from their seats, so Greig and I marched off towards Piccadilly, where a macabre sight awaited us.

In the street, the back of a car stuck out of a crater overflowing with water, and near this bomb-hole was another of even greater dimensions. Everywhere water squirted and flowed, and the street was littered with burnt-out incendiary bombs, sandbags, fallen masonry, broken glass and masses of different articles which had been blasted out of shop windows. "El Vino"—the tavern in which, only a few hours before, we had drunk sherry—was in ruins, and an adjacent house had practically vanished. In Leicester Square, fires were burning fiercely, and, here and there, bombs had made deep craters, in one of which members of a rescue squad were digging feverishly, every now and again calling down into what had been an underground shelter, "Anyone there?" But no reply came.

Shortly after dawn, upon approaching my home in Chelsea, I found the roads littered with broken glass and other débris, and although several buildings in the close vicinity had been demolished, or badly damaged, to my amazement, when I entered my flat, although one side of the house was blasted, I discovered that only one small window-pane in my study was missing. But marvel of marvels, although all the books had been thrown on to the middle of the floor from a flimsy, loose bookcase, on the top of it a delicate fluted vase made of Bristol glass remained standing. Among the many horrors and not a few humorous incidents, what will always remain deeply engraved in my memory about "blitzes" are the two stout and exceedingly prosperous-looking men, who, seated on antique chairs placed in the middle of a street near St. James's Square, calmly watched sparks fly through the open windows of the house in which they had their business establishment. I should not be in the least surprised if, one of these days, I again see the two gentlemen, probably lolling in a luxurious car, smoking outsize Havana cigars. In the meantime, farewell, ye two doubtful Bohemians of the open-air fireside seats.

Chapter XXI

War days in London.—Last visit to John Burns.—Return to the Argentine.—Submarine attack on convoy.—Priorities, and an American's experiences connected with them.—The adventures and travels of an exiled armadillo.—Once more, *adios*, South America.

AND so the war continued, until one became so accustomed to what it entailed that one only remembered times of peace as a kind of deceptive dream. Newspapers, magazines and occasionally glib politicians sang the praises of the unknown heroes and heroines of the back-room, queues, floating coffins, coal-mines, factories and kitchens, whilst black marketeers supplied the prosperous with luxuries the rank and file of self-sacrificing and patriotic citizens had forgotten. In London and other target cities, masses of houses and flats were deserted by their well-to-do occupants, who, for the "duration," sought safety in rural districts, where the prices for even tiny cottages soared sky-high, whereas in London many houses could have been bought for a pittance.

Thanks to officially sponsored entertainments—such as those organised by E.N.S.A.—and a variety of specialised war work, many artists managed to keep their heads above water, but others were not so lucky. In Chelsea, most of the studios were empty, many of the bearded, long-haired and be-sandalled sojourners of the palette, chisel and pen having betaken themselves elsewhere, mostly to Cornwall. Unemployed authors and journalists were driven to seek refuge under the protecting wing of officially subsidised publications, but in the case of others who were not so lucky, the only serious writing they did was when they filled in ration books and masses of forms, including the buff variety for tax on incomes they did not earn.

Suspecting all foreigners of being spies had become a mania with many people, and therefore anyone with a name such as mine fanned the flames of suspicion of snoopers and other little "busy-pants."

In view of the fact that my name looks and sounds as if it might be Russian, it was fortunate for me that, at the time, members of the Soviet Union—being brave, noble and extremely useful allies—were hailed as heroes and staunch defenders of democracy. Now, several years after the days of Stalingrad, whilst writing this, I tremble to think what might easily happen to me, if, owing to my name, I were taken for a Communist. What with spy, Fascist and Nazi hysteria raging all round me, as well as registrations and all sorts of official restrictions making me feel as if I were an arch-criminal, I longed to fly to some uninhabited island, and there to spend the rest of my days as a Robinson Crusoe. But, in London I was, and in London I had to remain; and, strange to relate, in some respects I was glad and even proud to be where I was.

So many things had to be done that most of my time was taken up, and in consequence opportunities to meet old friends were few and far between. Still, whenever possible I kept in touch with such. After a long spell, one Sunday morning I went out to Clapham Common to see how my old friend, John Burns, was getting on. Though he had lost none of his outward cheerfulness, I noticed a great change in him, for since our previous meeting he had put on years. He informed me that during one of the "blitzes"—when he happened to be reading in his kitchen—the blast of a bomb which fell near his house had stunned and thrown him on to a small circular stove. As it was alight at the time, and the old man fell on it, breast down, he was so severely burnt that he had to be taken to a hospital for treatment. Burns assured me that he owed his life to the fact that, once upon a time, he had been a prize-fighter, and to the boxer's instinct which had been dormant within him for many years. Apparently, upon regaining semi-consciousness, feeling an acute pain on his chest, he instinctively pushed himself away from the stove, with the result that he fell clear of it.

A few weeks after this lucky escape, when another bomb fell near Burns' house, he had another narrow escape from death. As on the previous occasion, again he was reading, when an exploding bomb hurled a kerbstone through the skylight. Fortunately, it missed him by inches, but shortly after, when I again visited my friend, he looked badly shaken. His stubbly beard and bushy eye-brows had turned white, but his dark eyes and sense of humour were as keen as ever.

When I made ready to depart, it was raining heavily, and as I was about to put on my overcoat, despite my protests, Burns insisted on holding it for me.

"Although I've never worn one of these contraptions," he said, smilingly, "I'm quite an expert at helping people put them on; for when I was a Cabinet Minister, this was one of my jobs, though, not infrequently, I felt like kicking departing callers."

Having assured me that I was not in this category, he warmly shook my hand, and as I walked towards the garden gate, he shouted after me, "Call again, soon. I'm always glad to see you."

That was the last time I met Burns, for shortly after this meeting he passed on. After his death, one section of his library sold for over £15,000, and his unique collection of books on London and town planning was bought for £6,000 by Lord Southwood, who gener-ously presented it to the London County Council.

Whilst writing this, in mind I am sitting with Burns on that rustic bench in his garden, but although I am curious to know, I dare not ask him what has happened to that Preface he wrote for my biography, *Don Roberto*, and I wonder where is to be found that small tattered copy of Thomas More's *Utopia*, which my departed friend bought, when a mere child, for 3*d*. Perhaps, for all I know, the auctioneers cast it aside as mere rubbish, and thus, possibly, it has found its way back to some second-hand stall. Should this be the case, I hope another boy has purchased the old volume, and that, influenced by its contents, some day, its new possessor will become another John Burns, or "Honest John," as he was often called.

.   .   .   .   .

During air raids the Brixton area suffered severely, and in every respect, my good friends in that part of the city had an exceedingly unpleasant time. For years to come, until the present generation of variety and circus artists has made way for a new one, many of its members who are scattered all over the globe will regret that, after having existed for close on a century, Price and King's huge training establishment in the Hartford Road was destroyed by a direct hit. Also, the little colony of circus people who lived in caravan wagons in a vacant lot, is no more, a stick of German bombs having written *finis* to the little cluster of romance.

Some of the Chelsea artists had deserted their studios, in order to seek refuge in the country, but others—probably followers of the impressionist and surrealist schools—found their *milieu* doing camouflage work for the Forces. Most of the majority who remained behind, enlisted in the Civil Defence, and on many occasions did sterling work. My voluntary task being that of fire-watching and, if necessary, to make myself generally useful during air raids, many of my nights were spent racing up to the roof, and down again into the street. Despite the lively sleepless nights thus spent, in the daytime I went to do research work in the British Museum Library, and thus, after having worked several months, I managed to complete a manuscript dealing with the Pizarro period, and the discovery and conquest of Peru. That was all very well; but how, and when, could the book be printed?

Realising that high living often means a long drop, I do not believe in recklessly throwing about money. However, despite this, what with nothing coming in, all sorts of commitments and liabilities, and everything getting more and more expensive, prospects for the future were anything but bright for me.

.   .   .   .   .

At the risk of being taken for a braggart, in connection with the war I will relate a short story about myself.

In 1938, whilst travelling in a train, I saw experiments being made with barrage balloons. Somehow, to me it seemed that, though efficient to ward off aircraft or to force them to fly high, such a barrage lacked mobility, and that it could not be used for naval purposes on the high seas. Remembering a kind of spider I had seen in tropical parts of South America, an idea struck me. This particular species of the order of *araneida* lays its eggs in a tiny, circular webbed bag which, attached to a kind of parachute by a long thread, is carried far by the wind. At different times I have seen masses of such spider parachutes, many of them with the young already hatched before they landed, maybe hundreds of miles away from the place where the little parachute was released.

Why not make a rocket, which, on exploding in the air, would release a parachute with a long wire, to the end of which is attached a small bomb? Such a contraption would remain in position for an appreciable time, and if an aircraft flew into the wire, the bomb would inevitably be drawn towards a wing, and, upon striking it, be detonated, thus causing its destruction.

Some weeks after having conceived the idea, I happened to be talking to a friend of mine who was one of the chiefs at the Admiralty. When I told him about my "spider-web barrage," he was so impressed that he asked me to submit the idea to the authorities. Accordingly, a few days later I did so, and shortly after received a card from the Under-Secretary of State for Air, acknowledging receipt of my communication, and stating that it would receive attention. Three weeks later, a letter reached me from the same quarters, informing me that my idea for combating enemy aircraft had been examined, that my scheme was not novel, and that in these circumstances the Department did not propose to take any further action in connection with my submission, for which, nevertheless, as well as for the trouble I had taken in bringing it to the Director's notice, he wished to thank me.

Five months later, the London Press published the news that a "parachute shell" had been invented in America, and in July, 1942, or be it, about five years after I had conceived the idea, the Admiralty revealed that one of the most successful devices developed during the war at sea was a rocket apparatus which shoots into the sky parachutes with long wires attached to them.

So much for a certain kind of South American spider and its life-propagating parachutes, and my idea to adapt wise nature's invention for destructive purposes.

.   .   .   .   .

As the war dragged on, and the only useful thing I could do was fire-watching, more and more I longed to go anywhere, and to do any kind of work, so long as I was not writing.

No one being allowed to leave Britain without official sanction—which was exceedingly difficult to obtain—when an opportunity presented itself to make a trip to South America, I fairly leapt at the chance, regardless of German submarines, which, at the time, made sea voyages anything but safe. Despite the fact that, in my case, evidently the chiefs of the British Council were not prepared to waste money recklessly, the agreement I reached with them suited me under prevailing circumstances. I was given to understand that in South America I would be expected to go on a lecture tour extending over a period of three months, whereafter I would be at liberty to look after my own interests. Salary I was to receive none, and the passage out and back was to be paid by me, but whilst actually lecturing under the auspices of the Council, my travelling and other incidental expenses would be met.

Thus, after having filled in masses of forms, and an exit permit had been granted me, at last, feeling as must criminals upon being discharged from prison, I sailed from Glasgow. On my way down the Clyde, I had a good look at Cunninghame Graham's house, near Dumbarton, where, before my friend's death, I had spent many happy days. A badly holed ship which was being towed up-river served as a reminder that the voyage out to South America would not be a pleasure cruise, and two days after having formed convoy, when we were off the north coast of Ireland, floating wreckage and a large abandoned ship, with her bows well down in the water, gave us further food for thought. A few hours later, the weather and seas became exceedingly rough, and at about 10 p.m., whilst I sat in the lounge, talking to the First Officer, suddenly there was a dull thud, and the ship shook violently. Rising from our seats, we hurried out on deck to see if we had been hit, and as I made my way through a J-shaped black-out door, a terrific icy blast and the rolling of the ship, made me catch hold of a hand rail, lest I slip and fall. It was a stormy, pitch-black night, but, by degrees, as my eyes became accustomed to the darkness, I could distinguish the

shapes of huge foam-crested waves as they came rolling towards
me.

Whilst the First Officer rushed up to the bridge, I went to my
cabin to fetch my life-jacket and identity papers, whereafter I
returned to the lounge, where the few other passengers were
assembled, ready, if necessary, to abandon ship. Though all looked
worried, no one showed signs of excessive nervousness, let alone
panic. It was only when one of them asked me if we had been
torpedoed that I realised that emotion, fear, or whatever it was, had
affected me. During the "blitzes," though on several occasions I had
felt apprehensive, I can't remember ever having been affected as I
was on board that ship; for when I tried to reply "No," a lump in
the throat so choked me that all I could do was to shake my head.

After a while, having put on my life-jacket, once more I went on
deck, where I arrived just as several thuds—this time in the distance
—slightly shook the ship. Presently, behind our stern, and on our
starboard side, several distress flares illuminated the cloudy sky,
indicating that ships were in distress. The sea was so turbulent, and
the icy wind so strong, that I doubted if any life-boats could be
lowered without being smashed to matchwood, so as I stood,
shivering, and staring into the darkness, my heart went out to those
who needed help we could not give. Orders having to be obeyed,
the convoy slowly steamed on, leaving rescue work to the corvettes
which shepherded us through the danger zones.

Here, in passing, I will relate something that once happened to
me in connection with fear.

People, especially ladies, often ask me if ever during my travels
through the wilds I was afraid. My honest answer to this question
invariably is, "Yes; often." It is all very well coming to us with
charming yarns about little Georgie Washington who is supposed
never to have told a lie, and trying to make us believe that Nelson
did not know the meaning of the word "fear." Whenever I hear
such and similar stories, being no credulous Marine, I always
"ha'e me doots."

One of the worst frights I ever had, came to me under most
trying circumstances. I was riding through a deep, narrow canyon,

with no idea of what lay ahead of me, nor exactly whither the canyon led; but, feeling hungry and thirsty, I forged ahead as fast as the rock-strewn ground permitted. I was half asleep when a peculiar, sharp and smack-like noise made me think a revolver cartridge must have fallen out of my belt, and that it had been detonated upon striking a rock. Naturally, my horse shied, and at the same instant a sound, like a minor thunder-clap echoing through the canyon, made me realise that I was being shot at from somewhere above. My intestines seemed to freeze, but fortunately I had the presence of mind to hug one of the walls of the canyon, where a slightly overhanging boulder afforded some shelter, provided, of course, I had chosen the side from the top of which the bullet had been fired at me, as I guessed, not by a friend. Luck was with me, for evidently my choice of canyon wall had been correct.

Whilst waiting to see what would happen next, in turns I felt either colossally big or very small; big when I thought myself to be the one and only live target in a hostile world, and small when I realised how far away I was from human help.

During "blitzes," when everybody in London was in the "show," and ambulances, doctors and other aid were always at hand, this gave one a certain feeling, if not of security, at least of comfort; for to be under fire *en masse* is one thing, whereas I to be shot at when all alone, and far, far away from home, and in a wild strange region, is a very different proposition.

Until darkness fell, I dared not move away from that canyon wall; but, whilst waiting I had ample time for making my plans. To proceed in the direction in which I had been travelling would be foolish, for, apart from the fact that I did not know the lie of the land ahead of me, most likely the bandit would be waylaying me further along my route. With this probability in mind, as soon as night fell I began to grope my way back to the place where I had camped during the previous night, and on the following day made a vast detour in order to give that ominous canyon a miss.

Did I feel fear during that ticklish experience? . . . "And how!" as Americans would say.

But to return to my sea voyage from Glasgow to South America.

Near the Canary Islands, once more we ran into minor trouble with submarines, but, fortunately, there were no casualties. Even if we had been torpedoed, the calm blue waters and the glorious warm weather would have given us every chance of saving ourselves.

Outside Freetown, the convoy split up, and, two days later, my ship, full steam ahead, steered a straight course towards Uruguay. Travelling in convoy, seeing the same ships every day, and sometimes even during nights, and moving at a snail's pace, gave one the impression of being in a port. But now, as we sped along on our own, everybody cheered up, and with pride some of the sailors pointed at the foam racing along the ship's sides.

We reached Montevideo as night was falling, and there beheld a marvellous sight that most of us had not seen for several years. Lights were shining everywhere; the black-out, attacks by aircraft and submarines, suddenly all seemed to have been merely part of a nightmare. The last reminder we had that war was raging in other parts of the world, came to us near the mouth of the mighty River Plate, when we passed the almost entirely submerged wreck of the scuttled German pocket battleship, the *Graf Spee*.

Next morning, brilliant sunshine and blue skies greeted us as we went out on deck to look at the skyline of Buenos Aires, and towards noon, after having gone through the usual passport and other formalities, I made preparations to go ashore. Before leaving the ship—in which I had been for over five weeks, taking care to spend as little as possible of the £10 I was allowed to take with me on leaving Britain—I called to the stewards who had attended to me during the voyage, and, emptying my wallet and pockets, asked them to divide among themselves what I offered them as a tip. Having borrowed 10 pesos from an old pupil who happened to come on board to deliver some documents to the Captain, I drove to an hotel in a taxi. By the time I had unpacked some of my belongings, banks were closed, so I went to a restaurant where the *patrón* knew me well. Upon seeing me appear, he showed great surprise, and when he asked me what on earth had brought me back to Buenos Aires, I jokingly told him that I had come all the way from London in order to borrow 100 pesos from him.

U

Without saying a word, my old friend went to the cash register, from which he produced what I needed, and after having given me the money, proceeded to open a bottle of champagne. Presently, raising his glass to me, he said, "I welcome you back to the land of the gauchos. If there is anything I can do for you, here I am, at your service."

To be brief, and frank, as far as my connection and activities with the British Council were concerned, I was both disillusioned and disappointed. But the joke of it all is that, to this day, many of my South American and English friends believe that for my "mission" I received a fabulously high salary, and that, therefore, like a few ladies and gentlemen of my acquaintance, I, also, "cashed in" on the war.

In reality, however, as already mentioned, I received no salary, and I had to pay my travelling expenses to the Argentine and back. Furthermore, upon returning to London, the income tax authorities charmingly informed me that, having been abroad for a period exceeding six months, automatically I became a non-resident, and as such—although, during my absence, expenses, such as rent and other commitments I had in London had to be met as usual—I had to pay full income tax, without rebates or allowances of any kind. Yes, it certainly was a grand war—for a few.

Having fulfilled my obligations with the British Council, I was happy to leave the city, and once more to return to the pampa, where gauchos ride broncos on their own merits, and whence no long reports have to be sent to headquarters in London, in order to give chiefs the impression that the nine muses and long dead poets have been resurrected in the flesh.

It felt grand to be out in the wide-open spaces, and to renew many old friendships; but work had to be done, so after a great deal of travelling afar, material for another book having been collected, I returned to Buenos Aires.

Owing to the war and sinkings by German submarines, passenger-carrying ships were few and far between, and accommodation in them—as well as in aeroplanes—was only reserved for people who were on official business. Of course, like a few others who were not in this category, but who nevertheless managed to "wangle" passages, I could have applied for priority, which, possibly, might have been granted; but hating to ask anyone for such favours, I much preferred settling down to waiting for a ship in which there might be room for me. Accordingly, I went to live in a small bachelor's hotel—called Casa Frossard—which was patronised chiefly by economical Scotsmen and not over-well-to-do ranchers and cattle-men.

In connection with priorities, in Buenos Aires I heard a most amusing story.

Some time after the U.S.A. had come into the war, a retired American colonel decided to return home in order to offer his services. Trained at the Westpoint Military Academy, and having served with distinction in the previous war, he thought that he might be of some use to the American Army. With this in mind, full of enthusiasm, the tall, square-set ex-colonel travelled from Buenos Aires to New York by plane, and when, in due time, he called on his old comrades-in-arms, and a doctor examined him, he was—to use his own way of putting it—turned down for three "b's," i.e. for being bald-headed, beer-bellied and bunioned.

With nothing to do, the disappointed volunteer booked a passage back to the Argentine, and after having been kept waiting for weeks, eventually he started on his long flight. But oh for the frailty of human hopes!; twice his plane landed in the U.S.A., and twice the colonel was "grounded" for several days, and subsequently, in Cuba, for nearly a whole month. When the unfortunate—and by that time exasperated—man began to think that the rest of his life would be spent seeing aeroplanes arrive and depart, without taking him on board, at last he was given a seat in a military transport plane which was bound for Rio de Janeiro. Upon landing at broiling Belem, situated almost plumb on the Equator, near the mouth of the River Amazon, when the Colonel saw the pilot and several airport officials go into a huddle, every now and again to cast sly glances in his direction, he looked on apprehensively, wondering if by any chance this secret pow-wow meant that the necessity of once more grounding him was being discussed.

u*

Indeed, the unfortunate traveller's suspicions and fears were well-founded, because, for three long weeks he had to kick his heels before he was rescued by a southward-bound plane.

But the humiliating reason why the colonel was grounded at Belem is best told in his own words:

"When I saw those guys at the airport go into a huddle, I said to myself, 'Boy, that means *you*.' Yes, and it sure did, and when one of the officials came to tell me why I was being grounded, for the first time in my life I got to know my real worth; for, believe it or not, I had to give priority to a consignment of plastic lavatory seats for aeroplanes."

.   .   .   .   .

Shortly before I returned to Buenos Aires from the pampa, I received a letter from a young Swedish friend, who asked me, if possible, to bring with me a young "de-skunked" skunk or some other suitable pet for his little boy who was very fond of animals. (By "de-skunked," he meant one from which, by means of a simple surgical operation, have been removed the anal glands from which skunks eject their fœtid defensive secretion.) Although I made every effort to oblige my friend, all I was able to catch was a young armadillo, which, after having been handled and hand-fed for a few days, became very tame.

It happened to be late evening when, with the peculiar pet bedded down in a small wooden box filled with straw, I arrived at my hotel in the city. An elderly Irishman immediately took such an interest in the armadillo that he suggested I take him out of the box, and turn him loose in a small *patio* outside his room, whence the animal could not escape, provided no one opened a shuttered door which connected his room with the tiled *patio* without. A saucer having been filled with milk and bread, and this placed in a corner for the armadillo to eat, we departed—I to sleep, and the Irishman to meet some friends.

Next morning, when I went down to the hall, the hotel proprietor and several guests seemed to be highly amused about something, and presently told me what had happened during the night.

Apparently, after having had a long session with his friends, the

Irishman returned home somewhat tired, and, forgetting all about
the armadillo, left open his door, with the result that the animal took
to wandering through the hotel. During its explorations, it entered
a room in which it awakened a woman, who, upon seeing the
strange apparition, screamed murder. From there the armadillo
made for the wooden stairs, down which it rolled, its hard shell
making such a clatter that the old Gallego night-porter, who slept
near the entrance door, got a terrible fright, wondering if he was
seeing things.

After much fussing and commotion, a guest caught the "dangerous" animal, and put it back into its box, and soon after I handed it
over to its new owner. But, as it turned out, the poor, inoffensive
armadillo's travels and adventures had hardly begun.

My Swedish friend was delighted with my gift, and when he took
it home and handed it over to his little boy, the youngster's joy was
great, but his mother was so terrified of the "huge, armour-encased
and rat-like creature," as she called it, that she bluntly told her
husband that, unless he got rid of it at once, she would leave the
house. This ultimatum led to a scene: Father and tearful boy siding
with the armadillo, and Mother dead against it. However, finally
the woman got her way, and Father decided to send the cause of all
the trouble to the Gothenburg Zoo as a present.

The captain of a Swedish ship undertook to deliver the animal,
and, in due time, with it on board, sailed from Buenos Aires. As it
happened, owing to the German blockade of the Skager Rak, the
ship and its cargo were diverted to a Spanish port, whence it sailed
back to the Argentine with the armadillo still a passenger. Having
become the sailors' pet, and being fed accordingly, in the meantime
it had grown to a tremendous size, and when the captain decided
that it would be kinder to send it back to the pampa to be turned
loose, he bumped up against a new and unexpected difficulty. When
he tried to take the armadillo ashore, the port authorities stopped
him, explaining that, for various official reasons, no live stock could
be imported without certain necessary permits and other documents.
Being refused entry to its native land, the poor animal had to be
taken back on board, where, after two more trips to Spain and

back, it finally died, not broken-hearted, but due to being overfed by the sailors. Thus, on the high seas, gave up its ghost what must have been the most travelled armadillo in history: a lone, exiled Bohemian of his ancient species.

What with these and similar happenings, masses of friends with whom to go here and there, and a lively revolution thrown into the bargain, time passed quickly. Fortunately, old-stagers, such as Dr. Primo and a few others, were still there, carrying on as usual, but, alas! most of the others had either died or disappeared without leaving clues as to their new whereabouts.

Every time when I happened to pass near a lunatic asylum, and certain memories were revived within me, I heartily laughed to myself.

Twenty years previously, when, before setting out on my ride from Buenos Aires to New York, I happened to pass that asylum, suddenly my two half-wild Indian mustangs started to dance their Patagonian war-dance. Whilst I made desperate efforts to remain in the saddle, and at the same time to hold the horse I was leading, several inmates of the asylum watched me from the top of a grassy bank behind a high stone wall. Even though I was having an exceedingly rough time, whilst my animals bucked, reared up, kicked and all but tried to stand on their heads, upon catching a glimpse of my interested spectators, it struck me that I, also, should be behind those walls.

·   ·   ·   ·   ·

Some of the semi-down-and-outs (or "stiffs" as they are called) of the English-speaking community in Buenos Aires, regularly met in what, at one time, had been the Deux Mondes Restaurant (formerly often called the "Ducks' Pond"). Situated in the heart of the city, after having been sold it was turned into a kind of cross between an *almacen* (grocery store), eating-place and bar. In this unpretentious establishment, sheets of brown paper take the place of linen table cloths, and, if desired, cheap wine is supplied by the glass. Naturally, as far as the majority of patrons is concerned, the bar is the chief attraction, so if anybody wants to hear big talk, the "Stiffs' Bar"—as it is nicknamed—is the place *par excellence* for such entertainment. As clients consume glass after glass of cheap *caña* (a kind of rum), their grievances against the world grow, and anyone who listens, wonders why all these great men are not prime ministers, presidents, field-marshals, admirals, managers of huge business concerns, or major-domos of ranches; for, according to the high opinions speakers freely and vociferously express regarding themselves, there is nothing they do not know or are incapable of doing. It is to be regretted that all these geniuses are being overlooked, but, fortunately, the "Stiffs' Bar" is there to serve them as a kind of forum. The establishment being open for twenty-four hours, at any time, day or night, groups of potentially great men assemble there, in order to drown their grievances, or to hold forth until sleep and empty pockets call for an adjourment of the session.

Thanks to a Scottish seafarer who is an old friend of mine, when his cargo ship arrived in port, upon hearing that I was waiting for a passage back to England, he immediately offered to take me with him. Hurried preparations for my departure having been made, I went to bid goodbye to many friends, among them Sir David Kelly, the British Ambassador, who, together with his charming wife, on several occasions had been my delightful hosts.

Early next morning, after cordial farewells on the part of Argentine Port and Customs House officials, dock labourers and policemen who happened to recognise me, and having waved *adios* to a few old friends who had come down to the docks to see me off, my ship slowly steamed out into the yellow vastness of the River Plate, soon after to head for Montevideo and the South Atlantic Ocean.

Chapter XXII

AFTER an exceptionally stormy, but nevertheless most enjoyable, passage, travelling as the only passenger in a cargo boat, it was a great joy once more to be back in dear old London. Though during my absence many things had changed, and I found something shoddy about the appearance of buildings and men alike, and little officialdom continued to make its weight felt, it was obvious that the core of England had remained eminently solid and sound. As far as little officialdom is concerned, it was Napoleon who once said that the corporal thinks himself to be much more important than the general. It must be borne in mind that the soul of a nation is not represented by its security-seeking civil servants—who in modern states have become as indispensable and almost as numerous as bacteria in manure-heaps—or by the vast majority of those who inhabit cities, but by the people of the soil and by independent creative workers; men and women thanks to whose initiative and toil, officialdom is kept in bread, butter and beer, or champagne and caviare, as the case may be. Come what may, it is my firm conviction that Britain, though temporarily "paper-bound," is not likely to change; for, as in the case of Bohemians, regimentation can never destroy what is inborn and deep-rooted.

Shortly after my arrival in London, I went to badly battered Brixton, in order to see how my friends, the variety and circus artists, were getting on. To my great joy, I found that, despite bombs and many sore trials endured, most of them are carrying on as usual, and that even the brotherhood of Brixton cowboys continues to flourish.

When seeking a change and relaxation from my sedentary and often wearisome task of writing, occasionally I make my way to that part of London, in so doing betaking myself, as it were, into another world. On the first floor of a long and roomy but rather dilapidated brick-built shed, in which are stacked up masses of stage props, I can sit for hours, chatting with friends, whilst watching others practise their respective arts and tricks.

Among the performers are two old American jugglers who, in the course of more than half a century, travelled all over the globe, working under the name of "Tambo and Tambo." A few years ago, when a countryman of theirs died (Curtis, the famous juggler), in his will he left the Tambo brothers 14,000 volumes he had collected during his long life. Books were Curtis' passion, and therefore most of his considerable earnings were spent on the acquisition of such.

The recipients being anything but book-worms, they did not know what to do with this legacy, but after having housed the books for some time, following a daring attempt on the part of robbers who, during the Tambos' absence, attempted to carry the valuable collection away in a furniture-removing van, they sold the lot to the highest bidder—who, incidentally, struck a rare bargain.

The Mexican *charro*, Carlos Mier, animal trainers, "cowboys," knife-throwers, trick and *haute école* riders, and many other artists continue to assemble in that to the vast majority of Londoners totally unknown and unsuspected corner of romance, where, every time I drop in, my friends, including performing animals, never fail to give me a hearty welcome.

As for the old *Maison Gristin*, even its tumbledown ruins have disappeared, a huge block of modern flats having taken their place. To-day, stream-lined cars glide along the concrete-sur-faced street which formerly was paved with rough but romantic cobble-stones, and in the "local" the quaint old atmosphere has been killed by chromium steel, fluorescent lights and platinum blondes, who, perched on high cocktail bar stools, make vain attempts to blow cigarette smoke haloes into the air. Surely, even the ghosts of some of our old "steadies" must have fled to other parts, where, I hope, these formerly earth-bound spirits are happily reunited in heavenly replicas of the Gristins' old lodging-houses.

Like many characters I had known and associated with, more

years ago than I like to remember, Bill and Ivy have passed on also, but Cockney family tradition being what it is, the male offspring of one of their three daughters followed in Granddad's footsteps, having taken to the buildin' and decoratin' trade.

Denny, the one-legged Irish newspaper-vendor, and spare-time street bookmaker, has also departed from his old pitch at the corner.

Work having to be done, most of my time was spent in my study in Chelsea, with occasionally a visit to the British Museum Library. During early evenings, members of the Savage Club often entertained me with interesting and amusing conversations, but, as often I did not walk as much as half a mile in a day, besides getting soft and flabby, I was beginning to get into one of those long and narrow graves known as a rut.

One day, when I felt listless and bored, suddenly an idea struck me: ring up old "Professor" Newton, the boxing and physical culture expert, who, thirty-five years before, had put me through the hoop, and sometimes through the ropes of his boxing ring. If anyone could lick me back into tolerable shape, the "Professor" was the man to do it.

When a voice at the other end of the line answered my telephone call, I immediately recognised it as being that of Andrew Junior, whom last I had seen, several years previously, shortly after his second eye had been removed. When I told him that I wished to speak to his father, he informed me that he had died shortly after the outbreak of war. When the speaker added that now he carried on the business, there and then I made an appointment to begin a reconditioning course with him on the following day.

As I approached the old brick-built house in Marylebone Road many memories came back to me, and after having rung the bell, in the doorway appeared the quick-moving, athletic figure of Andrew Junior. Having made myself known to the blind man, he led the way to a dressing-room behind the gymnasium. Whilst getting ready for my first lesson, I noticed that the place looked exactly as it had thirty-five years before, and when I asked my new instructor what had caused his father's death, he sadly told me that with the outbreak of war, and the consequent loss of pupils, he found it impossible to make ends meet, and that, finally, an eviction order was issued against him. Despite this bitter blow, and the dismal prospect of having to move out of the premises in which he had worked hard and happily since 1907, the "Professor" carried on until, one afternoon in his beloved boxing ring, he collapsed; not owing to old age or exhaustion, but from a broken heart.

Despite the seemingly unsurmountable handicap of being totally blind, I soon discovered that young Andy Newton is a first-class trainer, and that what he does not know about his job is not worth knowing. Should a stranger go to his gymnasium, and not be told that the mercurial instructor is blind, it would take the visitor some time to discover it. Andy is a wizard with various types of punch-ball, and his skill as a boxer is such that it would take a good man to beat him.

In the summer of 1948, when my friends, Gene Tunney, the former heavyweight champion, and Colonel Edward Eagan, the Chairman of the New York State Athletic Commission, were on a visit to London, I took them to see Andy. Shortly after Tunney returned to the U.S.A., in a letter to Newton, among other things he wrote: ". . . Seeing you work around your gymnasium was a most astonishing and inspiring experience. You are, indeed, a remarkable man, and I hope that the fates will give you many more years to impart to all who meet you some of the courage and steadfastness that you possess in such abundance. . . ."

One day, when Andy was busy making me do a series of exercises, a young man presented himself in the gymnasium, saying he wanted a little further training before taking up boxing as a profession. After having sparred with the would-be professional for two rounds, one of Andy's glass eyes fell out of its socket, with the result that his pupil stared, horrified, probably thinking he had done the instructor some serious harm.

"Do you know what's the matter with me?" Newton asked, and before the aspirant to championship honours in boxing rings had time to reply, Andy continued: "I'm blind; totally blind, both my eyes are made of glass. If what you've shown me in two rounds is all you know about boxing, just forget about becoming a pro.

Furthermore, let me tell you that I've pulled all my punches. If you don't believe it, and want proof, let's have another round, and I bet you a quid that you won't be standing up at the end of it."

The would-be professional was so bewildered and taken aback that he remained standing, puffing and panting, and unable to utter a word.

"Take my advice," Andy continued after a pause. "Don't waste your time and money on lessons. You'll never do any good in a ring."

Thus ended a young man's ambition to become a professional boxer, and I, after an interval of many years, once more enlisted as a pupil in Newton's boxing academy, where, in the course of fifty years, many famous men—both of the social and pugilistic world—have kept themselves fit.

With the passing on of the old "Professor," London lost a great character; perhaps a rough diamond, but nevertheless a fine type of English gentleman, who often was to be seen, almost bouncing through the streets of London, wearing a brown bowler hat, and on extra special occasions sporting a white "topper."

Vale, "Professor" Newton, and good luck to you, Andy!

.   .   .   .   .

One misty evening when I happened to be walking through a residential part of London, suddenly someone halted in front of me. I must have been daydreaming, for it was only upon hearing a mournful voice which sounded strangely familiar to me that I focused my eyes on the apparition. To my amazement, there, wearing a long, spreading patriarchal beard, and wrapped up in a flowing black cloak, stood Sophocles, staring at me with his large, black eyes.

"Good evening, friend," he said. "It is providential that we should meet again, and at this very moment."

Although walking had made me feel comfortably warm, as I looked at the reincarnation of Rasputin which blocked my way, a cold shudder ran down my spine. Before I had time to think of anything to say, save a curt, "Oh, it's you. Good evening,"

Sophocles told me that only two or three doors away from where we stood was the house of Lady So-and-So, and that he was bound thither in order to preside over a causerie on the fallacies of Greek philosophy. Laying a slender white hand on my shoulder, he told me that he and his friends would be delighted if I joined them, and with this tried to make me go with him.

I was on the point of shaking myself loose and saying something rude, when two elderly ladies arrived on the scene. Having greeted Sophocles, one of the newcomers turned to me, whereupon, simultaneously we recognised each other as old acquaintances.

"I see you are coming to our causerie. How perfectly wonderful!" she exclaimed enthusiastically.

With the excuse that I had an important appointment, I quickly took my leave, and hurried away. Throwing back a furtive glance to see if by any chance Sophocles might be chasing me, I noticed that a number of luxurious cars were parked outside the house in which the causerie was to be held, and, whilst quickly striding along, I passed several well-dressed elderly ladies who evidently were on their way to listen to the new prophet.

"It must have been written," as the Arabs say, for a few months after this chance-meeting with Sophocles, he crossed the Stygian ferry. With tears in her eyes, one of his female admirers told me that during the spell of Arctic weather early in 1947, despite warnings given to him by friends, Sophocles insisted on speaking at an open-air meeting, with the result that, an icy blast having got under his apostolic beard, he contracted pneumonia which led to his happy release from this wicked world, of which during his stormy lifetime he had seen much, and in which he had done many strange things.

.   .   .   .   .

No doubt, some of the characters whom I have introduced to the reader have led what formal citizens call "useless" and even "dangerous" lives, and a few among them were outcasts from society. And yet, seeing that example is a lesson we all can read, even the worst among them have fulfilled a mission in life, though, in most cases, unwittingly.

In a world in which regimentation, national prejudices and hatreds, and even dangerous forms of mass hysteria are becoming the order of the day, I find that only countries and cities—of which, as far as my experiences go, London is the one *par excellence*—in which individualism and originality are left to flourish comparatively undisturbed, have that "something" extra, the lack of which makes life in others so stereotyped and accordingly dull.

It has been said that a nation's culture can always be judged by the artistic merits of its monuments. With this snobbish statement I most heartily disagree, for wherever the breezes and currents of life have carried me, I have assessed the degree of a nation's culture, not by statuary, magnificence of cathedrals, contents of art galleries, and architectural beauty of Government buildings, but by the way the masses treat creatures and fellow men who are at their mercy, and also by the general attitude towards individuals who are outside the pale of conventional human society.

In writing these Bohemian memoirs and short biographical sketches, it was my chief aim to give readers glimpses into games in life with which he or she may not be acquainted. Unlike some of our highly advertised geniuses who freely hawk about their intellectual wares, I have no new doctrine, "isms" or theories of life to offer, but if the reader says with the old Roman poet, Ennius, "I am a man and consider nothing human outside my interest," I trust that among these pages he or she has found something that has struck a chord.

Life being like a stage, on the insecure foot-boards of which we are placed to act without our consent, and the dramas and comedies in which we have to take part being but as a wink in eternity, whenever I am in a light-hearted mood, I like to compare the span of human life with a certain gentleman's ride in a taxi.

In the company of friends, I had been dining in the West End of London, and as we were waiting to buy back our respective hats and overcoats from the cloak-room attendants, a well-dressed, middle-aged patron—who evidently had dined and wined exceedingly well—was also about to depart. Making valiant but futile efforts to appear sober, he steered an erratic course towards the street door, outside which was stationed a taxi. Assisted by the commissionaire, the tippler managed to get into the cab, but only to lurch in a forward direction, and with such bad luck that he tumbled out of the opposite door, which had been left open by the vehicle's previous occupants.

Having picked himself up, readjusted his clothes, and with great difficulty retrieved his hat and cane, in as dignified a manner as circumstances permitted, the victim of this little accident staggered up to the taxi-driver, and—evidently under the impression that he had reached his home—said, "Thanks, driver. How much do I owe you?"

And with this, to the gentle reader who has accompanied me all the way through these many pages, I also say "Thanks," and to members of Bohemia I exclaim, "Carry on, and may there be many more happy junctions!"

Index

Other titles in the Equestrian Travel Classic series published by The Long Riders' Guild Press. We are constantly adding to our collection, so for an up-to-date list please visit our website: **www.thelongridersguild.com**

Title	Author
Southern Cross to Pole Star – Tschiffely's Ride	Aime Tschiffley
Tale of Two Horses	Aime Tschiffley
Bridle Paths	Aime Tschiffely
This Way Southward	Aime Tschiffely
Bohemia Junction	Aime Tschiffely
Through Persia on a Sidesaddle	Ella C. Sykes
Through Russia on a Mustang	Thomas Stevens
Across Patagonia	Lady Florence Dixie
A Ride to Khiva	Frederick Burnaby
Ocean to Ocean on Horseback	Williard Glazier
Rural Rides – Volume One	William Cobbett
Rural Rides – Volume Two	William Cobbett
Adventures in Mexico	George F. Ruxton
Travels with A Donkey in the Cevennes	Robert Louis Stevenson
Winter Sketches from the Saddle	John Codman
Following the Frontier	Roger Pocock
On Horseback in Virginia	Charles Dudley Warner
California Coast Trails	J. Smeeton Chase
My Kingdom for a Horse	Margaret Leigh
The Journeys of Celia Fiennes	Celia Fiennes
On Horseback through Asia Minor	Fred Burnaby
The Abode of Snow	Andrew Wilson
A Lady's Life in the Rocky Mountains	Isabella Bird
Travels in Afghanistan	Ernest F. Fox
Through Mexico on Horseback	Joseph Carl Goodwin
Caucasian Journey	Negley Farson
Turkestan Solo	Ella K. Maillart
Through the Highlands of Shropshire	Magdalene M. Weale
Wartime Ride	J. W. Day
Across the Roof of the World	Wilfred Skrede
Woman on a Horse	Ana Beker
Saddles East	John W. Beard
Last of the Saddle Tramps	Messanie Wilkins
Ride a White Horse	William Holt
Manual of Pack Transportation	H. W. Daly
Horses, Saddles and Bridles	W. H. Carter
Notes on Elementary Equitation	Carleton S. Cooke
Cavalry Drill Regulations	United States Army
Horse Packing	Charles Johnson Post
The Cavalry Horse and his Pack	Jonathan Boniface
The Art of Travel	Francis Galton
Shanghai à Moscou	Madame de Bourboulon
Saddlebags for Suitcases	Mary Bosanquet
The Road to the Grey Pamir	Ana Louise Strong
Boot and Saddle in Africa	Thomas Lambie
To the Foot of the Rainbow	Clyde Kluckhohn
Through Five Republics on Horseback	George Ray
Journey from the Arctic	Donald Brown
Saddle and Canoe	Theodore Winthrop
The Prairie Traveler	Randolph Marcy
Reiter, Pferd und Fahrer – Volume One	Dr. C. Geuer
Reiter, Pferd und Fahrer – Volume Two	Dr. C. Geuer

www.ingramcontent.com/pod-product-compliance
Lightning Source LLC
Chambersburg PA
CBHW060314100426
42812CB00003B/781